The
Whole
Elephant

The
Whole
Elephant

Unlocking Solutions to
the Chaos in My Life and Yours

JO VANDERKLOOT
with Judy Kirmmse

Contents

Acknowledgements 7

Preface 10

Chapter 1: The Lure of Chaos 15

Chapter 2: What's Wrong with my Family? 31

Chapter 3: New Adventures—Old Tears 53

Chapter 4: The Dreaded Happens 66

Chapter 5: Orphans 69

Chapter 6: Becoming Who I Am 81

Chapter 7: College Interrupted 96

Chapter 8: The Crumbling Begins 108

Chapter 9: Family—at Home and Abroad 126

Chapter 10: Build It, Love It, Leave It 138

Chapter 11: Becoming a Therapist—The Path to Answers ... 151

Chapter 12: The Failure of Success 159

Chapter 13: Ex-Urbanites 168

Chapter 14: Father and Husband—Gone 180

Chapter 15: True Commitment—a Challenge 185

Chapter 16: Too Much to Bear 213

Chapter 17: Therapy In Action 254

Chapter 18: The Whole Elephant at Last 283

I dedicate this book to every member of my family—past, present and future. Thoughts, beliefs, and behaviors flow through families, generation to generation. We build on what worked for our elders: that's how we grow. It's essential for our survival.

Acknowledgements

Years ago my good friend Myrtle Parnell taught me a most important lesson: none of us accomplishes anything on our own. We all stand on the shoulders of others. *The Whole Elephant* was birthed with the help of many people, from those who pushed me to write a memoir, to those who read the manuscript and made suggestions, to others who gave it its final shape.

I wrote this book in collaboration with my business partner, Judy Kirmmse: together we decided we needed a story to wrap around the knowledge I acquired from figuring out my family and assisting many other families. We believe this knowledge can help readers struggling with their own families and that it offers a new and essential approach to solving the overwhelming global problems confronting us all. Judy and I work as a team; I could not do this alone.

Beth Wareham has been the perfect editor for us. She makes great suggestions, but she leaves the decision-making up to us. She's warm, she fits us into her schedule, she has extensive knowledge, and we can elicit her help at a moment's notice. She's amazing!

Throughout my life, people have showed up to support me when I needed them. Myrtle and Elsie Maldonado did that at the clinic where we worked in the South Bronx, at a time when I didn't know what to do with their acceptance and support. It was life changing, and I owe much of the knowledge I share in this book to them. They were my mentors. I had other mentors as well: Kitty La Perriere, one of the founders of family therapy, and Dorothy Gregg Scott, who started mentoring me when I was 17 and whose business acumen was revered. Kitty and Dorothy were legends in their own time. Three matriarchs were my life lines in different settings: my grandmother when I was growing up, Miss Sutherland at the Beard School, and

Dean Gertrude Noyes at Connecticut College. They supported me, reined me in, and prepared me for taking on tough situations.

I want to thank my entire family as well: my mother, both my fathers, and my sister Mac from childhood, and in adulthood my two daughters, son-in-law, and grandchildren. My original family provided the context for my childhood: it was not an easy life, but it gave me the lived experience of growing up in a complex family. That experience primed me for my career as a therapist, and I am grateful.

My marriage was a challenge, but from it came my two daughters, Katie and Pam, who are especially important to me, even though Katie is no longer alive. Pam's generosity in convincing me to live with her and her family during these most recent years is above and beyond what I believed could happen. Here in Colorado, I'm happier than I've ever been, and Pam and her husband, Bill, made that possible.

Of special importance to me also are my grandchildren: Nick, Alex and Grace, Zoe, and Zach, who buoy me up with their thoughtfulness, energy, and humor.

I am indebted to all my patients, both individuals and entire families. We worked hard together, and we learned from each other. I also learned from my students, who were interns at NYU School of Social Work, Seton Hall psychology doctoral program, and Smith College School of Social Work.

Throughout my life, friends have been like family to me. I want to mention in particular Johnny Dauvergne, whom I first met at age nine and who's still a phone call away; Margo Smith, my fellow team member and friend at the Beard School; Sue Vail Condon, my roommate for four years at Connecticut College, and even Sue's mother, who seemed to adopt me while Sue and I were there.

When you write a book, you need people to read the manuscript to keep you honest. I appreciate Pam and Bill; my grandson, Nick; Patricia Kiley; Pastor Felicia Smith-Graybeal; Michael Colberg;

Marsha and Jonathan Talbot; and Johnny Dauvergne for finding time in their busy schedules to do this, as well as a few others.

For helping make this book a reality, I appreciate Simon Hartshorne for taking our manuscript and turning it into the book you're reading.

Finally, I also appreciate YOU, the reader. I hope you'll join with us as we try to change the way people understand this world we're living in. We want to hear from you! Please share your ideas with Judy and me through our website, www.chaosinstitute.org.

Preface

In ancient India, three blind men came across an elephant as they wandered from place to place, but they had no idea what it was. They examined it, each taking a different part, and they started comparing notes, describing to each other this newly found, large, rough, strangely shaped thing.

"It's strong and thick, like a tree trunk," one said.

Another quickly disagreed. "No, not at all; it's wide and flat and flaps back and forth."

The third claimed the animal was like a long, thick snake with an open end. They could not agree. Their blindness prevented them from seeing the whole elephant.

Like the long, thick snake and the tree trunk, my life is full of extreme contrasts, each part different from the others. The parts of my life didn't fit together, and even as a child, I knew my family wasn't normal. I, too, was confronting a strange beast. I always felt like I didn't belong. When I tried to figure out what was wrong, I got nowhere. Later I became a therapist and was able to help my patients deal with their families, but it was decades before I finally understood my own.

But unlike those blind men, I knew there was more to discover. How could I not, when around every corner in my life there's been a whole new world? What I finally discovered is something so important I want to share it with everyone.

It all began during WWII in Queens, NY. My father left to fight in the war when I was two. With the blackouts, sirens, food rationing, and coal soot, I thought the world was a dark, tension-filled, scary place.

What I remember most about being a child is absence, loss, and illness. My mother was distant and out of reach, my father left, and my sister was often sick and always strange. I felt disconnected from everyone except my beloved grandmother, who tried to fill the void.

As I attempted over the years to make sense of this crazy life, my family and I experienced the highs and lows of a financial roller coaster. At first, we were a lower-middle-class immigrant family. When my mother joined forces with Bill Levitt, we became wealthy as they built Levittowns in the US and beyond. In stark contrast, when I worked as a therapist in the South Bronx I was immersed in the other extreme: abject poverty. The South Bronx was the poorest and most dangerous community in the country at the time.

Wealth didn't attract me: I was interested in people, not material things. Money separated people, while the poverty I saw in the South Bronx brought them together. People there were generous with each other as they all tried to survive. Survival was also my goal, so I bonded with both my colleagues and patients.

* * *

I'm an intense person. I was born that way, and losses I experienced as a child and adolescent amplified that part of me. I lived each day on high alert. That intensity set me apart in my family, but it made me determined to succeed no matter what, in athletics, in my work, and above all, in my quest to figure out the mystery of family. It drove me, and I'm glad it did. Without it, I wouldn't be here today.

When I went to the South Bronx to work, I fit right in. Everybody there had to strike that same high chord to survive amid the all-out chaos. You never knew what the next moment would bring, but you did know it would grab your attention.

* * *

Growing up, I was plagued by questions. Why was my mother never there for me? Why did my father leave suddenly without any warning? Who was that man who came to visit my mother? He said he was a friend of hers, but she didn't explain. She just told us to call him "Uncle Bill." Why did my mother have my grandmother's body taken away in the middle of the night right after she died? Why couldn't I have said goodbye to her? And why did they sell our house and get rid of our childhood belongings a couple of weeks later to move far away while my sister and I were in camp? In my family, the parts never fit together, like a random trunk or misplaced leg. These mysteries drove me to find the whole elephant.

Now I have answers to those relentless questions about family—not only my own—and I can ratchet down the intensity. I discovered why my family fell apart, and on a larger scale, I learned how people function in all kinds of groups, no matter the size. What I learned goes way beyond what I set out to understand, and it's important information for everybody, not just me. So I'm including it in this memoir with the hope it will be helpful to readers. Human groups of all sizes are becoming more complex, and people need help navigating through these complexities.

If you grew up in a family plagued by serious problems, like repeated losses, chronic illnesses, addictions, or the death of children, reading about my quest to understand my own family's problems may bring you useful information and some measure of comfort. In my case, culture played a role. The core pattern in my situation was loss and pain in a British culture that doesn't deal with either. My grandparents left England with no chance of going back; the pain of that loss of connection caused repercussions through the next generations.

* * *

My search for answers to questions about family introduced me to fractals, which are repetitions of the same design appearing in different sizes in the same larger structure. Fractals appear in nature: one example is the way blood vessels branch from major arteries to capillaries. I realized that human behavior functions with fractal-like similarity in groups of all sizes, and this discovery led me to create a way to solve complex problems that I call the "Fractal Model of Relationships." I believe this model can solve even our largest problems, including the ones threatening our existence. Humans behave the same way in complex families, workplaces, governments, and nations. Knowing how the smallest group—the family—functions leads to an understanding of human behavior in all types of different settings. This is critically important, because solving our major problems depends on it.

It's this discovery that human behavior is the same in all complex settings that compelled me to write a memoir, thinking that my life story could convey the knowledge I want to share. It's a different perspective, a new way of thinking about the threatening problems that confront us from every direction.

* * *

Our current situation calls for bluntness. We humans are not going to have a future if we don't learn to behave differently—if we don't get beyond our ignorance, greed, and aggression. We're killing our planet, the only place we can live. There is no planet B. All over the world, people aware of the danger are desperate for solutions. The doomsday clock is ticking closer to midnight. We can't stop the minute hand or push it backwards without understanding how to solve the complex problems we face.

But in spite of the despair and sense of hopelessness many people feel, I know there are solutions. My life and work experiences point the way forward. Without these experiences, I wouldn't have learned what I did. That knowledge is like the jewels on an Indian elephant dressed up to carry a Maharaja. It is treasure, and I want to give it away—to everyone.

There ARE ways out of the mess we're in, and it's up to us ordinary people to lead the way. Governments can't do it: they're stuck. My suggestions for bringing about massive change are in the final chapter, but they won't succeed without broad participation. We've never faced problems of this magnitude and level of complexity before, and we need everybody to become engaged.

Here is what we must do: we must bring a vast majority of people everywhere into a commitment to hold the planet and all the life it sustains as their highest value. This has to be our goal. If we miss the mark, we're headed for all-out destruction.

Chapter 1:

The Lure of Chaos

And what, Socrates, is the food of the soul?
Surely, I said, knowledge is the food of the soul.
—**Plato**

My family was a mystery to me, and I was driven to figure it out.
I knew it was different. I knew it wasn't the way it should be, but
nobody talked about it. Nobody talked about anything momentous
in my family. Important things happened, and nobody said a word.
That Indian parable about the elephant always resonated with me.
My life was my elephant, and I was a blind person trying to figure
out the parts, running my hands over its huge surface as far as I could
reach, limited in my abilities to completely perceive it. With all the
affluence I grew up in, there was also a poverty under the surface.
What was really going on? How did my family function? What was
my role in it? And most importantly, how could I heal it?

* * *

Me in the 1980s

My World Expands

It was 1982 and I was married with children when I offered my services as a Spanish-speaking family therapist at a neighborhood clinic in the South Bronx.

The South Bronx? In 1982? It was the most broken community in the city, and possibly in the country. Why would someone like me want to go there? Why would *anyone* want to go there? With my wealthy background—how could I fit in and what did I have to gain? Not salary.

My mentor at the Ackerman Institute for Family Therapy where I worked suggested I write to the Morrisania Neighborhood Family Care Center in the South Bronx to offer to work unpaid. I didn't need a salary. He knew they could use some help. They finally responded weeks after I wrote and gave me a date for an interview.

I wanted to work with Spanish-speaking immigrants, and this was the only opportunity suggested. But even if there were many, I would choose this one. My intense curiosity and determination always drove me forward, and those were stronger than any reservations I had about taking this job.

I had strong reasons for doing this. I saw it as a test: my training to be a family therapist was now finished, and if I could succeed in the South Bronx, I could succeed anywhere. Still more important, I wanted to know if I was as good a therapist as I thought I was even though I failed at helping my own family. The South Bronx was also beyond the reach of my parents' influence.

What I didn't anticipate was that this place, generally feared by people with backgrounds like mine, would be where I finally felt at home.

I was anxious about the interview. They took a long time to respond to my offer, which might mean they were reticent to consider me, and I also knew I would be thoroughly scrutinized. Spanish was like a second language to me, but would my Spanish be good enough? Furthermore, I knew my family didn't want me to work in such a dangerous place, and if I got the job, they'd keep the pressure on. That's how they were. I was breaking all the family and cultural rules to even consider this possibility. But I made the clinic a good offer—I was well trained, spoke the language, and was willing to work for free. So maybe I had a chance.

Jorge, our handyman, drove me there. We left my home in Sands Point, Long Island, and as we drove into the Bronx, I realized I'd never spent time in this part of the city—I knew just being there was especially dangerous for someone like me, a young, wealthy, White woman. I looked at the hollow buildings as we drove by. I saw inside through the gaping holes that were windows before the buildings burned. Clearly, for the people living there, this was a war-torn community full of loss. Looking down the street, destruction and desolation marked everything, from the stroller left on the street corner to the cars beside the curb with no tires. This was about as different from Sands Point as could be—in my house you could stand in the living room and look out through a glass wall at the sun setting over Manhattan. I told Jorge to drop me a block from the entrance and then come back to pick me up in an hour and a half. The last thing I needed was for people to see me get out of a chauffeured car.

Here I was, on the precipice. Jorge let me out two blocks away, and I went up to the doors. The entrance led into a huge open foyer with a high ceiling. I walked into a sea of people of color and tons of children playing and dancing, all kinds of movement everywhere, and suddenly, as if someone yelled, "Freeze!" it stopped. And they stared. I felt as if I had walked into a foreign country; I smiled and asked where the mental health department was, and they pointed upstairs. When I got there, I approached the receptionist and said I had an appointment with Myrtle Parnell. She smiled and said that Myrtle would be with me shortly.

As soon as I sat down, a man wearing a dress came over, sat next to me, and whispered in my ear in Spanish that he was a Russian spy. It was an out of body experience. "What do I do with all this?" I thought.

Then Myrtle appeared, and though she was smiling, I noticed her eyes were cold. She said, "Maybe we'll go out to the garden. It's nice out. I have a colleague who's Puerto Rican who'll be joining us." That was Elsie. It was the best interview I ever had: they both asked terrific questions and the conversation flowed. Myrtle was clearly in charge. Of the two, Elsie was more open, and she could see I was bi-lingual. Speaking Spanish was a requirement because there was a shortage of Spanish-speaking clinicians all over the city. Myrtle wanted to be sure I was self-sufficient: in this setting everybody had to be. Later she told me she was apprehensive about hiring me because they "didn't need any board ladies coming in to tell everybody how to do their job." They needed someone who wouldn't be deterred by serious problems—someone who could succeed in this tough setting. Working at Morrisania would be a trial by fire, that was clear. The self-possession and competence emanating from these two women reassured me. Was this clinic a real antidote to the chaos outside?

There was one thing about Myrtle: when she wasn't pleased, her face was blank. It was as if someone pulled a curtain over her eyes. They had absolutely no life in them. That's how she looked when she first came out to get me, but by the end of our conversation, she was more relaxed. She gave me a start date for a full-time, one-year position with no salary: September 3, 1982.

I had the position I wanted! But nobody at home was happy about it. That night my family rented the movie, "Fort Apache, the Bronx" to discourage me from going. The morning of my first day, my husband and two daughters—Fred, Katie, and Pam—were a united front; they were all worried about what I was doing, and Fred was angry I was going ahead with it. My parents were also opposed. In fact, police officers from the NYPD sent a message to my parents through a friend that I shouldn't take that job because there were places in that borough where even the cops didn't want to go. I was the only one in the entire family who thought this job was a great idea. This was not a good sendoff.

Years later I realized the unconscious reason my family didn't want me to work in the South Bronx. Loss. There had been a lot of that in my family, and they didn't want to risk losing me. My mother wanted me to become a physical trainer: a nice, safe occupation.

When I decided to get a graduate degree at the NYU School of Social Work, she didn't speak to me for over a year.

My family wasn't wrong about the risk; this job would put me in the red-hot center of a massive meltdown that was the Bronx. I was joining the therapy team in the crisis room at Morrisania, which was an affiliate of Montefiore Hospital. I would be working closely with Myrtle, who was the team leader, and alongside the other members of the team: Elsie Maldonado, other therapists, the community resources staff, and Dr. Don Brown, who was the Director of Psychiatry.

In the Midst of The Chaos, I Land Running

My first day at Morrisania was unforgettable. I drove myself there, got my car in the lot shortly before 9 a.m., and went inside. I would find out later it was a full moon: they were hanging from the rafters; you couldn't put another person anyplace. Many were in severe emotional distress. Out of the chaos walked Myrtle. I still remember her first words: "I hate to do this to you, but we have a woman who's psychotic and Spanish-speaking only; we have no more offices and nowhere to put her, and Dr. Brown asked me if you'd be willing to do an assessment right here in the hall and see what's needed, and we'll take it from there." I had no place to put my jacket and purse and no idea where my office would be or what I should do with this woman.

I gulped hard, because the woman was wailing and pulling her hair out in clumps, and there was all this other confusion in the hall. It was wild. This was my first introduction to real chaos, but it was only the beginning. None of the professional skills I learned at NYU were up to the tasks I would be asked to handle.

I just did my thing with this woman. She was psychotic and needed to be medicated, so I brought her to Don Brown, and in my nervousness, I didn't give her an appointment to come back. I went over to the reception area, which was totally cluttered, and Epi, the receptionist, said, "What are you looking for?" I said, "I'm looking for the Bronx telephone book." She asked me what for. I told her. She looked at me and said, "First of all, the Bronx is a very large borough with a very small telephone book. Second, her name will not be in it. She probably doesn't have a phone, and if she does, it's not listed in that book."

Who's Who?

The rest of the day was a blur, but I do remember they gave me an office—an office to share—and everyone said this other woman, Yvette, and I would be great together. Then they bring over this person, this other therapist: she was a White woman with wild salt and pepper hair, a French accent, and little feet that moved quickly for someone her size. From my perspective, I wondered what made them think this is a perfect match? Then Yvette went out to lunch, and I was briefly in the waiting area when a man walked by with a little beanie on his head and a portfolio like a model would have. I wondered if this was a patient or a staff member, and it occurred to me that I couldn't tell who was who. Next, an Italian woman, I think in her thirties, wearing jeans, came into my office and said, "Who are you?" I introduced myself and she asked if I'm new. I said yes, and she asked if I wanted some of her lunch, which was a bag of corn chips, and this woman was practically in my lap. Then she went out the door and said she's going to the roof. I thought, "If she's a patient, she might jump off." It was unnerving, but later Myrtle told me there was no way to get to the roof.

* * *

I remember that at the end of that first day at Morrisania, I met my husband and another couple at the Four Seasons restaurant in Manhattan. I felt like I was coming from a war zone, even though it was just a half hour away from the restaurant, and in this Four Seasons world, nobody knew anything about that war or that world. I was angry with every White person, but before I went to Morrisania, I, too, knew nothing about that world and that war zone. Nowadays we're all aware of it to one extent or another, but some people can afford to turn away and pretend it isn't happening. Some just don't care at all. At that earlier time, the South Bronx was the canary in the coal mine. Now the coal mine is everywhere.

Before I left for the Four Seasons, I went downstairs to get a parking permit for my car. Morrisania provided subway tokens to patients who couldn't afford them so they could get to the clinic. Two Spanish-speaking women were in the line to get their tokens, and I realized they couldn't read or write. They had to sign an X on the form to get their tokens. I had never met anyone before who couldn't read or write, but it was common in the South Bronx. Yvette told me later that influenced how therapists talked to their patients.

I was at Morrisania for only one day when I joined Fred and our friends for that dinner in Manhattan, but already I felt a strong allegiance to the clinic and strangely, to the South Bronx. Yes, it was dangerous there. The clinic had all sorts of rules to protect the staff, like you couldn't go into the community alone—you always had to be with at least one other staff member and sign out and in. Poverty breeds crime, and this community had disintegrated into extreme poverty, so yes, it was dangerous.

One would think fear would dominate my feelings about being there. It did not. I certainly took seriously my need to be careful, but I had to be careful my entire life. I grew up in a British "take no prisoners" culture, and I always had to meet its high standards.

Chaos isn't always as crazy, loud, and disorganized as it was in the South Bronx. Even when you live in a quiet, orderly environment with bountiful resources, things not said or done can stir up chaotic thoughts and feelings. When you're a child and nobody says a word when emotionally charged, life-altering things happen, you're left alone in a threatening wilderness. You sense imminent danger hiding everywhere under the surface—such a contrast to the veneer of normal orderliness around you. So fear was part of a familiar landscape, which left me free to focus on other responses to this new environment.

I have been intense and active my entire life, but during my childhood, no one else radiated that kind of energy. Here at Morrisania they did. It was everywhere around me. These people were alive! I loved it! They affirmed me. I resonated and connected with them. I knew their emotions because they were mine as well: the fear, the hypervigilance, the attention to nuance and subtlety. I was home; I knew it at once, despite the barriers.

Intensity is an important ingredient in my biological, psychological, and physical makeup. It's who I am. It made me different not only from other members of my family, but also from most of the people I encountered in my life. But I wasn't different from the people in the South Bronx! When I felt the energy there I felt at home for the first time ever. I immediately became a mother bear ready to protect this clinic and the people it served, which fueled my somewhat irrational anger at all the White people at the Four Seasons.

And I was determined, absolutely determined, to show Don Brown, Myrtle Parnell, and Elsie Maldonado that I could do this job very, very well.

* * *

That first day on the job I had a hard time distinguishing patients from staff. Staff didn't wear uniforms; everyone dressed casually. Velma, one of the community resources staff members, often came to work without teeth, wearing wild hats and occasionally her fluffy pink bedroom slippers. It didn't take long to discover she was a powerful asset. Another community resources person was a member of the Young Lords. He was about 40 and was a minister in the Santeria religion, a synthesis of the Yoruba religion of West Africa and Catholicism, popular in the Dominican Republic. He was a great guy but could also be a troublemaker. Staff members felt threatened if they found a feather on their desk; but since the cleaning staff used feather dusters, it could have come from that. He kept a glass of water on his desk to protect himself from evil spirits.

Later I found out the man with the beanie worked there and the woman with the corn chips was a patient. We ended up working with her, and she was off the wall. Myrtle later told me it was extra wild my first day because many of the staff were on vacation, and there was a peak number of people coming into the clinic. And then, of course, there was that full moon.

*   *   *

The crisis room was where patients came when they didn't have an appointment. They registered with the receptionist and then sat in the waiting room until a therapist came to usher them into their office. After finishing with one client or family, a therapist would go to the waiting room and decide who to bring in next. There were no time limits on sessions. To be effective in helping our patients deal with the extremely grave problems they confronted, we absolutely needed that time flexibility.

One day early on, Myrtle suggested I take two siblings nobody else wanted to deal with. They were a brother and sister, each close to six feet tall and each weighing probably 300 pounds. They were drunk and arguing violently, shouting at each other and making menacing gestures. These two patients would have been threatening to anybody. Although I was taught it was best for a therapist to sit close to the door in case they needed to make a hasty exit when dealing with potentially violent patients, my office structure prevented that. I was also told when I was being hired that each office had a panic button, but after I started my job there, I discovered that the buttons weren't connected to anything.

As I called these two patients into my office, Myrtle and I shared a look, and I left the door open. They were still arguing loudly, so I raised the volume of my voice to get their attention. I began loudly but calmly talking to them. As they started to listen to me, I gradually lowered my voice, keeping a calm tone. I couldn't help them solve their problem, but I de-escalated their conflict and brought them back to a normal level of conversation. Then they were ready to go on their way. As they left, Myrtle came in and asked me if I was trying to get help with them. When I told her I was, she said, "You have to come out and say it. You need to be obvious about it. There's so much going on here, you can't be subtle. We all help each other when we need to." That was good advice I never forgot.

Like Sisters

Myrtle, Elsie, and I went on to bond together like sisters, an odd little group. I came from a first-generation British family with a wealthy Jewish adoptive father; Myrtle was African American from a blue-collar family; and Elsie was Puerto Rican and grew up in abject poverty. During my first months at the clinic, Myrtle and Elsie kept close tabs on me in an unobtrusive way to make sure I was OK. Myrtle said she didn't want me to experience what she went through in social work school, where she was the only Black person in the agency during her placement. No one seemed to care how she was doing, no one checked in with her, and no one ever mentioned she was the only Black person. So, knowing how bad that was, she didn't want me to feel the same way.

Climbing with Myrtle, 1988

What pulled us together was our shared commitment to social work and our passion for helping the patients who lived in the terrible conditions of the South Bronx. As the crisis room's team leader, Myrtle had a strong vested interest in making sure my externship at the clinic worked. Early on, we talked about our cases, and I was very curious about how Myrtle saw things.

Then we sat in on each other's sessions, informally. But right from the beginning, the race issue was there, and Myrtle and I began to work through it. When I wanted to have a conversation with Myrtle, I'd go in and start talking about all this theoretical family therapy stuff, and I'd go on and on.

One day she said to me, "What are you doing? Are you trying to put me down or what? What's the purpose of what you're saying?"

I said, "Well, I'm just having a conversation. That's what we talk about."

She said, "Not me. I'm not interested in all that stuff. If I don't know who you are, I'm not interested in what you think about those things."

I was stunned. I didn't think I was doing anything to make her feel bad. I certainly wasn't trying to put her down. She knew more than I did. She'd been in the field much longer. I was trying to have a conversation in my typical White style, which was around abstract things that were out there, distant from the personal, rather than touching on things up close.

We were not good friends at this point. Later we realized we were acting out the cultural dictates of our racial and class identities. In general, Whites, especially from the middle and upper classes, like to start way at the outside and work their way in when they don't know people well. Blacks like to start by getting to know other people first and build relationships; then they talk about things less central.

Myrtle explained that because we worked with mostly Blacks and Hispanics, it was insulting for me—a White woman—to talk about our work from a theoretical and academic perspective when she lived it. She also told me she thought, and Elsie agreed, that Whites historically went into the Black and Latino communities and studied people like bugs under a microscope and then went and wrote about them.

She said, "You've studied us to death and haven't changed a damn thing, so why don't you just stop studying. It's like every generation has to come and do the same studies."

In a long, sometimes turbulent partnership, Myrtle and I learned so much about how cultural dictates make or break relationships.

Something happened during those early months that illuminates the relationship I formed with Myrtle and Elsie, and even Yvette. They assigned me to work with an extremely bright young African American woman, Sherelle, who was a police officer, and while they were supervising me, they were letting me work with her pretty much on my own. I told them about our sessions and so far, they were excited about what I did with her.

However, one day Sherelle showed up and started wreaking havoc in the clinic. Don Brown got involved and went after Myrtle, Elsie, and Yvette, asking them how they were supervising me. This disturbance shouldn't have happened, not if I were properly supervised. Then Yvette asked me point blank, "What didn't you tell us about her?" I had described her behavior to them, but I downplayed the seriousness of her symptoms. What set her off was that she wanted to see me and couldn't take no for an answer when they told her I was busy. She went bananas.

This blow up (that's how I thought of it) devastated me. I felt terrible that my colleagues were chastised because of my omission. I didn't sleep that night and kept wondering how I could show up the next morning. I was upset with myself beyond belief, not about my treatment of my patient, but because Myrtle, Elsie, and Yvette felt I betrayed them by putting them in an awkward situation. Unconsciously, I was protecting my patient by not disclosing her worst tendencies. That was wrong-headed in this situation where the therapists, in that dangerous environment, knew their lives could depend on everyone knowing the full picture of the patients they

CHAPTER 1: THE LURE OF CHAOS

dealt with. I was confident about my work with Sherelle. I just hadn't realized how important it was to share everything with my colleagues.

The next morning, I got there early as usual, went in, and dragged myself down the hall. There were Myrtle and Elsie sitting in my office with a huge bouquet of flowers, waiting for me. I couldn't take that in. I didn't know where to put that, and I probably didn't truly thank them then. I was startled, confused, and overwhelmed. In my world, when you make a mistake, people don't let you forget it—they beat you up endlessly.

In this beautiful world where I now worked, it was understood that everyone makes mistakes, and because relationships were so important, you supported your friend or colleague when they got something wrong. You didn't devour them. My colleagues valued my work with Sherelle—my intense amount of care and concern with her—and they respected my abilities even though I was a new therapist. I couldn't be appropriately appreciative at the time because I didn't understand what happened. Later we l talked about it. It was a huge deal to me.

This was such a big contrast with my harsh, unsympathetic culture, where you weren't allowed to make mistakes.

*   *   *

What a relief it was to find myself in a world where everything was real and alive! Until I got there, I didn't realize I'd spent my life holding my breath. In my family, the British rules and the hidden emotions were like a strait jacket. My survival strategy as a child was to be quietly defiant when I could get away with it and to play as many sports as I could. That quiet side of chaos is a killer. I'd tell you to go ask my sister about it, but she died young.

The South Bronx expanded my world immeasurably. It was as if I left a gray place and found color everywhere. Here people showed you how they felt; they talked about their feelings; and they didn't mince words. Here people cared about each other. You're in trouble? I'll help you. And when I'm in trouble, you'll help me. We staff members did that too. If our patients needed a loan, we'd give it to them, and they'd pay us back. And bring us presents. It seems ironic that I found the home I was looking for in the war-torn South Bronx, after leaving my life full of big houses, chauffeurs, and private planes.

My experiences in this beautiful, broken, loudly chaotic, disintegrating community were one part of the elephant. I'd found its trunk and mouth! It fed me, and the sound of its trumpeting was loud and clear. That trunk smelled nourishment, and it smelled danger. And when it smelled danger, it let everyone know.

Chapter 2:

What's Wrong with my Family?

"The night is always darkest before the dawn."
–John Galsworthy

"It is during our darkest moments that we must focus to see the light."
–Aristotle

It Started When I Was One

~ I am a one-year-old, and I'm practicing how to walk. I took my first steps three months ago. I'm holding on to a huge wooden thing, stepping sideways carefully, with my hands on the rim. The grownups aren't talking much. Nanny is quiet. My mother just sits. My grandfather isn't here. I feel the heaviness all around me. ~

This is my earliest memory: I can revisit the confusion I felt holding onto my grandfather's coffin, with my mother already retreating into herself, and my grandmother absorbed in her grief in her stolid British way. My mother was close to her father, but not her mother. As my mother melted away into some distant, vacant place, I began to rely only on my grandmother, my most steadfast source of light and strength in the dark world of World War II.

When I was born on May 23, 1940, in Queens, New York, World War II was beginning to tear Europe apart, but the US had yet to join in the fight. Nevertheless, everyone in this country felt its threat. Queens was a dark and depressing New York City borough at that time. My family lived in one of the small two-family houses crowded close together on our street. Inside the house it was cold and dark during the winter months. In the evening, as soon as night began to fall, my mother and grandmother pulled down the blackout shades and turned on the dim lights. They didn't want any light to seep outside—houses had to be invisible at night.

I remember the coal stove in the kitchen, my grandmother lighting the fire and the way it smelled, and the fumes from the coal furnaces in our neighbors' houses. Trains whistled as they slowed down to pass through our neighborhood, trailing their smoke. In the nearby harbor, foghorns blasted, trying to protect us against the German submarines. I didn't understand what was going on, but I absorbed those sounds and smells along with the grownups' fear and tension. The train whistles and foghorn blasts embodied that fear for me. I was terrified every night alone in the dark. Later in my life I always made sure to be surrounded by light; I think this comes from the darkness of these early years.

I have a visceral memory of the tension in our house before my father left for the war. The nightly blackouts and the siren announcing them made me feel helpless and vulnerable. I was so afraid that I would lie in bed holding my eyes open trying not to sleep, and I needed to have the door open. Later, when as an adult, married with children, I lived on the water in Sands Point, NY, the foghorn on the nearby lighthouse triggered that latent fear.

I felt alone during this early time in my life because people in my family were either not there or busy. My father left to fight in the war when I was two, and after he left, my mother was often out. When I understood that my grandfather had died, I was afraid my grandmother would follow. I somehow knew she wasn't in good health, and she was my everything. Around the time my father left, my sister, Mac, was born, and she cried a lot and was often sick.

Children know how dependent they are on adults, and it can be terrifying when they understand their parents are missing in action. Thank goodness for my grandmother. She was the only one who was there. Shadows of these early impressions of loneliness, sadness, and fear stayed with me and are present even now, despite all my training and work.

It took a physical toll on me then as well. While my father was at war, I was sick a lot. I had pneumonia when I was five and couldn't keep any food down. I heard the grownups worriedly talking about me, so I knew they thought it wasn't likely I'd make it past my current age. Even at that young age, I knew people could disappear because of my grandfather's dying. I was too young to understand what death was, but it seemed to cause generalized fear and anxiety to those around me. I remember being in my bed in a dark room, with the doctor sitting beside me on one of my little chairs. I later learned he gave me penicillin, which was just then available for non-military use. My fever broke; I remember him saying to my grandmother and mother: "She's going to make it."

Aspects of my childhood increased the intensity I was born with. The coldness and loneliness, my parents' absence, along with the generalized fear—all these added anxiety to that intensity. Pneumonia was another layer: it made me aware of my own mortality, my fragility.

* * *

Then on a special fall day in 1945, I felt as if the darkness blew away. I was five years old, and it was beautiful and sunny. My mother, my grandmother, my sister, and I were driving on the Northern State Parkway through Long Island, and it was jammed, which *never* happened. I could see the cars on the road so close together I thought people could walk across their tops. We left Queens and were headed toward the city. It was a big, big day, and I was excited. When we

33

arrived at the place where the ship docked, there were hordes of people, and everyone was as excited as I was. After we stopped in an endless line of cars, I ran and crawled under the ropes to get to where the ship was. A policeman stopped me and said, "Honey, you can't go there." "But my daddy's on that ship," I told him.

The ship was the USS Missouri, just back from Tokyo Bay where it was the site of Japan's surrender at the end of WWII. It was in New York to participate in the Navy Day celebrations. Of course there were speeches, and the sailors couldn't leave the ship right away, so we went home to wait.

The next thing I remember is all the men in uniform running down our street, and I had no idea which one was my daddy. He was gone three years, and I remember thinking, "A little girl should know who her daddy is." Little did I know that would become a lifelong question.

My father, Bill Habermehl, was finally home. Now I had a daddy again, in addition to my mother, Alice Habermehl; my Nanny, Mary Kenny (my mother's mother); my sister, Mac; and our black and white cocker spaniel, Kilroy.

This was my little family before all the complexity that came later. But looking back, I can see the seeds of that complexity already in place when I was very young. It never really felt like a family to me. Instead, it seemed more like a random bunch of people somehow thrown together. That becomes even more clear when I think about each member of my family as if they were characters in a play.

My Parents, Supporting Actors; Nanny, The Star

Which came first, my mother's silence about anything distressful or her depression? I believe that in some ways, she never recovered from the shock of her father's death when she was only 24, when the US was being drawn into the war. She retreated so far into herself she never completely emerged again. I think that trauma prevented her from seeing me as her daughter. Many years later she told me she always thought of me as her younger sister. She left the parenting up to my grandmother, and only with Nanny did I have an emotional bond. My mother observed me from a distance, detached it seemed, as if she were regarding a piece of furniture that sometimes needed to be moved around. Was it the trauma of her father's death that kept her from ever discussing anything emotionally threatening? Or was her silence also due to the British culture she grew up in?

The war pushed many young lovers into early marriages they might have postponed otherwise. I'm sure my parents' extended separation during that time damaged their relationship. My mother must have been devastated when my father joined the Marines and left soon after her father died, while she was so depressed. During his absence, she grew out of their marriage as she built a life on her own, and when my father returned three years later, my sister and I were strangers to him. My mother was focused on her job at Sperry's doing war-related work and then in a better job as a secretary at Levitt & Sons, a real estate development company on Long Island. These jobs gave her a sense of her independence and ability to take on responsibilities. Through work I think she saw a way out of the gloom surrounding her life in Queens. Perhaps she saw my father as an extension of the part of her life she wanted to leave behind.

However, for me, our family was a lot livelier when my father was with us. He hadn't been back from the war long when I remember he came home in his car with some friends one night and parked it in the garage. He didn't realize a lighted cigarette was left in the car. An hour later it seemed like the whole place was on fire. My father ran to get into the car and drive it out, and my mother yelled at him, "Don't get in that car or you'll explode, too!" My sister and I were put in our room so we couldn't see what was happening, and Nanny stayed with us. The fire department came, pulled the car out of the garage, and put out the fire. It all worked out: my father didn't get hurt and our house didn't burn down.

After he came home, my father and I got to know each other again. I loved being with him! He would dance with me on his shoulders and sing with his beautiful voice. He could charm the spots off a leopard with his warm smile and twinkling eyes. I had never known such happiness.

When my father was home for a while, I went to church with him every week, which was expected for the eldest child of a Catholic father. He was always late, which for some reason made the nuns angry with *me*. I also went to Catholic school, but not for long. The Church had a deleterious effect on me. I became terrified; I was saying prayers all the time, and I was afraid of the nuns. I wasn't eating or sleeping, so my mother took me out of the school. But I was still supposed to go to church on Sunday, and I made my first holy Communion.

However, after a time, I went to bed one night and said to myself, and to God if he was listening, "I'm not going to say another prayer, and if I'm dead in the morning, that's ok." I woke up in the morning, somewhat amazed and quite happy with myself. And as weeks went by, I thought I was really on to something. After that I went to the Episcopal church with Nanny, which calmed me. I even carried the cross for the children's services and sang in the choir. I loved going to this church with her. It was beautiful with its pageantry and uplifting music. And Nanny was happy to have me with her. It reinforced the bond between us. The Episcopal Church became emblematic of my grandmother to me.

My experiences with Catholicism set up a dynamic between me and religion that played out in later stages of my life. I told no one about my little experiment with God. In spite of turning my back on Catholicism, I believed the concept of an almighty power, and religious services with my grandmother were fulfilling as long as I could go with her.

I don't think my father was angry about me not going to church with him anymore. I think he understood; he had an easy-going personality.

Enter Bill Levitt

Bill Levitt came into my mother's life after she started working at his family's company. He returned from the war when my father did; he was in the Seabees. When he met my mother, he decided he wanted her to be *his* secretary.

Some months after the war ended, I learned we were moving into a new house in Albertson, a small town in Nassau County, Long Island. A house was being built for us there. When we finally moved into it, the exterior hadn't been landscaped yet. One day I was sitting in the dirt behind the house, and a nice man came around the corner and said, "Hi honey. Is your mommy home?" I said she was, and he said, "I'm a friend of hers." Enter Bill Levitt, who was to become father number two. My mother told my sister and me to call him "Uncle Bill." After a while, we knew that term of address was a mask over something complicated. He was much more than an "uncle."

We lived there for several years, and during that time, another new house was built for us in Old Westbury, a town about 10 miles away. The few years we spent living in Albertson were an important time because of what happened there.

And Just Like That...

When I think of that house, I remember coming home from school one sunny day when I was six and running into the house. We had lived there for only six months at the time. Suddenly, I knew: my father was gone. I ran upstairs to my parents' bedroom, threw open the doors to their closet, and saw that all his things were gone. No one said anything to us children. This was my first experience of the pattern of adults not sharing important information with my sister and me. I later came to realize this kind of non-communication is a clear sign of a broken family system. Not talking about serious things that were about to happen or had already happened generated a state of anxiety and hypervigilance in me; it eroded my trust in most adults.

Even though he disappeared, I knew my father loved me and my sister, Mac. After he no longer lived with us, and when my mother's relationship with Bill Levitt became firmly established, my father occasionally tried to see us. We went to a small public elementary school on Long Island. I liked it, but there was one troubling thing: my father tried to come at lunch time to give me money. Nobody else's father did that. My friends would ask me, "Who was that?" While I was happy he hadn't forgotten me, I was embarrassed when he showed up at my school. Divorce wasn't commonplace during that time, so what was I going to say? I don't know if he was doing the same thing with my sister because I never talked to her about it.

With him being gone and my family reorganized around Bill Levitt and his business of home building, I didn't get to know my father until much later, after I became an adult. I didn't even know much about him, so when I realized he didn't have many years left to live, I tried to get to know him better.

When he was in his elder years, I asked him to tell me what his childhood was like. In response, he wrote me a long letter describing his life. He gave it to Carol, his eldest daughter from his second marriage, who was intensely jealous of me. She kept that letter a secret; I didn't know it existed until I received a typed version of it from my youngest half-sister, Lizzie, just a few years ago, about a quarter of a century after he wrote it. In it he talks about how the sudden death of my grandfather "left a terrible scar on [Alice's] life which she never quite overcame." And he describes how my grandfather was laid out in his house (in the coffin I was holding onto when I was one year old). He said that after the funeral he took my mother and me on a trip to Virginia Beach to help us forget. He was a lovely, kind, and thoughtful man.

He also described in his letter how he met my mother. When she was in her late teens, she met my father during activities in a Catholic Club for boys and girls; they felt a mutual attraction. In that letter, my father describes going to my grandparents' house to ask if he could take my mother out on a date. He said, "I knocked on the door and her father answered. He was very gruff and asked me what I wanted. I told him that I would like to take his daughter out. He said he didn't think so and closed the door."

I remember more about this: I remember hearing that my father was wearing a shirt and a bathing suit when he went to ask permission to take my mother out and my grandfather told my father to go home and put his clothes on. My father probably didn't know any better, and my grandfather probably thought my mother could do better than that. But my father went on to say that a week later, my mother and her sister threw a scavenger hunt and invited him. "Alice and I were paired together for the hunt. When we came back, I spent most of the evening in the kitchen discussing politics with her father. After this session he gave his permission for me to date his daughter. This was the start of a very special time in my life."

Later in the letter, he also described how he felt about my mother's relationship with Bill Levitt. He said, "…I discovered accidentally that Bill Levitt was in love with Alice… I can understand in retrospect how this happened. There was a Village Bath Club which was owned by Levitt & Sons. This contained a fine restaurant which served the community. They had a swimming pool attached to it. You could dine and overlook the pool if you so desired.

"Alice would take the children over so that they could use the kiddy pool. I was working seven days a week so naturally I could not accompany her. I was devastated by what had happened, but I have always been a fatalist. Gradually I began to accept things as they were. I did not blame Alice. Bill Levitt in addition to his wealth could be a very charming individual. Very few women would have been able to resist the temptation. He was alive and I am afraid I was very dull."

That was my birth father being self-deprecating. He certainly was not dull: like Bill Levitt, he was also a charming man, but he was satisfied with an ordinary life, while Bill Levitt craved the excitement of reaching challenging goals. Bill Habermehl grew up in poverty in a poor neighborhood in New York City, so he accepted their living conditions as normal.

His family lived in an apartment on the second floor of a brownstone building: a hall ran between the two apartments on that floor. Living in that apartment were his mother, father, two half-sisters, two aunts, a cousin and five children. My birth father worked hard to succeed. He mentioned in his letter that when he was growing up, there was no such thing as welfare. He said, "You either worked for what you got or you starved." He found a lot of creative ways to earn money to contribute to his family's income throughout his boyhood and beyond. His notion of success was to earn enough money to support himself and his family in comfort. In contrast to Bill Levitt, my birth father had to scramble throughout his childhood to contribute to his family's earnings; he learned to expect limitations whatever he tried to do.

Bill Levitt, on the other hand, grew up in a middle-class family, and he was determined to become wealthy. He always said he wanted to live like the robber barons. Having started out higher on the income ladder than my birth father, he aspired to far greater achievements. He had an expansive personality, with an interest in everyone and everything. He was filled with optimism about his ability to achieve great things, to push through any barriers he encountered.

Bill Levitt's ambition appealed to my mother. After her father's death, as she emerged from depression, she became restless, and she didn't feel constrained by any attachment to her mother. She and my grandmother were never close. My mother took care of Nanny, but she also used her as a caregiver for my sister and me. I think she longed to break away from the depressing environment in Queens; there was nothing there for her. In contrast, the entire country was opening. It was an exciting time, and Bill Levitt's ambitious, action-oriented personality was in tune with the mood of the country and my mother's goals.

I too resonated strongly with Bill Levitt, and he with me. We were alike: give us a challenge and we couldn't say no. We were both always reaching for something greater. He told me once I couldn't be more like him if I were his biological daughter. However, I was also like my birth father in important ways. He was athletic, finding time to play golf, basketball, and tennis, and succeeding well in all of them even while grasping at every opportunity to earn money. For me, sports were my way of coping when things got tough. Like my birth father, I tried a lot of different sports and succeeded in them all. I'm sure that ability is linked to my genetic inheritance from him.

Both my fathers were kind and generous people, and I loved that in each of them. Bill Levitt hired my birth father to work at Levitt & Sons, and later hired the other members of his family. My birth father writes extensively about Bill Levitt in his letter to me. He says, "Bill Levitt knew that I was unhappy with my former job. He arranged with the man who handled his mortgage business that he give me a job as solicitor for the business." Later he writes, "Several more months passed and one afternoon Bill Levitt came into the rental office and dropped a bombshell. He told me that he wanted me to take over the entire Service Department. He told me that although I wasn't broken in to handle this I was to do my best and if I made mistakes he would back me up." And still later, "At the end of the year I sent a letter to Bill Levitt and reported the good job that had been done and without the help of the service men the job would have been impossible. He responded in his usual fair manner and gave each of the servicemen a very generous increase."

These were my two fathers. I think they genuinely liked each other. I usually refer to Bill Habermehl as my birth father and to Bill Levitt as my father. Two fathers named Bill is just the beginning of my family's growing complexity. My mother always said having two husbands of the same name was a good idea because she couldn't call them by the wrong name.

She Went Her Way, And I Went Mine

My sister, Mac, and I were not at all alike. For one thing, she was outgoing, and I was so introverted I wouldn't even say hello to people. Mac's real name was Mariellen, but she quickly became Mac. (Mac and Jo—can you tell my father wanted sons?) We were only 18 months apart, but it might as well have been 20 years. She was strange right from the beginning, and that's not just my sisterly opinion. She had migraine headaches beginning at age four or five that would completely do her in.

Mac and I always shared a room, which was torture for me. She was very messy, and I was obsessively neat. She threw her clothes on the floor and wore the dirty ones. None of the adults made it clear to her that this was a bad idea or that anything she did was wrong. This is one reason she never got the help she needed. My grandmother was the only one who said anything. When I was nine, I marked a line down the center of our room, and if any of her stuff found its way across it, I tossed it back to her side. Life long, she was messy and disorganized.

Mac and I also responded differently when we were told to do something. Mac could sit there forever and not do what was expected, but I always bent over backwards to avoid the anxiety of no response. My frustration would turn into anger with her because she didn't even try, and she got away with being obstinate. All her acting up worried me: I was terrified Nanny would die, and then my sister would be in big trouble, given our parents' busy lives. Little did I know that would portray the future.

I realize now that Mac couldn't help some of the ways she annoyed me. It seemed to me that whenever we went somewhere to do something exciting, she'd get sick. One time we planned to go to Macy's in the city on the train. I really wanted to go, but she got one of her migraines again and the trip was cancelled. That was typical.

When I was eight and we lived in Albertson, my mother went out one day and left us home alone with our German shepherd. Mac needled me as she always did, so I slugged her and knocked her out. I was on my way to get a bucket of water to revive her so I could knock her out again when our mother came home. I don't remember what happened after that, but the living room was in complete disarray with the furniture upended. Despite wanting to hurt her, I scared myself with my own rage, and I determined this was no way to go. I needed to do better. Shortly after this incident, we moved to Old Westbury.

Another time, Mac pushed me down the stairs. She was like that. She'd pick a fight. She and Jimmy Levitt, Bill Levitt's son who lived with us for a while, got into a slug fest in the bowling alley when they were 17. I want to make this clear: I didn't walk around looking for trouble with my sister. I was always doing my own thing. But I typically got punished if Mac and I got into it. My grandmother tried to treat us equally. Unfortunately, we had different needs, and equal treatment doesn't cut it in that kind of situation.

In some families, parents bend over backwards to treat their children the same to be fair. That can cause major problems when equal treatment is unfair to one. It's better for parents to be in close communication with each of their children, helping them understand they're always paying attention to each child's individual needs.

I somehow intuited how disturbed Mac was, but I couldn't put all the pieces of my family together. I was always helping her, just like I later tried to help Bill Levitt's son, Jimmy. I talked to her, encouraged her, and problem-solved with her, but she became increasingly more unavailable to me. The more I tried to help her and couldn't, the more frustrated I got, because I knew the implications of that were dire.

Recently I became aware of the emotional process I experienced when I tried to help Mac. I got balled up in frustration that then turned to anger toward her. I stayed stuck there for a while, until I realized what was happening. Then I could accept those feelings, but I needed to understand why this was happening. Understanding the behavior doesn't get rid of the pain entirely, but the anger dissipates. Then you can respect the fact that things happen, and that we're all trapped in our behaviors to a certain extent. This awareness gives you a glimpse into the complexity in your life. When you can't understand the behavior, your frustration can lead to repressed anger.

When Mac was 13 years old, she was playing field hockey one day, and the ball hit her in the jaw. It wasn't a terrible injury, but it was bad enough that she was prescribed pain pills. Her physical pain wasn't all that bad, but her emotional pain was enormous; she became addicted and remained so until she died. The drugs sealed the deal: they put a growing distance between me and Mac, and after that injury, I never felt as if I could get through to her. It was another big loss for me, because despite our fights and disagreements, she meant a lot. We'd been together since I was two, and with my family being so fragmented, my sister helped me feel rooted. We depended on one another.

When Mac was an adult and the mother of young children, our parents bought and decorated an apartment for her: sadly, it was typically littered with dirty diapers, toys, dishes, and clothes. Her outward chaotic messiness was a manifestation of her inner turmoil. My sister was mentally ill; her drug addiction was an attempt to cope with the losses and trauma we both experienced. She was what I came to know later as a MICA—a mentally ill, chemically addicted person. Really, the deck was totally stacked against her with all the traumas. She never had a chance. She died at age 46.

Me with Mac, 1970s

Our parents paid a lot of attention to Mac and continually tried to protect her because of her erratic behavior and the chaos she caused in our family. In contrast, they assumed I could take care of myself. Mac was always all over the place, while I focused on achievement, trying to win my parents' approval and recognition, which was rarely expressed because they didn't want Mac to feel jealous. My sister gave me my first experience with chronic mental and physical illness and the way it functions in a family. I'm sure this was one of the factors that propelled me into a career as a family therapist.

When Living Gets Hard, Immigrate

My maternal grandparents, Walter and Mary Kenny, brought English culture rooted in the Victorian era with them when they immigrated to the United States. Our family was a closed circle. My grandparents didn't mix with Americans other than my father: they kept to themselves. They thought Americans were heathens who didn't speak properly.

Nanny never challenged male authority, but under the surface she was the boss. My grandfather, a furniture maker, was smart and a tough guy. During the summers he quit his job and drove the family across the country to get acquainted with it. He was the one who decided he and my grandmother should leave Birmingham to immigrate to North America, leaving her family and their friends behind. Nanny missed them; she knew she wouldn't see them again. Most members of my grandfather's family were no longer living, except for his brother, who immigrated to Canada. My grandfather went with him and stayed there for a few years before going to the US.

My grandfather and his brother ran away because their family fell apart. Their mother, named Mary like Nanny, was in a mental institution; their father, an alcoholic, couldn't handle raising them, so they were put in a boys' school. Subsequently, both my grandfather's parents died within a month of each other when the boys were young teens. The loss issues in their family were great, and families at that time could rarely afford to return home after they immigrated, so there was little discussion of what they left behind. It was too painful.

Walter and Mary Kenny, late 1890s

Nanny's life wasn't easy either. She and my grandfather had their first daughter, Kitty, in England in 1902. One year later, in 1903, my grandfather immigrated alone to Canada, to join his brother, leaving my grandmother and my aunt Kitty with family members in England. Finally, after a six-year separation, my grandmother and Kitty immigrated to the US, arriving in Philadelphia in 1909, where my grandfather joined them. Their next daughter, Agnes, was born in 1913, and my mother in 1917. My grandparents left behind family, friends, and culture.

Aunt Kitty died of osteomyelitis in 1949. I remember seeing her in her hospital bed in her living room making jewelry and plastic crosses with shells. Her sister, my Aunt Agnes, was a 4'10," nervous, volatile person who didn't leave home often and couldn't eat with anyone. She had emotional problems. But she married, had two children, and she and her family later lived in a house on an estate owned by my mother and Bill Levitt.

I should mention that my grandfather banished Aunt Kitty from the family because she violated his command that my mother not be baptized in the Catholic church. He was vehemently opposed to Catholicism; my Aunt Kitty decided it was more important to have her little sister, my mother, baptized in the faith she believed in than to obey her father. After my grandfather found out, he would not allow Kitty in his home and never spoke to her again. When people refer to a "take no prisoners culture," this is the kind of behavior they're referring to.

After my grandfather died, all the burdens in our household fell on Nanny's shoulders. She was challenged by the grief and loneliness of being a widow living far from her original home and the terrible toll the war was taking, particularly on Birmingham, England, which endured the worst bombing in WWII except for Dresden. She also had to cope with my mother's nervous breakdown and then her long workdays, and on top of that, the responsibility for raising me and my sister. When I was about two or three, my mother started leaving for work at seven a.m., and she wouldn't return until midnight. Thus it was that Nanny raised Mac and me. She carried it all without complaint, in the good old English tradition.

When we were older, Mac and I became too much for my grandmother, who was 73 when I was 11. That became obvious, even though we had a live-in English couple working for us who also took care of my grandmother. That couple was good company for us all. At some point, because it got too hard for me to share a room with Mac, I ended up sleeping in the other bed in my grandmother's room.

Her snoring scared me because I was afraid it meant she was dying; the noise of her gasping for air between the snores was terrifying.

My grandmother took on all those responsibilities even though her health was poor. She had a heart condition, which meant she needed rest. It must have been hard for her to put up with the shenanigans of two little girls who didn't get along well a lot of the time. But sometimes Mac and I had fun together. I remember we were playing "going fishing" one day when I was about five and she was about three.

First, we pushed the kitchen chairs away from the counter: they ended up partially blocking the door, but that was unintentional; they were just in our way. We kept one chair near the counter to climb onto it. I climbed up first and pulled Mac up beside me. We used broom handles for our fishing poles, with string tied to the ends. We sat there having a great time when the landlady pushed open the partially barricaded door. She was surprised by what she saw and must have asked why the furniture was pushed all around. I told her we were moving. We weren't of course, but she went back home aghast. Later, when she was ill and dying, I had to go see her with my grandmother to say goodbye. I felt guilty; I thought my little lie was enough to kill her. I can only imagine how my grandmother managed with all the things we did.

During my childhood, Mac and I were two little girls home alone with our elderly grandmother. Even though my mother sometimes hired caregivers, I felt I had to try to manage things because I didn't trust those hired strangers. What did they know? With Mac being difficult and my grandmother old and frail, I had a tremendous concern that we were in a precarious situation. I knew it didn't have to be that way, so I struggled to make things better. In my mind, I was the real caregiver, and the job was endless.

* * *

These were the members of my family. I never felt as if I belonged to this group of people, except to my grandmother. We were all loosely tethered together. By the age of six, I had faced serious challenges, and my life had too many holes in it. First my grandfather died. That loss ricocheted through my family, causing my mother to retreat (my second loss) and deeply affecting my grandmother, who, despite her poor health, had to step in and take charge. My sister arrived, and she claimed some of my grandmother's attention. My father left to fight in the war (my third loss), when I was only two. Then, at age five, I was so sick with pneumonia my mother and grandmother feared for my life. Add to that my disastrous experience in Catholic school, and the fact that six months after the joy of my father's return, he disappeared, and NOBODY EVEN TALKED ABOUT IT. This accumulation of emotional assaults traumatized me, and I became withdrawn and shy, reluctant to speak to anyone outside my family. However, I took my cues from my very British grandmother, my only consistent source of love and affection: she taught me by example that no matter what happens, you keep on keeping on.

I attribute my survival to Nanny. Years later I co-authored a book chapter with Myrtle, who by then was my business partner, about how some children survive traumatic childhoods. Our research, as well as our experience as family therapists, indicated that if a child has one competent, enabling adult in their life (who doesn't have to be a family member), that can be enough support for them to survive. My own experience attests to that: my grandmother was that person. She held my life together before I was old enough to take on that task.

But why did I survive, while my sister, also raised by our loving grandmother, succumbed to drug addiction and chronic illness, both mental and physical? We had the same biological parents and the same adoptive father. Early on, we went to the same schools. Did it make a difference that I was two years older? That I had some time with our father before he went into the war? Probably. But I also think our DNA differed. Our mother was pregnant with Mac while she was suffering from the shock of her father's death, and that may have affected the fetus that became my sister.

The pneumonia I had when I was five deeply affected me. It brought me close to death, but I was lucky to have access to penicillin. I later found out Bill Levitt was able to procure it. In hindsight I believe that illness presented me with two alternatives: to wither and die, succumbing to it, or to find the determination to survive, to hang on to the light, wherever it was coming from, and build myself on that foundation. That determination against the odds made me focus intensely, and it honed the intensity that's been a hallmark of my entire life. Throughout my childhood, I had to pay attention to the subtleties in what was going on around me in the absence of communicated information. I had to become a spy, a detective, a connector of the dots. That would prepare me for my future career.

Because care and affection were shown to me primarily by one person, the importance of that rare commodity was clear. I treasured my grandmother and was determined to safeguard her values. Perhaps that's why I've focused on trying to help others. My grandmother was holding our family together, much the way the matriarch of a tribe of elephants protects the herd and helps adults care for their offspring. She bequeathed that responsibility to me, but for me, it went beyond family. For me, as with a herd of elephants, my extended family includes all the people I'm traveling with through my life. Caring for people became the purpose of my life. Nanny gave me my first glimpse of the whole elephant, of what I was seeking: relationships built out of reciprocal caring and protection—strong, nurturing, authentic relationships in which the well-being of the other person matters deeply.

In my family of origin, I was able to have that type of relationship only with my grandmother, and later, to a lesser extent, with Bill Levitt. No one else was capable of that type of reciprocity.

But I began to learn much more about relationships as I entered the larger worlds of sleep-away camps and schools. And I was able to find the protective guidance of a few other matriarchs along the way.

Chapter 3:

New Adventures—Old Tears

"Where should I go?" – Alice.
"That depends on where you want to end up." – The Cheshire Cat
–Lewis Carroll

Going to camp and school helped me come into my own. Unlike Lewis Carroll's Alice, I didn't choose where to go, but my parents found good places. At that time I had no idea where I wanted to end up; I was just trying to survive. When I was 13, Mac and I were sent to Brown Ledge Camp for Girls in Malletts Bay, Vermont

During my first year, I learned the hard way about the camp's rule that you had to eat whatever you were served. One day, breakfast was Wheatena cereal, which I hated. I wouldn't eat it. I thought it looked like bird food. They told me to sit there until I finished, but somebody had to stay with me. Obviously, they didn't know anything about oppositional people. I sat there all day! This is what I now call a "worser alternative." When evening came, I politely asked if I could eat dinner, and that was the last time anybody there told me what to do.

The Crying Didn't Make Sense, Did It?

While Mac and I were sent to excellent schools and camps, the hard part was leaving home again, and again, and again. I was always going somewhere. Even though home was like a ghost town, I didn't want to leave. Bill Levitt and my mother were busy building Levittowns, and my grandmother was too frail to take care of us full time.

Those leave-takings were so hard I would cry or throw up as we pulled away from home. That went on for years, starting when I was nine and first went away to camp. The big departures were to sleep-away camps almost every summer and boarding school starting when I was 12. Even when we went to a local school, I cried every day when we left home. I couldn't help it, although I knew crying was a violation of our British code of conduct.

Home was difficult, so why would I cry when I was going to a place where I'd have a wonderful time? I almost always did have a wonderful time, because I was learning and growing, finding the courage to talk to people, reveling in sports, getting good grades, and coming into my own.

I think my birth father's ongoing and never-discussed absence and my mother's emotional distance kept me continually aware I was abandoned: that's what my tears were about. The question in the back of my mind was always, "Would anyone come to claim me?" I knew my grandmother couldn't, and my parents' minds were on their business. Those nauseating leave-takings were an expression of how real the abandonment felt to me.

Being aware I was discarded made me want to get everything right. I think I was unconsciously attempting to win over my parents, who didn't pay much attention to me. At the very least, it might give me a place at the table.

So, although it was painful to leave home, I usually overcame the homesickness quickly once I got to school or camp, and then I threw myself into what was going on around me. I loved challenges, especially athletic ones, and after I overcame my intense shyness, I discovered I loved being part of a real community.

Brown Ledge was my favorite camp. It allowed us to go to whatever activities we wanted and stick with them as long as we wanted. The camp calls this their "Freedom of Choice Program." There were four "bunkies" in each cabin with no counselors: instead, the counselors patrolled the grove where the cabins were located. My friends and I had a game of trying to beat them going from cabin to cabin. All the sports offered challenges at different levels—beginners, intermediate, and vanguard. My favorite activities were horseback riding, archery, canoeing, waterskiing, and tennis. We also did a lot of singing, and I loved it, especially the songs from Carousel and the war songs.

The freedom we experienced at Brown Ledge was what I needed. It was an escape from the expectations weighing me down at home, and I could soar. I spent a lot of time doing all the sports, especially waterskiing and tennis, and my athletic skills improved tremendously. Because I loved being active, this camp was heaven for me. Athletics allowed me to express my inborn intensity in acceptable ways, and being active kept that intensity from building up inside me.

Before Brown Ledge, Mac and I went to day camp, and that was in some ways worse than sleepover camps because the leave-taking happened relentlessly every day. It was during these summers that I learned to ride horses, and my parents even bought one of the cow ponies for me from one of those camps.

His name was Calico Fury, and surprisingly, he could jump; we boarded him right down the road from our house. I would take him over the steeplechase jumps on the Phipps' estate (which is now Old Westbury Gardens, a museum of life in the Gilded Age). To this day, I have no idea how a cow pony could take those jumps.

During this time, around 1948, my mother was living with Bill Levitt during the week as they were building Levittown, PA, and on the weekends they would each go home to their families. Bill Levitt's family included his wife (he was still married) and his two sons, Bill Jr. and Jimmy; my mother was divorced, so her family was Nanny, Mac, and me.

Soaring at Brown Ledge camp in 1955.

When I was 12, I didn't go to camp because my mother rented a place called Echo Farm for the summer in New Hope, PA. It was an artsy community about 20 miles from Levittown, where we had chickens and horses, including Calico Fury and my sister's horse, Chief. I was allergic to horses and a lot of other things, but I didn't care. I mucked the stalls and curried the horses and rode every morning at sunrise, which was amazing, and I didn't care because I loved them so much.

During that summer my sister and I were racing across a field, and my horse's foot went in a hole. I kicked my foot free from the stirrup as I flew off the horse. My head hit a rock and I got a concussion. Because my foot was free, I didn't get dragged. My 10-year-old sister managed to hoist me up, sling me over the horse like in the Westerns, and lead me home to my mother. The next thing I knew I was in bed with a headache that felt like someone hit me over the head with a meat cleaver. The doctor came (those were the days of home visits), and I was under observation for a week.

But I brought the worst thing on myself. The farmhouse had a low, wide veranda. The English couple who lived in and worked for us was cooking dinner early one evening, and I was bored. I thought it would be great fun to ride my horse up the few stairs and into the kitchen to surprise them. So I did. The couple was more than startled, and they didn't share my sense of humor. Neither did my mother, who was silently furious.

Calico Fury was gone the next morning, and I cried the rest of the summer. She never said a word about it, just like she didn't tell me my father was moving out. Loss issues. Interestingly, my sister's horse, Chief, was "stolen" that summer, the first time a horse was stolen in that area in 100 years. I'm sure my mother sent Chief away and lied about it to Mac and me. We were both unsaddled for the rest of the summer.

About my mother: reading this, it would be easy to think my mother was cold and cruel to me. I have to say, even as a child, I knew she didn't relate to me as a mother, and I accepted that. I accepted her as she was. Now, after all my years as a therapist, I can see how deeply wounded she was by her own early life. I know she was doing her best, even if she couldn't give me what I needed. Her own losses, and being first-generation American in an immigrant family, were what caused her to pull a cover over the losses in our lives, hiding them as best she could from me and Mac. I think fear and sadness were familiar companions to her, and she typically responded with a determination to move on and get out ahead of them. I know that in immigrant families who had no hope of returning home to their countries, there were often multiple generations of sadness or depression, often unconscious.

Musical Homes

Not only did I leave home often, but home moved around as well. When I was six, we moved from Queens to our new house in Albertson, Long Island; and about three years later we moved to our second new house in Old Westbury, ten miles from Albertson. Between leaving Albertson and moving to Old Westbury, we had a memorable stay in the Garden City Hotel. After living in Old Westbury for some years, we moved to an estate called "Landia" in Pennsylvania, overlooking the Pennsylvania Levittown. Still later we moved to a huge estate near Philadelphia my parents called "Albidale" (Al for Alicia, as my mother now called herself, and Bi for Bill). Next my parents bought a penthouse in NYC and my father had the French chateau "La Colline" built for them. By then I was out of the nest, and it was crisis time.

These moves were a different kind of leave-taking. I didn't cry about them because my family was moving together. That is, my family, including father number one, moved from Queens to Albertson, and my family, without any live-in fathers, moved to Old Westbury, and my family with father number two moved to Landia and beyond.

These houses were important to me, almost like members of the family that came and went. Albertson was the place etched in my memory as the site of my father's permanent disappearance. I liked that house, but that's like the famous question, "Other than that, Mrs. Lincoln, how was the play?"

After my father disappeared and while we still lived at Albertson, our family consisted of me, Nanny, Mac, my mother, a Norwegian couple who helped at home and took care of Nanny, and our first German shepherd. I say "first" because since then, I've always lived with a German shepherd or two. That changed only recently. This German shepherd didn't last long though because she ate the kitchen table. My mother said this dog was crazy, but I thought she was cute.

Even though my father no longer lived with us, building the house in Old Westbury continued. We moved out of our Albertson house before our new one was ready, so our reduced family had to stay in The Garden City Hotel, which was six miles from our new house. This is who moved into the hotel: my grandmother, Mac and I, our German shepherd, and two birds. My mother was in Pennsylvania with Bill Levitt. Here is what life was like there: our dog loudly greeted people at the door, the birds made noise and mess, and my sister and I rode the elevator up and down, pressing the buttons on every floor. I also rode the banister down two flights of stairs, and the dog lifted his leg on it at the bottom. I was like Eloise, in *Eloise at the Plaza*. We stayed for two months. They were so glad to see us leave.

Life Among The Mansions

Old Westbury is an incorporated village in Nassau County on the North Shore of Long Island. It was and is a beautiful village, even now quite wealthy. In 2011, it was the second richest town in the U.S. after Palm Beach. Wealthy families lived in magnificent estates surrounded by carefully tended gardens and lawns.

Our house was not an estate. It was a beautiful ranch house on five acres, three of which were in a grove of white birches, across the road from Corey's racing stables. I would get off the bus, put my books down, go in the field, launch myself onto one of the racehorses, and ride it bareback. Or I would walk up to a horse and sit on the base of its neck while it was grazing. I would hold onto its mane and fly like the wind when it put its head up. I was fearless, and I loved horses. But one day as I walked into the pasture, I saw a horse baring his teeth at me. I ran like crazy with the horse coming after me, and I vaulted over the fence in the nick of time. That was the end of that adventure. That didn't deter me in my love for animals. I love them all, and I'm very calm around them; they sense that and seem to trust me.

Our house was built by Bill Levitt, but I didn't know that at the time. I just accepted the fact that we had a new house to live in, and I made friends with the children in the neighborhood, who were mostly boys. I ran around with them; our favorite thing was to put rocks in our pockets and roam the neighborhood looking for houses where no one was home. We called windowpanes "lights," and we threw our rocks at them aiming for the center. It was fun, and I was good at it, especially for a nine-year-old. But one day the police came to see my grandmother and told her someone who looked like me was doing this, but they thought I was too sweet and shy for it to be me. My grandmother was so upset I couldn't live with myself, so I stopped. One of the boys I knew well during that time was Johnny Dauvergne, who is still my close friend.

Even at Albertson, when I was six or seven, my friends were mostly boys. That made sense: I was a tomboy—I was all about action. That's how I expressed myself. I didn't talk much; I just played rough and tumble with these friends. We'd roll in big cables we found down a nearby hill, or we'd stand on them and try not to fall off before the bottom. I could beat all these boys up, and sometimes I did, when they picked on my sister. Then I went after them with a fury. I was the sand lot pitcher on their baseball team, and I joined them in all their daredevil stunts. Because I was tough, they accepted me as part of their group. How odd my mother was upset that I was the only girl invited to their parties, even though she was the one who pushed me to stand up to them and take care of myself.

My mother hired a woman, Rose, to help my grandmother: she seemed like a real beast to my nine-year-old self. But my mother wouldn't listen to any complaints about her, so my sister and I decided to drive her crazy to get rid of her, and it worked! We made her so upset she threw up all the time and couldn't come to work. Again, I was always ready to protect my grandmother, no matter what that entailed. My mother explained later that she hadn't fired Rose because it was hard to find people she could trust to be with Nanny and my sister and me.

Living in Old Westbury was a calm time in my life, and I was immersed in nature. I would go into the three acres of birch trees on our property and spend time there reading. We had a swimming pool, too, which I loved.

I remember being in my mother's bedroom in Old Westbury, lying on a chaise longue. My mother was puttering around, and there was no tension between us. It was a fleeting moment of happiness, so rare I've never forgotten it. I never had moments like that again, because either we children or my mother were gone most of the time.

During the time we lived in Old Westbury, my mother continued to work with Bill Levitt in Pennsylvania during the week. She was home a lot of weekends, but she was still emotionally distant. Mac and I were at boarding school then, so on the weekends, we were all back home together. But not for holidays—that's when my mother and Bill Levitt often traveled, and my sister and I were left at home with my grandmother.

Starting Out

Some children go to the same school from kindergarten through 12th grade. Not Mac and me. Just as our summers were moving targets, so were our school years. We started out in a small public school that I was SO eager to attend. A big Irish family lived next door to us in Queens. They had six children; their name was O'Hara, and I wondered if they were related to Maureen O'Hara. Their school was down the street a few blocks; I thought it was far, far away. I used to practice going to school by walking with them carrying an empty lunch box and then come home by myself. Those girls taught me how to read when I was four. No one else read to me, although my mother loved fairy tales and she would tell them to me. I don't think my grandmother could read; she had very poor eyesight. She could see to knit, but I can't remember ever seeing her read.

After my disastrous experience at St. Aiden's, the Catholic school, my schools were secular, except for one year in an Episcopal school. I was relieved when my mother took me out of St. Aiden's and enrolled me at the North Side School in East Williston Park, NY, near Old Westbury, but I had to repeat second grade. It's easy to understand why a skinny, shy child who had a lot of early traumas to deal with, especially her parents' divorce, would fail second grade. Divorce cast me as a pariah with some people and further confused me about who constituted "mother" and "father" in my family. After I repeated second grade, I never had any academic problems.

One day at North Side, I went to make a 10c phone call at the pay phone. When I hung up, the coin box emptied out all over the hallway. Unbelievable. I was pushing it into a pile as I called the operator and asked how I could put it all back. She said, "Are you crazy? Put it in your pocket and go home."

When I think about it, going to three different elementary schools wasn't a good thing for me. It contributed to my sense that my world was unstable and in constant flux, which helped cause the intense homesickness I experienced later whenever I went away to another school or to camp.

Me, age 9, Old Westbury

Fledging

Before my first summer at Brown Ledge camp, I was deemed old enough at age 12 to go to boarding school, and my mother sent me to Friends Academy, a day and boarding school in Locust Valley, Nassau County, NY. Since I was going, Mac was sent there too, and I was charged with taking care of her. That was hard.

At this time in my life, my shyness prevented me from speaking unless I had to. It's hard to make friends with other children if you don't talk, but sports gave me a way. Because I was a good athlete, I made friends with the children on my teams. I made the varsity basketball team in eighth grade; I was the youngest team member. I also played field hockey and tennis.

My sister and I often went home for weekends, since Friends Academy was only seven miles from our house in Old Westbury. We were driven back and forth by my parents' chauffeur. I made a pact with him to stop a mile away from the school so we could walk the rest of the way. My sister agreed. We didn't want anyone to know we had a driver. If we were driven up to the school, the other students would ask about it, and that would lead to a lot of questions we weren't prepared to answer. It would make us seem different, and there were already enough things setting us apart.

The summer after seventh grade I vowed to talk even if I made an ass of myself. I was a strange child: I sometimes tried to get in trouble, because taking risks was exciting, but I was pathologically quiet. I was an anomaly, and in some ways, I've never fit the given molds.

At Friends, after I got over being silent, I got into my usual trouble making. I was friends with the boys in the boys' dorm, and we made a walkie talkie out of pieces of tin and a long string. After the lights were out, the other girls gathered in my room, and we talked to the boys. One night, one of the boys climbed up to the window in my room. The housefellow discovered him as he was arriving. There was an old-fashioned fire escape ladder there. I guess she was afraid the whole boys' dorm would show up, even though my room was on the second floor. The housefellow was not at all happy.

Another time, my friends and I put a huge sign on the school's entrance saying, "Nudist Colony." On April 1st, the headmaster was going to be speaking at a school assembly, so we all got up early and went into the auditorium and turned every chair so its back was to the stage. The headmaster's name was Mr. Brown; we didn't like him. We chanted as we turned the chairs around, "What's the color of horse manure? Brown, Brown, Brown." The two sides of me, having to be perfect, and being an imp at heart.

My three years at Friends Academy were good for me. I began to come out of my shell and made friends, the academics were good, and I could focus on different sports. I loved boarding at school; I felt I belonged, and all the parts seemed to fit together there, unlike at home.

When I left Friends Academy at the end of my third year, I had no idea I wouldn't be returning.

Chapter 4:

The Dreaded Happens

"Sometimes we need to be destroyed by a situation,
before we understand how bad it was for us."
–Karen Waddell

"It is not how long we spend with someone that matters. It's
the effect of that encounter that makes the difference."
–Mimi Novic, Guidebook To Your Heart

Nanny and I almost shared the same birthday: ours were one day apart in May, and we always celebrated together.

In the first week of June 1955, I came home from Friends Academy for the last time, though I didn't know it then. I had just turned 15. Nanny and I were sitting together on the screened-in porch in Old Westbury on June 19, Father's Day, and she was knitting baby clothes for the child of a friend. We didn't tell her the baby was dead, not wanting to upset her.

Suddenly, my grandmother grabbed her chest and said she thought she was having a heart attack, the event I dreaded my entire life. It was clear she was in a lot of pain. I called for my mother: my sister and I helped get her to bed while my mother called the doctor.

I went numb as we put her on her stomach, and I started rubbing her back and shoulder. I heard her whisper, "Kiss me, I'm dying," but I couldn't do it. The kiss of death was never far from my consciousness. Soon the family doctor sent an ambulance with a hospital bed and oxygen.

Toward nightfall, we said goodnight to my grandmother from her doorway and she waved to us. My mother shooed us upstairs to bed after we watched this unfold, and then she stayed with my grandmother, who died during the night.

Mary Kenny, my Nanny, 1947

My mother called the ambulance to take her body away before morning. Again, when something terrible went on, she hid it from us as much as possible: my father leaving with no communication; Calico Fury disappearing; my sister's horse, Chief, being reported "stolen;" and now my grandmother's body being taken away in the middle of the night, before we could see it and begin to process what happened, or to say our final goodbyes. Was she trying to protect us, or herself?

The next day people began calling our house, and I heard Bill Levitt saying, "Yes, Mary passed away last night." I was afraid of this my whole life, and I tried to protect her every chance I got. She was the one person I could trust to be there for me—the one person who really cared.

My grandmother's wake, funeral, and burial in the cemetery are a blur in my memory. It was a horrible event. Bill Levitt and my mother knew a ton of people, so the funeral was huge. There was an open casket, and I thought, "This isn't her." She was stone cold. I put a gold cross in her casket and told myself I was done with God. Why would I need a God who could take away the only person who deep down cared about me? Later, when I was in college where chapel was required, I had other girls sign me in. I took a religion class taught by the chaplain; he always started it with a prayer, and I would stand outside the classroom until he finished it and then go in.

After the funeral, my mother, Bill Levitt, my sister, Johnny Dauvergne, and I had lunch at the Village Bath Club in the Strathmore community, a part of Manhasset, LI, near Old Westbury. This was one of the communities Bill Levitt built, and this was the club where I learned to swim. We were quiet, and we were all taking things from each other's plates we knew the other person didn't want. Johnny said, "Is this a family affair, or may I have that tomato." That made us laugh despite our sadness. Within two weeks or less, my mother sent Mac and me back to Brown Ledge camp for eight weeks. She didn't tell us her plans.

We never went home again.

Chapter 5:

Orphans

"Maybe only an orphan can understand this, but we had been
cut free from our anchor and the blow was crushing. We didn't
know who we were, and more importantly, we didn't know whose
we were -- forever proving that identity precedes purpose. You
can't know who you are until you've settled whose you are."
–Charles Martin, The Record Keeper

The Grief of an Elephant

In their natural environment in the wild, female elephants and
young males up to the age of 12 through 15 live and travel together
in a herd of 6 – 20 members, led by their older female matriarch.
Adult males (bulls) roam alone or band together in unstable groups.
The matriarch knows how to get to the watering holes and feed-
ing grounds; she's like a grandmother to the members of the herd,
assisting them as they care for one another and the babies. Social
relationships and interactions are strong in elephant herds, just as
they can be in extended human families when members live near
each other.

When a member of a herd dies, the other members show their
grief. "Elephants do grieve, and they are one of the few animals
who are similar to humans in mourning patterns. Believe it or not,
elephants cry. They bury their dead and pay tribute to the bodies and

to the bones. Scientists have observed that elephants feel empathy: they toss dust upon the wounds of fellow elephants, they help others climb out of mud and holes, they even have been seen plucking tranquilizing darts from one another with their trunks. Researchers have observed elephants trying to help dying friends, lifting them with tusks and trunks, crying out in distress." (Animals Growing Up: The Five Animals that Grieve, Harper Collins Publishers, 2023, online.)

When the member of a human family dies, grief takes many forms. Some people close to the person who died cease participating in normal activities and find it hard to stop crying; others bottle up their emotions and go about their lives; and others spend time in prayer and retrospection.

In my British family, grieving was not encouraged. In fact, it was hardly allowed. Mac and I suffered after my grandmother died, but our emotions were barely acknowledged. My parents seemed not to know how to create space for them. We also suffered from my mother's emotional absence, but it seemed as if our parents were not aware of that. Their response to grief or any of its cousin emotions was to ignore the problem and get back to work. So Mac and I were expected to keep on keeping on.

When it comes to nurturing family members, and when it comes to grieving, elephants do a better job than my family did.

Moving On?

Mac and I were at Brown Ledge camp for eight weeks that summer, both of us numb, on our own to grapple with Nanny's sudden death. That summer, the counselors came to get me just about every night because Mac was having nightmares, and she needed me to comfort her. At summer's end, someone came to pick us up, I can't remember who. But, unbeknownst to us, we weren't going home to Old Westbury or even back to Long Island. They took us to a large house they called Landia overlooking Levittown, PA, where my parents worked. This new house was convenient for them: no more long commutes to spend weekends with their separate families.

My parents' convenience—moving to Landia—came at a price for Mac and me. We were sent away a bare two weeks after Nanny died; now our home was gone too, and our community: all the familiar landmarks of our childhood. Our belongings were gone as well, discarded as part of the move, perhaps in the name of efficiency. Gone were the riding boots Nanny gave me, which I treasured, along with all our books (surely, we'd outgrown them), and even our dog—gone. I did manage to rescue a white cable-knit sweater Nanny knitted for me that my mother overlooked; if she saw it, she might have thrown it out.

Brown Ledge camp was important to me because it bridged my old life as a child with my grandmother and my new life alone, without her. Even though Mac and I were numb, it was at least a familiar environment after Nanny died. Without that link to Brown Ledge, it would have seemed we were dropped into outer space. We had no rudder, no anchor, and no grounding.

At Landia Mac and I had a room with two twin beds in the servants' quarters. We shared it. I said to Mac, "We're orphans now, you know." She nodded. Having a home and a dog was always so important to me. Those were my other anchors, along with my grandmother. Now, overnight, they were all gone. I realize now I was more of an orphan than Mac. My mother thought of me as her sister, but Mac was clearly her daughter. Even so, we both felt completely undone by Nanny's death.

The recognition, when you're 15, that you're an orphan, is an overwhelming feeling, unlike any I've had. I was alone, unprotected, bereft, insecure, and too numb to be frightened.

Here is what I realize now: My mother and Bill Levitt were "living in sin" according to the cultural norms of the time, because

71

Bill Levitt was still married to his first wife. But at this point he and my mother wanted to live together full time, and this house allowed them to do that. Bill Levitt's youngest son, Jimmy, came to stay with us for periods of time as well, joining the household of his father and his father's divorced mistress, which is what my mother was, at a time when divorce was not at all common and certainly not talked about. Jimmy was a 14-year-old boy who'd had a lot of trouble in school, not because he wasn't intelligent, but because he was spoiled, and he'd been neglected like my sister and me.

The whole time we lived there, my parents' focus was on their development business, and they worked hard at it. They paid little attention to us kids.

We had a French cook at Landia. She was an excellent cook, but perhaps a little too free-spirited. She went out to get the milk from the milkman without wearing a stitch of clothing. She did this not once, but several times; I thought she might have been too hot in the kitchen and just took off her clothes. When the milkman complained to my father, threatening not to deliver milk anymore, my mother fired her. How do you explain this stuff to friends, especially in the 1950's? No wonder I kept trying to figure out why my family wasn't normal. Throughout the years, this need to understand my family grew in intensity.

Because it was awkward for my parents to have Mac and me with them after we moved to Landia, places were found where we could be sent—good schools and camps where we could be educated and find experiences that would nurture us.

My parents had neither the time nor inclination to provide those experiences. There was no place for us in their daily lives: we were more than they could manage. After all, Nanny was our real parent. It was better for them and for us that we were sent off to schools and camps designed to give girls good solid educations and opportunities to explore athletics, make friends, and learn new skills. Now

I understand my parents were doing their best. They were totally incapable of tending to our emotional health at this precarious time. They were not *able* to be there for us.

True to pattern, my mother and Bill Levitt never talked to us about why they were now living together at Landia full-time, or why they threw out all our things. I didn't expect it to be different, although Bill Levitt and I could have serious conversations at times.

I've learned that even when people do their best, the outcome isn't necessarily rosy. What made sense to me was that when it was bad, I needed to understand that's the way it was and rise above it.

My parents' painful neglect of us had a silver lining for me: it taught me resilience. Out of the two apparent choices—first, to blame them and fume away in anger, or second, to accept it and move on—only the latter made sense to me.

I tried so hard to help my sister understand that, but she couldn't. For her, the first option was the only one. But I said to myself "I better excel, or I'll go the way of the house, the dogs, the horses, and everything else."

I recently found more silver linings to all that neglect and dismissal: my parents' lack of communication about anything emotionally threatening is what made me value communication so much. And that's why the South Bronx was such an important place for me. The patients there were desperate to talk about what was happening to them, and I was desperate to listen.

To be fair to my mother, I must mention that she decorated the Landia house: Mac and I were each given a room of our own, and they were nice. It was the beginning of a glamorous, but almost soulless life. And when the school year began, we were sent to St. Mary's Hall in Burlington, NJ, which was a short distance from Landia. St. Mary's was a small, high Episcopalian, and very religious private day school for girls. We attended chapel every day wearing white veils.

Throughout our early childhood, up through the year at St. Mary's, Mac and I were in the same schools and because we were close in age, we were part of the same group of friends. Being older, I was expected to look out for her and take care of her when necessary, and I did, not just because it was expected, but because she was my little sister and I cared about her. Early on, when she was in trouble, I'd talk to her and try to get her to "fly straight." She wouldn't, or couldn't, listen to me, and that was frustrating. When I finally realized this wasn't going to change, I knew we would be in different worlds from then on, and I felt sad and alone.

It was at St. Mary's that Mac got hit in the jaw with a hockey ball and was prescribed the pain pills that dominated her life. From the time Mac was 13 or 14, whenever I tried to talk with her, it was clear she was stoned. There was no way I could get through to her. Meanwhile, I focused on what I *could* do rather than on what I couldn't.

Mac's life expressed more openly than mine the emotional desert we both inhabited after our grandmother died. At St. Mary's, she was disorganized and self-absorbed, with a kind of unattractive mess around her. She often looked disheveled and out of focus. I covered over my feeling of being unmoored by striving to achieve, which was sometimes successful and acknowledged and sometimes not. I was organized, focused on helping other people, and at times a magnet for other people's attention. Underneath all that, I floated around in a kind of limbo. In the portrait below, you can see how straight forward I look and how tentative Mac's expression is.

Portrait of me and Mac, 1947 or '48

I particularly remember one friend at St. Mary's Hall because she invited me to her house for an overnight, and the experience was odd but enlightening. Mimi was in my tenth-grade class, and I was happy to visit her. Her home was large but also cold; I'm sure the temperature was under 60 degrees. I think they told me that. Dinner was most unusual: tomato aspic is all I remember. I didn't like it, but I ate it all and then her parents gave me more. In the morning, suddenly there was a guy wearing a white stocking cap and granny gown in the room; he ran to the window wielding a gun and shot something. I was in shock—I asked Mimi, "What just happened?" She said, "Oh, he does that all the time. He shoots the pigeons off the roof." It turned out it was her father.

I thought her family was strange at dinner and even more so in the morning, but it was all normal for her. Experiences like this gave me a beginning understanding of complicated families. Like mine, her family was odd too, but unlike mine, there was the normalcy of living with her real parents.

During the end of that year at St. Mary's Hall, my then boyfriend invited me to the senior prom at the Choate School for boys in Wallingford, CT. He called a few days later to tell me that the school administration was having trouble letting me come because my last name was different from my mother's—after she separated from my birth father, my mother reclaimed her maiden name, Kenny. My sister and I used Habermehl or Kenny as our last names depending on the situation. The concern went up from the headmaster all the way to the board of trustees because divorce was so unacceptable, and different last names signaled divorce. Many people aren't aware that not so long ago, things were quite different. I was considered a pariah.

After that year I took a speed-reading course, which has proved to be helpful my entire life. I love to read, and there are so many books I find interesting; I devour them as fast as I can and go on to the next one. There was a lot going on in my life during that time, and I read to remove myself from the craziness.

I basically liked St. Mary's, but something happened that made it untenable for us to stay there. Unfortunately, all the student leaders were lesbians, including the student head of the athletic association; someone found out and they were all expelled. Homosexuality was not acceptable, but I never had a problem with it. Straying from the norm of heterosexuality could ruin your life. I was angry: they had been good student leaders. I hated this violation of my values and felt terrible for the girls.

I asked my parents to find us another school, and they found the Beard School, a boarding school for girls in Orange, NJ. I went there for my junior and senior years. My sister's grades at St. Mary's were bad, so she was sent to another school. We were never in the same school again and rarely together after that for the rest of her life. This separation was a significant loss to me. Even though I sometimes couldn't stand her, Mac was my sister. We'd been together her whole life, and we went through everything together. We experienced the losses and abandonment, and the good times as well, together. No one else shared that.

* * *

Mac was lost to me not so much because we went separate ways after St. Mary's, but because we responded to all that happened to us in opposite ways. Mac kept re-creating the trauma in some form or other. She just couldn't make her life work.

I saw Mac's ongoing despair play out in her life. Later, after she married, she and her husband had four children, three boys and a girl. I tried to be a presence in their lives, but Mac's whirlwind kept me at arms' length. As her marriage began to fail, she had a lesbian relationship with a woman who was herself a problem. They were both abusive to their children. Mac and her husband eventually divorced. I always intuited Mac's sexual orientation. That was another strike against her. She was at St. Mary's with me when the student leaders were expelled because they were lesbians, so Mac got the message that her sexual orientation marked her as unacceptable.

Just like my mother, but in her own way, Mac couldn't be there for her children. When she drove them somewhere, she'd sometimes have to pull the car over and sleep off the effects of the drugs. Children are fortunately resilient; I imagine Mac's children were aware their mother was impaired and learned to manage on their own when they were being neglected, just as I did. It's a family pattern. Mac's life steadily spiraled downhill, and her children had a rough time.

When Mac's children were still small, our mother and father offered to buy her a house near mine, but she categorically refused. Later I realized she didn't want me to know about her drug addiction and abusive behavior.

When Scottie, Mac's oldest child, was about 17, he was killed in a single-car crash on Mother's Day, as he went out to buy her a gift. She was driving right behind him.

I can remember when my sister called to tell me that Scottie died. He was killed outright. It was like the bottom dropped out. Mac was sobbing so much I almost couldn't understand her.

Scottie's death was horrific on many levels. I never knew if it was truly an accident or what I might call a "wished-for-death," not quite a suicide. Deep down, he knew he couldn't leave his mother, so there could have been an unconscious wish to die. But on the other hand, the tires on his car were bald, so maybe it was an accident.

Mac always had a room in the hospital where she went for bleeding ulcers and various problems; she was chronically ill and frequently hospitalized. She died there; the doctors never told us the cause of death. It could have been AIDS from a blood transfusion. I know she had gangrene toward the end of her life; just before she died, they amputated her right arm. I'll never know what took her life. Maybe it was life itself.

When Mac was dying, my mother, my birth father, and I went to see her. This was in 1987. It was the first time our original family was together in 40 years. After spending time with her, we returned to our hotel. My mother was inconsolable, realizing she would never see her younger daughter again, and I crawled in bed and held her the rest of the night. My birth father was also having a rough time. The three of us kept trying to console one another.

*　*　*

Back to Landia: Living there worked well for my parents because it was close to Levittown, PA. But this house was owned by Levitt & Sons—and my parents longed to buy a place they could call home. In fact, I found out later that as soon as they moved to Landia, they started looking for their dream home. They found it and moved soon after I left to board at the Beard School for Girls. After my first year at Beard, I came home to a whole new life at the estate my parents called Albidale, the name they created using the first initials of both their names to reflect the merger they felt in their marriage—it was truly beautiful.

* * *

Throughout this part of my life, I was painfully aware of the way the pieces of my life and family could not come together. I was searching in vain for the whole elephant. When I think of that animal, I see an intelligent, caring, capable being who lives easily on the earth in harmony with everything in its environment. All the parts of the elephant work together

- as it moves around on its thick, sturdy legs;

- as it uses its trunk to gather food, break through dense brush, sniff the air, give itself a shower, pluck up a blade of grass, and caress the babies and other adults;

- as it fans itself with its ears while listening for important sounds; and

- as it freely feels the emotions evoked by whatever is going on.

I wanted to find the wholeness of this being. I wanted to become that whole elephant. And I like to think of Albidale as a place where a whole elephant would feel right at home. (It was certainly big enough.)

Chapter 6:

Becoming Who I Am

"You know how sometimes, your life is so perfect you're
afraid for the next moment, because it couldn't possibly
be quite as good? That's what it felt like."

–Jodi Picoult, Handle with Care

Before Albidale, Another New Beginning

I was 16 when I left Landia to go to the Beard School. The night before, I ran away because I didn't want to go. I was beside myself and completely torn apart; I couldn't deal with yet another separation. To make matters worse, this time it was just me leaving because Mac was going to a different school.

In the middle of that night, I sat in the rose bushes blowing my nose because of my allergies until I ran out of tissues, and then I moved to spend the rest of the night huddled on the floor in the back of my mother's Cadillac, hoping the plane would crash the next day. I forget who uncovered my hiding spot, but my parents ordered me to clean up, and they took me to the airport.

Bill Levitt owned a DC-3 plane he called the "Redhead" after my mother; it was a WWII plane that was redone inside to look like a living room. A pilot and co-pilot retired from Trans World Airlines (TWA) were always on call. The plane even had a red bathroom. Sometimes we flew to Washington, DC, just to have dinner.

A DC-3 plane like the one Bill Levitt owned

It was a short flight to the airport near the Beard School. My parents both came; they wanted to tell the headmistress, Miss Sutherland, that I ran away. When she heard that news, she put her arm around my shoulders while walking me to my room and said, "If you want to run away while you're here, use the front door." That was the perfect thing to say to an oppositional person—with permission to run away, who wants to do it?

Miss Sutherland was just the person I needed when I was suffering the loss of my grandmother. She was smart and tuned into the students. At the end of my first semester, I got a C in one of my courses. When she complemented me on it, I got mad and became determined I would get good grades. I think she was oppositional herself since she understood me so well.

On the way to my room with Miss Sutherland, I noticed the beautiful, long banister curving down from the second floor to the first and thought, "I'm going to wake up in the middle of the night and ride that thing to the bottom!"

When a fire drill awakened us during the night at Beard, we had to gather in the hall below the floor where we slept. One night during a drill, getting up in the middle of the night made me think of the banister. So, another night soon after that, I got up giggling around two or three and went out to the stairs, got on the banister, and rode it to the bottom. Then I noticed a pair of large feet there—the headmistress! I first thought I was in big trouble, but she laughed and said, "I've always wanted to do that!"

My usual homesickness started after I moved in, and I was trying hard not to cry. I remember my roommate, Joy, saying to her parents when they brought her to the school, "Don't worry, I'll be fine." She was 5'10", a big girl, and she was jovial about being there and easily dismissed her parents' concerns. Ironically, she was the one who cried. All that joviality was her putting up a good front. She cried a lot for a month until her parents came for her. So, the typical drop-off-day crier stayed, and the girl who was supposedly happy to be there lasted only a month.

After Joy left, I didn't have a roommate for a while, but then a girl named Fran said she wanted to room with me. She lived not far from Levittown, PA. We got along most of the time. However, Fran's habits reminded me of my sister: she would leave her clothes all over the room. Because I was on the dean's list, I could study in my room, so I was there a lot. I kept asking her to clean up her mess, multiple times, nicely, getting more and more frustrated, but she wouldn't.

One day I picked up all her clothes and threw them out the window. She never left her clothes lying around again; instead, she threw them on the floor of her closet. She wasn't mad either, which helped me understand it was good to take action to make a point when talking failed. I now realize it wasn't just the mess that was getting to me: the reminder of my sister, who didn't come to Beard, triggered all my loss and family issues. And Fran was an only child, so she wasn't used to thinking about someone else's needs.

As usual, what gave me a place at Beard was sports. I was center forward in both field hockey and basketball during fall and winter my junior year. In the spring, I wanted to play lacrosse. One of my classmates, Margo, said she'd get to school early every morning to teach me the game.

Margo was a delight: she bridged a gap for me between the day students and those like me who boarded. Boarders had reasons to be there; there were often problems at home. Margo had relatives and friends at the school, and she made it easier for me to be there. We were both Athenians, one of the two athletic teams. She was a good teacher, too. I learned the game and played third home as the position was called: I was the attack. The first game we had with another school, I was running with a clear shot on goal, and in my excitement, I threw the ball all the way over the three-story school building into the street on the other side. Everybody cracked up. Fortunately, it wasn't the only game ball. Margo and I are good friends to this day. Maybe because my birth family seemed so fragmented, all my life I was able to accumulate good friends, as if I was filling those gaps and building my own "family."

Scoring! 1957 or '58

While I was at Beard, Bill Levitt came to the Father's Day celebration, which included a competitive basketball game. I won the game for my school with a hook shot from mid-court—for a girl, that was unusual. The fathers came running to congratulate me and my father, who looked like he would happily disappear if he could find a hole to crawl into. He was truly mortified. Even the boys in his family were not athletes, and girls of my era were not supposed to be.

Athletics for girls ran counter to the stereotypes of females being passive objects to be controlled. I was nothing like that stereotype. When I was dating guys in college, they would often invite me to play tennis. That stereotype was so much the culture they would never ask if I knew how to play. They assumed they would teach me. When I beat them, they'd say, "Why didn't you tell me?" "Tell you what?" "That you're a good tennis player." "Well, did you ask me?"

When I was at Beard, sports helped me break my long practice of silence and got me talking to my teammates, just as it had at Friends Academy. From there, it was easier to talk in class and in the dorm, but easier is a relative term. It was hard. I had to screw up my courage to talk. Once I got going, I was ok. Perhaps my silence was a response to the lack of communication I experienced at home.

At Beard none of the students had cars on campus. My first year there was my junior year; I was 16 and had my license. I decided it was important to have my car there so I could drive home if I needed to, and I got permission to do that. No student before or for years after was given that permission, but I negotiated it. I learned the important developmental skill of negotiating during my childhood and knew it was more effective than lying or sneaking around. That's what I teach adolescents now.

While I was at Beard, the imp and caregiver parts of me dovetailed. In the second half of my first year, I met an eighth-grade boarder—Jackie. Her parents wouldn't allow her to come home for holidays because her behavior was a problem everywhere, including at Beard. She broke out of the school and vandalized local homes. We had strict rules against leaving school: we couldn't even walk five minutes to the nearby store for a snack. Of course, we did, occasionally.

One time, five of us went to the store, and we were sitting at the counter with sodas. Our lookout called, "Teacher coming!" We split, leaving the sodas on the counter. We never did anything like vandalizing homes. I outgrew that type of activity after my grandmother got upset over my tomboy rock-throwing with the neighborhood boys.

The headmistress talked to me about Jackie: she told me the school was expelling her. I suggested I could help. I ran what amounted to a group therapy session every evening, even though I didn't know that's what it was. I got a bunch of the girls together, and we talked about our issues and supported each other. The headmistress suggested to Jackie that she talk to me, which she did.

Jackie knew she needed help. She told me, "I want to be just like you, Long Neck." (For some reason, that was her nickname for me.) I said, "Instead, let's see how you can be the best version of yourself." Together we changed a lot of things for her and then her parents invited her home for holidays. I heard from her on and off through the years, and when she was in college, she wrote to let me know she had her act together. I always tried to help people: my grandmother, my sister, Jimmy, and Jackie, trying to set the world right.

Another student needed help also. Gerry sat next to me in study hall, and she absolutely stank of body odor. When I worked with Jackie, I had to tell her the facts of life. No one ever did. I don't know why Gerry didn't bathe, but I had to do something. I told her I needed to talk to her after study hall one day. I explained that she smelled bad, and she was appalled. She told me she took a shower once a week before church. I said to her, "God can't smell, but the rest of the girls are dying! You play sports with us, and you work up a good sweat!" She got it. It was the kindest thing I could do.

Helping Jackie and Gerry drew on my instincts to make the world a better place. But there was also that part of me that liked throwing rocks at windowpanes and terrorizing the women my mother hired for my grandmother if Mac and I thought they were mean. Sometimes I listened to my better self and sometimes to the devilish one!

No one liked our housefellow at the Beard School. She reminded me of some of those women my mother hired. She was an adult who had no idea how to work with mischievous young girls. Our first retaliation was short sheeting her bed. Then we put Saran Wrap under her toilet seat. We all heard the howls from her bathroom. We were proud of ourselves, and she left soon afterwards. My devilish self was often successful in what it tried to accomplish; but then so was my better self.

My birthday came in May just before the summer break between my junior and senior years. My parents were sorry to miss my big day, but they had plans to be in Europe. They arranged with friends to take me out to dinner. I knew the restaurant where we were meeting. When I arrived, I walked through the dining area so intent on finding them I walked right past a big table where my parents and other family friends were seated. None of it registered. That was one of the few times in my life when I was completely surprised. That was a happy birthday.

At the restaurant, I got little splits of champaign to take back to school. I gathered everyone in my room and handed them out. We also had cigarettes, so after the lights were out, we smoked and drank the splits. The window was open to let the smoke out; suddenly we heard a huge racket and saw a lot of police officers searching around along under our windows. We thought they were after us. Douse the lights, shut the window, everybody in her own room! We all went to sleep, and in the morning, we heard a pedophile had escaped from prison. It was odd feeling joyful about a visiting pedophile. But he certainly took the heat off us.

During spring semester, junior year, I decided to run for president of the boarding school; if I won, I would be president my senior year. There was one girl running against me; her whole platform was no one would vote for me because I was "too pretty and too rich." They didn't believe her, so I was elected president at the end of March, which meant that the first week in October, I would have to speak before the entire school during the ceremony introducing the student leaders. This gave me diarrhea for six months. That old fear of talking still lurked deep inside me.

I met with Miss Sutherland in September of my senior year just after school started, and she said, "Hah! Now you'll have to obey all the rules." I smiled sweetly and said, "Well, only the ones that make sense." I was very cognizant of what those should be, and which ones should be tossed. One to toss, for example, was the silly rule that everyone had to wash their hair on Tuesdays. There wasn't enough hot water for even half the boarders on Tuesdays, so we did whatever we pleased. I thought we should spread out hair washing throughout the week. One good rule was that no one could have cigarettes, matches or anything that would put the community at risk. I thought it was a good rule even though I'd broken it.

The housefellow we terrorized didn't come back, so Miss Sutherland put me in charge of study halls every night. The students were quiet and there was never a problem. I was also in charge of social events, like dances with boys' schools and other weekend events. Students were allowed to have only three after-school activities, but we could exceed that number with permission. I signed up for nine, which included varsity basketball, hockey, and lacrosse. They let me do it.

During my first year at the Beard School, my parents called me all the time, whenever they felt like it, even though that was against school rules. They did it so often Miss Sutherland told them that if they didn't stop, with that on my record, no good college would take me. Parents were often afraid of her, but my parents wanted to control her as well as me. My mother needed surgery that year, but of course she didn't tell me beforehand. She and Bill Levitt flew to the hospital in the DC-3. There was no contact with them for a few days—just dead silence; this was before Miss Sutherland reminded them about the calling rules. When I didn't hear from them, I thought maybe the DC-3 crashed. Even after the surgery, they didn't tell me about it. Later I surmised my mother had thyroid surgery, but nobody said what it was. She was OK, but this was another instance of adults hiding important information from Mac and me.

If you don't trust your parents to tell you things, it turns out you worry all the time. It's much better to tell kids what's going on; when you do, you're showing you trust and respect them. Then they're apt to trust and respect you in return and stop worrying non-stop.

All seniors were encouraged to give a talk to the whole school during their last year, but as the student president of the boarding school, I really had no choice. This would be my second big speech at Beard. That shy part of me I had largely overcome reared its ugly head again as I anticipated this talk. I signed up for the very last date before graduation so if I made an ass of myself, I wouldn't have to return to the scene of the crime.

I had to meet with the head of the English department for weeks before I did my presentation, as did each of the seniors giving talks. The night before the dreaded day, I was so terrified I stayed up all night rewriting my speech under my bed with a flashlight. It was a bit crowded under there, but lights out was 9 p.m. and I didn't want to be discovered. I went to the auditorium exhausted and pale as a ghost, and I delivered my spiel. Instead of slinking away in disgrace as I imagined, I got a standing ovation. The head of the English department came up to me with a big smile and said, "That was wonderful!!! But it certainly wasn't the talk we worked on together." The Beard School gave me a major leg up in becoming who I am, starting with Miss Sutherland. With her help I rose to the challenges I encountered, growing beyond my initial debilitating shyness. When I think back on those experiences, I'm amazed at the latitude she gave me: permission to run away the first day, permission to take on six more extra-curricular activities than allowed, asking me to supervise study hall, and allowing me to have a car on campus. All these experiences, along with the sports, gradually built my self-confidence.

In addition, my education between the ages of 15 and 21 was in schools for girls and women; that structure contributed to my self-assurance. These single-sex educational settings were important at that time. They were a tacit acknowledgement that women were second-class citizens who didn't have a seat at the power table. In a segregated environment, we girls had opportunities to become leaders in our own right and to learn how to wield power effectively. Because I am oppositional, knowing society closed doors to people like me made me determined to show that my life mattered. This was another drive that amped up my intensity.

When I graduated from Beard, there was a special celebration for the boarders and their parents. The celebration was to recognize me for helping others, but before I arrived, I had no clue the gathering was for me. It was an unanticipated validation of who I was and what I did. That celebration put the perfect cap on those special two years at Beard, which broadened my sense of the wider world beyond my family. This school showed me there were other matriarchs out there who were caring and nurturing, just like my grandmother.

Normal at Last?

My parents moved to Albidale during my first year at Beard. It was such a beautiful setting for my family as we all came together in a new way. My time there was the happiest period of my growing up years. I think my parents' relationship was also at its best. Levitt & Sons was growing fast, my mother was the interior designer for the model homes, and my parents were contemplating expanding their reach by developing Levittown, NJ.

Albidale, around 1956

Albidale was a large, beautiful estate in Bryn Athyn, PA, outside Philadelphia. The 12,000 – 15,000 square foot mansion was surrounded by 355 manicured acres, with an indoor quarter-mile racetrack and a half-mile outdoor track for the 40 or so horses previously living there. Included on the grounds, in addition to stables, were several houses for people who worked for my parents and a five-car garage.

We bought three non-racing horses after we moved there. One of them was my Arabian, Rudi, a bay. I had a special relationship with him; we understood each other and riding him was magical. Before living at Albidale, we owned a few horses the whole time I was growing up, and I rode with two hunts on Long Island before we moved to Landia. After my mother got rid of my first pony, Calico Fury, as punishment for my bad judgment, she never interfered with my horses. I took Rudi with me to college.

The estate grounds afforded my mother the perfect opportunity to start an organic farm, which became the largest one in the Philadelphia area. She was a fan of *Silent Spring* author, Rachel Carson. It was a real farm with chickens, pheasants, black angus cattle, and a 75-foot-long greenhouse for veggies and flowers. There was also a gigantic compost pile. My father bought a herd of cattle from Senator Wayne Morse (I-OR), a rare and now endangered breed called Devon cattle, but he didn't keep them long. My parents turned Albidale into a "losing farm," which meant they could claim the losses on their taxes for seven years.

My mother supervised the greenhouse planting; she wanted us to have year-round flowers in the house and fresh vegetables to eat in winter. She brought some wild "fraise des bois" plants home from France, those delectable French strawberries. They survived the flight home even though she sat on them the whole way, since bringing in plants was not allowed. Once they were planted, they spread for several acres. Those strawberries were delicious.

There were several children living in the various houses at Albidale. Their parents included my aunt Agnes and her husband, who was an employee of Levitt & Sons; James Edwards, my father's butler, and his wife, Vivian; and the farm manager, George Bourdette, and his wife, Jane. Also, during the summers, a crew of local people worked for us, many with children.

Christmas was a special season there. We put on a wonderful event for the children, including those of the summer workers. I was charged with buying Christmas presents for them; first we'd have a hayride, and then refreshments and the gift-giving. I absolutely loved buying those presents, picking out gifts I thought the children would like, and seeing the delight on their faces.

Bill Levitt was at last divorced, after all those years of being married to his first wife while living with my mother. He and my mother finally got married, and Bill Levitt adopted me and Mac. Earlier, when I was about seven or eight, he thoughtfully asked me how I felt about being adopted, which meant I would have a Jewish last name. Given what happened to Jews during WWII, he wanted me to be aware of how the last name of Levitt might affect me. He wanted to be sure I was willing to take on any anti-Semitism I might experience if he did adopt me. I loved him, though, and I thought of him as my father, so I very much wanted to be his legal daughter. I was 18 when the adoption was finalized.

* * *

Now that I had a family that seemed more normal, it was as if the whole elephant was taking shape before my eyes. But perfection is mythical. And Albidale, while wonderful in so many ways, was not perfect.

Soon after getting back from Beard one summer vacation, I stood looking around at my beautifully decorated bedroom with its marble fireplace. My room was as big as some people's living rooms, and I even had my own elegant bathroom. Then I looked out of my window at the expanse of carefully manicured acreage, and I told myself, "This is not good for people. It's not healthy." I was suddenly acutely aware that this whole way of life was an anomaly.

Furthermore, the beauty of this estate could not hide the reality that our family still had problems: I had to face the fact that Mac was disturbed; she would sleep all day in a pitch-black room, and she was almost always nervous and stoned on her drugs. Jimmy

Levitt was also having serious problems: he lived on the third floor in a room full of guns.

Growing up, I was considered one of the children and was expected to sit with Mac watching TV during my parents' cocktail hour—we were joined by Jimmy when he lived with us. By the time I was 18, I was working at Levitt & Sons during summers and vacations, but I was still treated as one of the children. I couldn't stand being with Mac and Jimmy, listening to them constantly biting their nails. Their problems were so unavoidably obvious, it would make me want to run away screaming. I told my parents, "I cannot sit with those two while you have your cocktails because I'm not a child anymore. I'll either work late and eat on my own, or I'll come home just in time for dinner." They agreed I could join them instead.

Also, our cook was a little crazy, or at least I thought so. She was a good cook, but one night I heard someone turning the knob on my locked bedroom door. I opened it and looked out; she was in a granny gown, holding a lighted candle, walking down the hall with her hair unbraided and streaming behind her, trying all the doors. It was eerie. I told my father, and he told my mother because she was the one who disciplined staff when necessary. The cook had been deteriorating, and my mother let her go.

All these troubling aspects of our life at Albidale did not mar the experience for me to any great extent. What was most important was that my parents were married, and we seemed like a real family doing normal things. I was going to a good school and had summer jobs like my friends did. My parents were busy working and managing our farm; we behaved well and interacted more normally than ever before. That my parents were married was a big factor in this new feeling of having a normal family.

* * *

Elephants also live in a beautiful setting in the wild, wandering through extensive plains called savannas. These are undulating grasslands featuring an open tree canopy, or clusters of trees, and spotted with watering holes. Elephants, who are vegetarians, may travel for 16 – 18 hours a day, covering up to 30 miles, as they dine on the grass and tree branches. Their territory is stored in their matriarch's memory, and she guides them along their way.

Albidale, my version of a lovely, peaceful savanna, was the backdrop for my adolescence and emergence into the world of adults. We lived there while I was in my last two years of high school at Beard and while I was in college. After our marriage, Fred and I lived at Albidale for a couple of years as well. In some ways, this beautiful estate was a catalyst for my becoming who I would be as an adult. Now I was more on my own, separated from Mac by our different schools and temperaments, and while I was still dependent on my parents, I was learning to be more objective about them. During the time my family lived at Albidale, and after I left Beard, I was venturing out beyond the reach of any matriarchs. I would now have to rely on the guidance I imbibed from my grandmother and Miss Sutherland as I went on my way. Perhaps one day, I would become a matriarch myself.

Chapter 7:

College Interrupted

*College is a place to keep warm between high
school and an early marriage.*
−George Gobel

New Grazing Lands

Younger female elephants learn from their close connection with
the matriarch: they absorb her knowledge of geographic landmarks,
and they learn the importance of caring for the herd. Through her
example, they develop skills of leadership. When the matriarch
ultimately reaches old age, a younger female is primed to ascend
into that position. I was lucky; I was taught by two women, each
extraordinary in her own way. My grandmother and Miss Sutherland
nudged me along, supporting me through difficult times, preparing
me for more independent learning environments. All along the way,
I was exposed to the skills of the matriarch, while still much too
young to become one myself.

* * *

Fortified by the self-confidence I gained at Beard, I was ready for
the kind of independence and distance from my family I would find
in the safe community of a women's college. I loved that type of

environment in my previous schools. I was interested in Wellesley, Goucher, Vassar, and Connecticut College for Women. Although it was unusual, I visited these campuses without my parents, traveling on the DC-3 with the pilot and co-pilot, who also rented cars and drove me from the airports to the colleges. Those car rides were the scariest part of these trips. My parents were, as usual, too busy with their business to come with me.

At Wellesley, the admissions office was in the basement, which was uncomfortably dark. I raced to get there on time, but they told me I didn't have an appointment. They asked for my name. My last name was Habermehl, but they had no appointment under that name. I tried Kenny, my mother's maiden name. Nope. I tried Levitt. The admissions person looked at me as if I had three heads. Who is this student who doesn't know her own last name? Do we want her? I got out of there as fast as I could, and I didn't apply.

I ended up going to Connecticut College for Women; in 1969 it dropped the reference to women when it began to admit men, and now within its community it's often referred to as Conn. Being allowed to go there is a story in and of itself.

I first learned of Conn from my boyfriend, Dick, when I was a senior at Beard. He was a year ahead of me, and he was attending Wesleyan University in Middletown, CT, an hour away from Conn. He wanted me to go somewhere close enough for us to see each other, and he told me he'd heard good things about this college. I wanted to be close to Dick as well, and I was impressed with Conn, especially after my visit to its beautiful campus. It was my first choice.

When I told my parents I wanted to go there, I met with unexpected resistance. I was accepted easily, but that didn't make a difference.

My father wanted me to go to Goucher College in Towson, MD. He owned the Woodward estate near there. But since Connecticut College was my first and only choice, I put up a fight. He told me he would pay to send me to Goucher but not to Conn. My grades were good enough that I was pretty sure I could get scholarships and loans to go to Conn if he wouldn't pay. I said to him, "Why do you think I'm at the top of my class? I'm planning to go to Connecticut College and if you don't pay, you'll deprive someone else who really needs the scholarship money. Are you sure you want to do that?"

Then he told me they would pay for me to go to Conn if I stopped seeing Dick. That was the real reason behind his refusal: even though my parents could see that Dick and I loved each other, they didn't want this relationship to blossom. I was heartbroken by my parents' objections, but with all the losses I'd endured, I desperately needed to avoid a total break with them. They were basically all the family I had. Dick was so sick about this turn of events he lost a lot of weight during the rest of that year. But we both knew we couldn't win this battle, so we ended our relationship. Another major loss to say the least. Over the next twelve years, we often met at the annual National Tennis Tournament in Forest Hills, NY. We never stopped feeling connected.

Dick and I had so much in common. We were both athletes and had similar personalities. He was a junior national tennis player, and I played as well. When he and I played doubles with my parents, they never saw the ball coming. I'm not sure if that was part of it or not, but whatever it was, they didn't want me to marry him. I think they were afraid they couldn't control him any more than his tennis ball.

My first semester at Conn was in the fall of 1958. Freshmen had "senior sisters" to help them adjust to college; mine fixed me up with her boyfriend's roommate at Yale. This guy's father was John Charles Daly, the moderator of the TV game show, "What's My Line?" and my date was also named John Daly, as were his four brothers, each of whom had a different middle name. I thought that was strange.

He came to pick me up on our first date in his new Thunderbird, and as we're driving to the main gate from my dorm, he told me how rich he was. I told him that if that's all he could talk about, he could take me back to the dorm. But he protested that he could talk about lots of things, and he could. He took me to dinner at The Wagon Wheel, a local restaurant. His other roommate, Fred Vanderkloot, joined us for dinner with his cousin, who was another Conn student. I was wearing an elephant pin (how ironic), and Fred kept commenting on it. After dinner John took me back to Branford, my dorm. When he pulled up in front, Fred drove his car up beside John's on my side and tried to talk to me. When he went home, he told his family he met the girl he was going to marry.

A few days later, Fred called me on the phone in the hallway of the third floor of Branford. He said he wanted to take me out for my birthday in May—somehow he knew it was then. I agreed, and he took me to the Lighthouse Inn, an iconic inn and restaurant overlooking Long Island Sound in New London. I continued to date him on and off, even though he was volatile. He was constantly having fits over things, and he had a lot of trouble with himself. But he was affable, smart, and had a good sense of humor. On the other hand, he was easily bored, and if he was with people he didn't connect with, he'd be yawning in the corner.

Fred graduated from Yale in 1959 while I was ending my fresh-man year, and he went to work on Wall Street, but I continued to date him, along with other boys who were still in college. He didn't want me to come to his graduation because he was afraid if I met his mother, who was very controlling, that would end our relation-ship. While he was growing up, any time he did something wrong, she would say, "Watch it. You're already a half orphan." His father died when he was four. She was expecting him to come home and take care of her after he graduated. He had to tell her that was not happening. Fred always refused to tell me anything about his family except that it was awful. Knowing what I know now, his refusal was a huge red flag, but I knew nothing then.

Illnesses: Near Disaster

My time at Conn was fraught with a lot of difficulty, much of it due to illness. In 1958, during my first semester, doctors found cancer in my father's vocal cords. After surgery, he slowly recovered his ability to speak, albeit hoarsely, and in February, he and my mother finally married. That was when he adopted me and my sister. After they married, my parents took a trip to Europe: I was supposed to meet them in NYC when they disembarked from the Queen Mary.

I got there and they were nowhere to be found. I was frantic. In that time before cell phones, you could panic in an emergency because there was no way to connect to anybody. I went back to my car and started driving. My plan was to go to one hospital after another until I found them. But on the way, traffic was stopped because someone jumped into the river to commit suicide, and someone else tried to rescue that person. Now people were trying to rescue the rescuer. I got back in my car after finding this out, even more numb. I went a few blocks more, and the car in front of me hit a pedestrian. By this time, I figured I was on a fool's errand, and I drove back to Conn College.

I was not about to go back to New York City. When I got to Conn, I called family friends, and they told me my mother was taken by ambulance to the hospital. I finally found out what hospital she was in and that she would be ok. She was hemorrhaging and was having a hysterectomy.

My sister was also sick that year: she got a sinus infection so severe it could have impacted her brain, and so she was hospitalized.

During the summer vacation between my sophomore and junior years at Conn, back at Albidale, it was my turn to get sick. I passed out from heat exhaustion after a tennis match: the doctor came and thought I had leukemia. Of course he didn't tell me the diagnosis. I overheard him in the hallway outside my bedroom whispering with my parents. I was terrified, especially since nobody said a word to me about it. Ever. That same old silence again. Here I was trapped in my room at Albidale, not knowing what would come next. I thought this was curtains, that I wouldn't make it to my next birthday, when I'd turn 21.

My friend, Charlie, gave me John Galsworthy's book, *The Forsyte Saga*. I was so frightened I couldn't sleep—I read instead. I remember the line from that book that goes: "At midnight the tears run into your ears." That captured what I was experiencing. This illness triggered memories of being sick with pneumonia when I was five. I was losing weight, and the exhaustion continued. That's when, because I thought I wasn't going to live very long, I made a bargain with God: I never wanted to face death again feeling I hadn't contributed anything. I've been trying to make my life meaningful ever since.

I have to admit I was terrified by a leukemia diagnosis, but that isn't what I had. It was osteomyelitis in my lower jaw, also very serious and potentially lethal, but somehow it seemed less threatening. However, my aunt Kitty died from osteomyelitis several years before, and Betty Davis, the famous actress, who had the same disease and the same surgeon who would operate on me, experienced a recurrence two years after the surgery. That surgeon became famous for being able to operate in a way that didn't leave an enormous scar from your ear to your chin. Knowing about such outcomes, I had reason to be scared.

I still remember the surgery and what led up to it. When I was in his office, the surgeon was examining my jaw with an instrument when it suddenly went right through the bone, and he said, "You have to go to the hospital now." He called to reserve a room in New York Hospital. I got in a cab and went to the hospital by myself—it was an enormous place—I took the elevator to the room and sat on the bed waiting for whatever would happen next. A nurse came; she was nice, and she said, "Honey, you can't stay here. You have to go downstairs to register, and you're underage, so we have to notify your parents."

After the hospital called my parents, they came and checked me in. It hadn't occurred to me to call them. It always seemed to me I did all the hard things by myself from when I was an adolescent on. My parents were too busy. That was a painful realization, but I always pushed it aside and did what needed to be done. Maybe I was also learning from them not to tell anyone about scary things.

The Critical Moment

That surgery was a big deal: the surgeon removed most of my jawbone down to the marrow, and they used a new anesthesia that would allow a patient to recover quickly. I remember being in the recovery room, with six to eight other patients, and it seemed dark. Suddenly I felt the blood spurt up my nose as I started to hemorrhage—I couldn't breathe, and I was drowning. The two nurses were across the room helping someone else. My mouth was full of packing to stop the bleeding, so I couldn't cry out. All I could do was stare hard at the backs of the nurses, and finally they must have felt it: they turned around, saw the blood, and came running over. It was clearly a medical emergency.

My osteomyelitis surgery with its near-death experience had repercussions beyond the physical. When I recovered, I remembered those two nurses were speaking Spanish, and I realized I wanted to become fluent in that language. Who knew when it might be a lifesaver? I followed through on that goal: I learned some Spanish when we built a Levittown in Puerto Rico, and when I went back to Conn, I took enough courses for a minor in it. That's how I became bi-lingual, which in turn led to my job in the South Bronx and my deep friendship with Myrtle Parnell. I always hired Spanish speakers to help with my children so that they would grow up bi-lingual.

Isn't it interesting the way things in our lives can be strongly and causally connected? An accidental occurrence can completely alter the arc of our lives.

You're probably wondering how I could remember all this. Many years later when I was in hypnotherapy training and in a trance, I went back to that experience. When I came out of the trance, everyone in the room was totally shocked by what they witnessed, and I was drained. I remembered what I re-experienced in the trance, but no one would tell me what they saw, not even Myrtle.

I know I stayed in the hospital for ten days after the surgery, and the nurses kept giving me shots of Demerol every four hours, which barely touched the pain. One of the nurses told me that in her 30 years of nursing, she never saw a patient my size being given so much Demerol. Each shot lasted only one hour, and then the pain was so bad I mentally removed myself and floated above my body. Somehow, I knew how to hypnotize myself without ever being taught.

After the operation, the doctor filled the open space in my jaw with 24 inches of half-inch packing. The first time the packing was replaced, they gave me 21 shots of Novocain and it hurt like crazy anyway. The doctor told me, "Don't yell! This is going to hurt worse than anything you've ever felt." He offered me Demerol to ease the pain of subsequent changes of the packing, but I didn't take it. I went home with some, but I flushed it down the toilet. I would rather feel the pain than become addicted like my sister.

The doctor wanted me to go home to recuperate, but at this point, school was more home than anywhere else, so I went back to Conn. I had to go into New York City by train several hours each way to get the packing changed three times a week. I moved carefully wherever I went on campus because my jawbone was down to the marrow and could easily be broken. I finally recovered, but I'd lost so much weight that when I went to see one of my professors, Prof.

Ely, she took one look at me and cried. I was 5'5", weighed 90 lbs., and a size two swam on me.

The whole osteomyelitis episode traumatized me for decades. I was afraid it would come back. As a frequent reminder, my jaw ached whenever the weather got bad. Doctors exhibited alarm every time I told them about it because it does sometimes recur. It did with Betty Davis, as I mentioned. It's an infection that can lie dormant for long periods of time.

I subsequently realized something about the off-the-charts excruciating pain I experienced throughout that ordeal. I believe it wasn't just physical: I think the pent-up grief I wasn't allowed to express during early losses was finding an outlet.

My surgeon told me he operated on a young woman soon after he did my surgery: in her case he had to break her jaw and move it significantly because it wasn't properly aligned. She had no pain during that procedure. He told me about her experience because it contrasted so much with mine. Her lack of excruciating pain suggests to me that part of my suffering was emotional. I think I was conflicted during this whole experience. A part of me desperately wanted to survive, which is why I tried so hard to get the nurses to turn around and notice what was happening to me in the recovery room. But part of me was also willing to die because the loss of my grandmother and the absence of her emotional support was still too painful to bear even five years after her death.

For most of my remaining time at Conn, except for when I was recuperating, I was busy with athletics again. I played center forward on the field hockey team. Then there were also lacrosse, basketball, tennis, and riding. I boarded my horse, Rudi, at the college stables and rode him frequently with the riding club. Of course I also went to class, majoring in economics. Bill Levitt's influence pushed me toward a career in business after graduation.

I now understand that illness is an important pattern in my life, beginning with the pneumonia I had when I was five. That was a big one; I could have died. In between that and the osteomyelitis, illnesses were happening to my parents, my sister, and my grandmother. Some were major, some minor. I see illness as a fractal-like pattern, similar episodes of different magnitudes happening over time. Stay tuned for more about fractals—the amazing patterns that occur in nature and in human behavior.

My college years were basically a happy time for me, except for the illness. The Conn campus was beautiful, the people were nice, the sports were great, and the courses were interesting. I had the same roommate for four years, and I'm still in touch with her. She's another part of the family I built over the years. Every weekend I went away on dates to Yale, Wesleyan, Harvard, and Princeton—all men's colleges at the time. Although I met Fred my freshman year, I dated a lot of other guys, and my relationship with him went up and down because of his temper tantrums.

While I recuperated from the surgery, Charlie, the friend who brought me *The Forsyte Saga* earlier, was sweet to me. He visited me in the hospital and brought me a huge bouquet of gardenias, my favorite flower. He stayed in touch and showed he very much cared about me. He was related in some way to my father, but even so, my parents broke up this relationship in the same way they stopped me from seeing Dick. They couldn't control Charlie either. And they thought he was too short. Fred, in comparison to Charlie, was terrible while I was sick. But he was tall, and he was malleable, so he was OK in their eyes.

My parents were happy when Fred proposed to me and I accepted. I think my decision to marry him was influenced by my conviction that I didn't have long to live. Also, my parents finally liked someone who wanted to marry me. And he very much did want to marry me.

The year before I married, while I was a junior at Conn, my parents gave me a wonderful 21st birthday party at a fancy club in NYC. Several of my former boyfriends and Fred were there. We all stayed at the Waldorf Towers. In the garage was my birthday present, a Renault Caravelle, which I was to drive back to college in CT the next day. But I wasn't familiar with stick shifts, and at the first light, I rolled back into a car. Fortunately it was my parents' car and there was no damage to anything. My classmates had a rather lurchy ride, but by New Haven I was ok.

My senior year was even more momentous for me than it is for most college students. I married Fred in March that year, two months before graduation. I did not want to be a June bride.

Early in May, during the end-of-the-year award ceremonies, I was given the Charlotte Pyle prize, a sterling silver bowl given each year in memory of the Pyle's daughter, Charlotte, to a member of the senior class who displayed qualities of leadership and did the most for the athletic association. In making this award, Dean of the College Gertrude Noyes said, "I'm about to give this award to the only person who's had three last names in the last four years. We'll be spending a lot of time untangling the records." The three names were Habermehl, Levitt, and finally, Vanderkloot. I was hardly paying attention, until my friends started poking me and saying, "It's you!"

Dean Noyes was a wonderful woman who reminded me of Miss Sutherland. I began negotiating after spring break freshman year to have a car on campus, and I did that every year. At the beginning of my senior year, she said, smiling, "I can't wait to hear the reason you want a car on campus this year." I had one there all four years: normally no one was allowed to have a car on campus until after spring break senior year. Dean Noyes was widely respected and beloved on campus—another matriarch.

So there I was, married and graduating from college. I survived a life-threatening illness; I won many athletic victories; I met and married my husband after having been forced apart from the person I loved, and now I was ready for the next chapter in my life. My parents were living a glamorous lifestyle; Mac was essentially lost to me for many reasons; and I was now clearly advancing into adulthood. But I had no idea where my life was going.

My wedding, in some ways, was a reflection more of where I was coming from in my life than where I was going. And I couldn't even begin to imagine then that life was taking me in such an interesting and important direction.

Chapter 8:

The Crumbling Begins

"Marriage has no guarantees. If that's what you're looking for, go live with a car battery."
–Erma Bombeck

"The only question with wealth is, what do you do with it?"
–John D. Rockefeller

Final touches before the ceremony, 1962

My wedding

My wedding was a fairy tale affair that took place March 24, 1962, toward the end of my senior year at Connecticut College. We were married at Albidale in a lodge Fred and I later lived in. My parents hired a well-known events planner to orchestrate all the elements of the wedding. He worked his magic on the lodge: it started out as the chapel where we took our vows, became a fancy restaurant for a formal dinner, and then shape-shifted into a nightclub. The ceiling was hung with tens of thousands of baby rosebuds. A hundred people were in attendance, mostly my parents' friends and Fred's and my college friends. Aside from his mother, Fred didn't have much family.

My wedding gown was designed by Norman Norell, a well-known au couture American designer. My parents didn't start with that; I was still very skinny from the osteomyelitis, and I kept trying on a lot of gowns. I had in mind what my wedding gown should look like—a Josephine Bonaparte empire style, even though I hadn't seen a picture of it. It was a psychic thing. Norman Norell recently completed this design, and when I saw it, it was the one! My parents agreed to buy it, even though it was expensive.

Flowers everywhere! Even on the ceiling. 1962

Fred and me with one of the musicians

I felt numb throughout the whole wedding ceremony and reception. Fortunately, I have a lot of photographs of it to supplement my actual memories of that day. After it was over, Fred and I took off for the airport; we flew to Mexico City, and at the airport there Fred was hysterical when he thought there were no seats on the plane to Acapulco, our destination. I spoke to the agents at the gate in Spanish, and we were OK. When we boarded, there were only two other couples on the plane. I plunked down in my seat in relief, and as I leaned on the armrest, it fell on the floor. "Oh no," I thought. "I've come this far, and the plane may crash."

Acapulco was undeveloped at that point. We stayed for two weeks in a beautiful home owned by a doctor who was both a friend of my father's and the surgeon for his cancer of the vocal cords—the house was perched on a cliff overlooking the bay. It had an open-air living room and a swimming pool and came with maid service and a pink Jeep. We spent our time there riding around in the Jeep and on the beautiful beach. I also did a lot of waterskiing. But all was not peaceful and calm, and maybe what happened was alerting me to the nature of the adult world I was entering. Fortunately, the house was on very strong stilts because we experienced a major earthquake that threw everything on the floor, including me. But all's well that ends well! The house, and we, were not harmed.

Newlyweds

Fred and I continued to remain within my family's orbit for quite a while. At first, we tried to live apart from them: shortly before our wedding, we rented an apartment in the Wyncote House in Wyncote, PA, bordering Philadelphia, about seven miles from Albidale.

We settled in there after we returned from Mexico, but we didn't stay long before moving back to the lodge at Albidale where we were married, down from the main house. Right after we moved in, I cleaned it and hired one of the cleaning ladies to come and tell me what I missed. She said I got everything except the top of the lamps. I was practicing for married life with less money.

After graduating from Conn, I went to work at the Albert Finkel advertising agency as a secretary to the number two guy. Fred was working for Brown Brothers Harriman, a private bank on Wall Street. We each had an economics degree: Fred was hired on Wall Street, and I got to play secretary in an ad agency. That's how gender worked in those days. I was considered "pregnancy prone." It was also ten years before Roe v. Wade.

At my job I had to put up with too much attention from my boss, who followed me everywhere. One evening he even followed me home. I parked my car in the driveway, and he pulled up behind me. He got out and approached my car. I said, "See that car in front of mine? It belongs to a very large and jealous husband." He left and I quit the next day.

I was pregnant.

The lodge was where we were living when our first daughter, Katie, was born. When I was newly pregnant with Katie and went to the doctor to make sure, he thought I had a tumor—he didn't think I was pregnant. He asked if I ever had any life-threatening illnesses, thinking the answer would be "no." As soon as I mentioned the osteomyelitis, he raced me down the hall to take X-rays. We were both relieved to discover there was no tumor—and there was a fetus in there.

We lived in the lodge for a year before buying and moving to a house on Windmill Drive, in Huntington, LI, 23 miles east of Old Westbury, my old stomping grounds. We paid $27,000 for that house. It was a cute little ranch, and while we lived there, our second daughter, Pamela, was born.

Our house at Windmill Drive, 1965

We were still caught in my family's sticky web, which was both seductive and disempowering. At about this time my father offered Fred a position at Levitt & Sons, which I didn't want him to take. In fact we had a big fight about it. I knew my parents' objective was to control me by bringing Fred into the family fold that way, making him (and me) dependent on them for our income. Controlling me was their constant goal.

We didn't take any money from them aside from Fred's salary: we lived on what we made, unlike my sister, who took for granted or didn't care that my parents would buy her apartments and decorate them whenever she wanted them to. They could never own her, but they weren't trying to do that with her in the same way they tried to control me.

I was their pet cow. I tried so hard at everything to earn their acceptance, and where did that get me? I was not so much accepted as someone to be owned, so I didn't achieve my goal. I wanted to be valued for myself, but to both my parents, I was more like something they could show off. With all the troubles they had with my sister and Bill Levitt's son, Jimmy, I made them feel like they did a good job. Then some of their friends would say to me, "How did somebody like you come out of a family like that?" That message was unpleasant and confusing to me.

Living like the Robber Barons

My father always said he wanted to live like the robber barons. He liked the idea that he and my mother could buy whatever they wanted and that luxury would be their norm. This was his goal, and he made good on it, but along the way, he also provided well-built affordable housing for young veterans and others who didn't have a lot of money. My father was a good man—a generous man—but he did have an obsession with wealth. At this point in his life, wealth validated his success.

As building Levittowns made my father and mother increasingly wealthy, they enjoyed their opulent lifestyle. They had a 150-foot yacht named *The Lady Alicia* after my mother. We sailed around Europe and the Caribbean and had many a party on its decks. I remember being on it with them once when we were docked in St. Tropez: we were having a formal dinner when suddenly the boat tilted sharply toward starboard. At first, we didn't know what was happening, but then we saw Bridgitte Bardot and her sister sunbathing in the nude on the boat docked next to ours. It turned out this was their hangout. Our crew was intrigued, to put it mildly...

The Lady Alicia, 1960

Fred and I almost never had the yacht to ourselves and our friends, but we did once with three other couples, including my tennis doubles partner and her husband. She indiscreetly got herself intimately involved with the captain, a very good-looking German who had been on a PT boat during WWII. I was upset with her; my father was upset with both me and the captain. Entertaining on the yacht, which meant being responsible for the meals AND the guests, was too much for me— that's why we didn't do it more often.

* * *

Elephants in the wild live a simple life, wandering through the savanna grazing on grass, shrubs and lower tree branches and looking for water. Their lives are not without danger; in fact, danger is increasingly present as climate change threatens their habitat and poachers hunt them for their tusks. But they don't cause these dangers themselves. We humans, in contrast, often bring the challenges we face into our own lives. We create many of the complexities in our lives that ultimately bring us down. I see that happening in my patients' lives, and it was certainly true in my family.

* * *

In the early 1960s, my father bought an estate in Mill Neck, LI, tore down the old mansion, and built a grand French chateau, La Colline, surrounded by almost 70 acres. La Colline is still there and was for sale again in 2021, advertised as having 33 rooms. It evoked the period described in *The Great Gatsby*: the long, two-story French chateau overlooks a reflection pool centered in an oblong paved courtyard that lies between the house's two wings. La Colline has a brick exterior with floor-to-ceiling small-paned windows on the first floor. Arched windows grace the second story.

Inside, in the foyer, a beautiful mural depicting the history of the building industry surrounded you as you walked in, covering the dome as well as the walls. I doubt that has survived. The house is nestled among lush gardens on all sides, and a curving driveway leads through them up to the house from the main gate.

La Colline, 1965, which was then surrounded by 70 acres

My parents moved into La Colline the night of the 1965 blackout in New York. It was October and the days were short. Fourteen moving vans brought my parents' belongings from Albidale. My mother labeled all the boxes and furniture so the movers would know exactly where each piece was to go. But with the blackout, the only working lights were on the van, and it was all the movers could do to get the belongings into the house and find a place to park them. My parents stayed in the Waldorf Towers during this move. Of course the Towers had no electricity either, so the elevators weren't working. That night as my father was going up the stairs, a hotel employee was coming down with a tray. My father asked if he could get some drinks. The guy said, "Hell no, I'm out of here."

Bill Levitt and my mother lived at La Colline for a while, but at the same time, they had their penthouse apartment at The Dorchester on 57th and Park in NYC. At this point in their lives and marriage, they were getting restless.

The Tipping Point and a Downward Spiral

A lot happened while we lived at the Windmill Drive house. Big changes were in store for us, and they began to unfold.

First and foremost, Bill Levitt entered into agreement with ITT to sell Levitt & Sons to them in what was at first a very secretive transaction. Fred figured out what was happening. The sale became final in 1968.

My mother and Bill Levitt, 1960s

Because my father was fixated on living large, he thought if they sold the company, they would garner more wealth and power than if they retained it. He was also probably bored with Levitt & Sons and ready for a new adventure, which meant he was somewhat bored with everything in his life. His desire to live like the robber barons was becoming particularly obvious. I'm sure my mother shared his mood.

They sold the bond that since 1946 held them and the rest of us together.

The Crumbling Begins

Around this time my mother and father planned a big party and invited celebrities. For some reason, my father never showed up, and although my mother was annoyed, she danced the evening away with Fred Astaire.

Before the company was sold, my father took 14 family members and friends to France and Monte Carlo, and at the casino he started a craps game. He was very good at craps, and people came, stood around, and watched. He won and broke the bank. Then he paid to put the 14 of us in five-star hotels for two weeks.

During that trip, in Paris, we went for cocktails at the apartment of a couple, Simone and Barney. I don't remember how my father met Barney. Simone was Greek and was an art dealer in Paris. Fred and I went with my brother, Bill Levitt, Jr., and his first wife, Elaine. As we were leaving, Bill Jr. asked, "Do you have a feeling that everything in that place is for sale, including the two of them?" I said yes.

My father started an affair with Simone soon after he met her. Contributing to his restlessness was the experience of loss. His father died in 1962, his mother in 1965, and his younger brother in 1966. His family was important to him, since they not only shared their personal lives, but were also in business together. His life started to get frazzled even before the sale, but everything in my family unraveled after it happened.

In 1967-68, just preceding the sale, my mother owned a designer boutique in Manhasset called the Country Duchess. I was the manager and model for it. One day while I was there and my mother was in the back room, in walked Simone. I could not stand her. I simply could not abide her. She was only nine years older than I was. So I went in the back and said to my mother, "Your friend is in front. I will not wait on her; she's all yours." Simone was at this time still married to husband number one, Barney. They had three young daughters. My parents and Simone and her husband were pretending to be old friends. My mother went out and waited on her.

My mother tended to make it the other guy's fault when something went wrong so she would be in the clear, and she would do that to get out of a marriage as well. She was on board with what was going on with Bill Levitt and Simone at some level.

Around this time my father was building a large new office building in Lake Success, a village in Great Neck, LI, and he put on a huge party. It was a big deal: the architect, Edward Durell Stone, who designed the Museum of Modern Art, was there, along with hundreds of people, including my birth father and his family members, all of whom my father hired at Levitt & Sons. (Everyone complained about one of those family members. They told Bill Levitt, "We can't stand this guy." I don't remember why they didn't like him: I just remember he was mild-mannered. And my father, who was so good at being diplomatic, told them, "But he has the best handwriting in the company!" He kept the guy.)

At the party, Simone was standing behind me. I was wearing spike heels. I aimed very carefully, stepped back, and got her on the instep. She screamed, and I said, "Oh, I'm so sorry!" I would have slugged her if I could.

Felix Rohatyn, the man who rescued New York City in the 70's when it was teetering on the brink of bankruptcy, brokered the deal between my father and Harold Geneen, president of ITT. While it was being culminated, my mother disappeared into Europe for a month. None of us, including my father, knew where she was. At the end of that time, she called me from Germany, and she said, "How would you like to talk to my next husband?" I said, "I wasn't aware you got rid of your last one."

Then I spoke to Walter von Kees, whose English wasn't good, and my mother told me she was planning to come back. My father tried to explain what was going on, trying to get me on his side. I told him, "I don't want to be in the middle of this. You're both cheating." I knew I couldn't abandon my mother because she was more vulnerable. He had all that money, and my mother's money was entangled with his.

My mother and Walter came back to New York, but right after they arrived, Walter disappeared. My father had people out looking for him. Separately, my mother and father each went to their Dorchester apartment to see if he was there. Walter wasn't there, but then he called my mother, and she told him it was safe for him to come back. I think he hid because he was afraid of Bill Levitt's power. Maybe he thought Bill Levitt was angry with him for having a relationship with my mother.

The first time I saw Walter was at the beauty salon in NYC where both my mother and I were regulars. I went there for a haircut, and an attractive man about 39 or 40 years old who looked like he might have a drinking problem was in the waiting area on the ground floor. When I got upstairs to the salon proper, I saw my mother and asked if the man downstairs belonged to her. She said, "Yes, that's Walter."

After Walter returned, my father wanted my mother and Walter to come back to La Colline with him and Simone. The house was certainly big enough for them all with its 33 rooms. During this period, when the divorce conversations were happening, my sister called and said she was going to come and put things back together again. She didn't understand. I told her, "No, Mac! No. Just stay out of the way like I'm doing."

But no matter the circumstances, my parents were always polite and friendly, so meanwhile, back at La Colline, all four had dinner together, and then my father took Walter to his room to show him his watch collection. He had a drawer of valuable watches, and he wound them every day. He opened the drawer and asked Walter to take his pick—he could have whichever one he wanted as a gift. The next day, my mother and Walter went to the Dorchester apartment to stay for a while.

While my parents were talking about divorce and consulting with lawyers, I became suspicious of Walter. I knew nothing about him, and I thought he might be interested in the money that was part of my mother's world, so I had him investigated. A good friend of ours was in the European/American import/export business, and he knew how to have Walter investigated in Europe. It turned out he was OK—one of the few good things in this mess.

I don't remember how quickly after that they made their divorce plans. What I do remember is that this polite, friendly little group— my mother and Walter, my father and Simone and Barney—all traveled to Mexico together to get my parents' divorce. Around this time I said something about my father to my mother in a conversation, calling him "my father," and she said, "He's not your father anymore." And I said, "Oh, yes, he is! Walter is on you!"

After the Mexico divorce, my father went back to New York City and bought another penthouse apartment in the Sherry Netherland building on 5th Avenue where he and Simone could live, and my mother stayed at La Colline with Walter.

While my father was still married to my mother, they sold the Lady Alicia and contracted to have a larger, fancier yacht built for the two of them. Not long after my father married Simone, he named the new yacht, which was still being built, "La Belle Simone." We called it "La BS." What he was doing made me sad. He was becoming an old man trying desperately to hang onto his youth, and I knew I was losing him before he was old enough to die.

La Belle Simone, 1971 or '72

Why my Parents' Marriage Unraveled

Selling Levitt & Sons ended my parents' relationship because their whole lives together were built around that business. Why did Bill Levitt sell? I would say that the seduction of money can be absolutely corrupting. ITT offered him $92 million in 1968 dollars ($760 million in 2022), and he couldn't refuse that. Also, he thought Harold Geneen would put him on their board, but Geneen had no intention of doing that. My father realized right away the sale was a mistake. He tried to buy the company back, but ITT refused. Levitt & Sons was so much a part of his identity that losing it broke him emotionally, and he no longer had commercial use of his name for future development projects.

The sale also ended Fred's ability to function. Now he was destabilized, and because his father's early death cast its shadow on his entire life, he was ill-equipped to handle other losses as an adult. Fred did well surrounded by the double insulation of the business structure that was also the family structure. He tried to hang onto the familiar by continuing to work at the company under ITT's ownership, but after a year he left because it wasn't the same. Fred lost direction being on his own, even as he began consulting with other corporations. In response to these unsettling changes, I again became focused on athletic achievement. It was my way of coping.

Bill Levitt was my father from 1946 until he died on January 28, 1994. During the years between 1957 and 1969 our lives were, more than ever, smooth and happy, interesting, and exciting. After he sold the company, his restlessness and all that money drove him in a downward spiral, helped along by Simone's need for public attention and extravagance.

When I took Katie and Pam to visit my father at La Colline after his marriage to Simone, the girls would say as we drove there, "OK, two hours and counting." On one occasion Pam indignantly said, "Simone thinks she's Edith Piaf." They couldn't abide her any more than I could. One time when we went there for dinner, I think it was around 1980, Simone was drunk, and we were having dessert in the den. While we were eating, she picked up the bowl of whipped cream and threw it in my face. I wiped it off and laughed, and she staggered off to her bedroom.

After he sold his company, my father started to become increasingly vacant; I believe dementia was setting in. From when I first met him and all during my growing up, he and I had a warm and connected relationship. For 20 years, I had breakfast with him for three hours or more on weekends talking and laughing—he was often funny. I wouldn't give that up for anything. That person wasn't there anymore after he sold his business and married Simone. And he became more irrational as well.

Years before the divorce, my mother began to have chronic headaches. Her doctor told her that if she divorced her husband, the headaches would stop. He was right. My father refused to pay that doctor. According to my mother, my father wanted to get back together with her within a year after marrying Simone, just as he wanted to buy his company back after selling it. I think he realized that by selling Levitt & Sons and divorcing my mother, he sold his soul, and he wanted to put the pieces of his old life back together. But he couldn't.

* * *

Thank goodness I had my athletic interests to distract me from the family mess. Early on when we lived at Windmill Drive, I joined the Huntington Racquet Club. I was a competitive tennis player, so I challenged the woman at the top of the tennis ladder. Other players told me I'd never win. I asked, "Why not?" They said, "She cheats."

I went out to play with her, and I had an American twist serve, which had a nice spin, like a left-handed slice. As we played, I noticed that everything close to the line but in the court, she called, "Out." So I waited until she hit the ball and it landed smack in the middle of my side of the court, and I yelled, "Out!" She threw her racquet on the ground and yelled, "What do you mean, out?" I said, "Honey, you call 'em on your side, and I call 'em on mine." She was never number one again, and I took her place.

Everyone could see that my name was number one on the ladder, and others came up and asked me, "How did you do that?" I told them the story and they said, "Damn, why didn't I think of that?" For the rest of the time we lived in Huntington until we moved in 1980, I remained number one on the ladder without cheating. I also played number one singles, doubles, and mixed doubles on grass at the Crescent Club in Huntington, where I was seeded number one in the town. After that, when we moved from Huntington to Lighthouse Road in Sands Point, I took up long distance running in training for the NYC marathon because tennis was no longer a challenge. Pam told Katie, "I don't want to watch Mommy win anymore. It's boring." I couldn't disagree.

* * *

This was another challenging period in my life, but having faced obstacles all my life, I didn't shy away. Tennis was now a no-brainer, so on to running marathons; they were more difficult. The challenges posed by my family were not as easily conquered.

My father overcame obstacles to master two goals: figuring out how to build homes more quickly and inexpensively than anyone else and amassing great wealth. But then he lost his way and made the misstep of selling his business, causing everything in his life to unravel. My mother, understanding that the life she built with Bill Levitt was collapsing, moved on; she seemed ready for the challenge of finding another man to focus on—her next adventure.

In the elephant world, it is the adolescent males who leave the herd to travel alone or to loosely band together with other bulls. In my family, it seemed as if all the members of our herd were moving on separately. My father, stymied in his attempts to build more housing developments, tried to build a life with Simone. My mother moved with Walter to Europe; her way to create distance between herself and her past. I, too, was searching for my next challenges, in addition to running marathons. Fred and I were thinking about moving, but it would take some time before that became a reality. In the meantime, we gradually began consulting with other companies, using the skills we learned from our involvement with Levitt & Sons.

Chapter 9:

Family—at Home and Abroad

"Loving life is easy when you are abroad. Where no one knows you and you hold your life in your hands all alone, you are more master of yourself than at any other time".
    –Hannah Arendt

A Lull in the Middle

This period of my life, when my parents' and sister's lives were topsy-turvy, was an in-between time for me, almost a lull. I welcomed the stability of being married with children—a structure I thought I could rely on. Although Fred's job situation was a bit insecure, and I was working only in the capacity of helping him with his consulting, our financial situation was not precarious at that time. It was in flux, I would say. We had enough money to do what we wanted.

My traumatic childhood was behind me, and I accepted Mac's incapacities and the tumult of my parents' lives. My focus was on making my life, and the lives of my husband and children, stable and harmonious. The challenge of my athletic adventures kept me focused as well.

My future was unknown, of course. I was at home in the world of affluence to which I was accustomed, and I had no idea this was a down time between past personal traumas and intimate involvement in the chaotic, complex lives of others, as well as eye-opening experiences in a community of extreme poverty. I particularly enjoyed the adventures in foreign lands that characterized this time in my life.

European Odyssey

After the divorce dust settled down, my mother and Walter moved to Italy. They were to sail on the Raffaello, a large Italian ocean liner built in the early 1960s, one of the last ships to be built primarily for liner service across the Atlantic. My mother had a lot of belongings to move: they were to be shipped in those large cargo containers. She worried about safety, but we had a friend, Sirio, of Le Cirque, the famous restaurant in the city, who would protect my mother's belongings through his connections with the Italian mafia. It fell on me to get the movers lined up because my mother was upset after the marriage-go-round, and I'm always trying to take care of everybody. My mother and Walter stayed in Europe for the next ten years.

I remember the evening before they were to sail. Fred and I went to see them off, and Jimmy Vanderkloot, one of Fred's cousins, joined us. Fred ordered a case of Dom Perignon to be sent to the ship. We hired a limousine to go to New York and had a fancy dinner and drinks in the city with my mother and Walter. During dinner my mother casually and quietly told us that she had over a million dollars' worth of jewelry in the satchel between her feet. None of us worried about that. We went from there to the Raffaello, where we continued to celebrate until the last gangplank was being pulled up.

I was sad, because it was the first time my mother was moving away, and she was moving FAR away. She and I were closer then. Our departure celebration turned into a funny evening. We went back home in the limo, and Fred and Jimmy drank brandy all the way home. When we got there, Fred went to dive into bed but missed it completely and went splat on the floor. I helped him up, got into bed and slept until morning.

127

When I woke up, I was still sleepy. I wiggled around and felt funny. Then I noticed I still had my hat on, along with my white dress and shoes, and a Raffaello flag was lying between Fred and me. I was thirsty, so I had a drink of water, not realizing that would make me high all over again. I called Hilda, our pharmacist friend, who had a good formula for hangovers. I got three doses of it, one for each of us, took mine, and put the others near Fred and Jimmy. I had to take care of the girls, but Fred and Jimmy kept sleeping.

That was the last time I had too much to drink, and there were only two times before. The time before this was when my sister was engaged, and we had a party to celebrate at Albidale near the pool. My father made scotch stingers that night: the next day they had to drain the pool to rescue peoples' wallets and jewelry from the bottom.

Spain

When my mother and Walter were getting settled in Italy, Fred and I traveled to Spain. This was in the 1970s after Fred quit his job at Levitt & Sons following its purchase by ITT, and I was helping him with some consultancy jobs. We signed a contract with Colgate Palmolive to find a golf course in Italy, France or Spain and do a comparative study of the options: the company wanted to build a course in Europe like Pebble Beach in California. I was the translator in all three places. In France we got lost in the countryside, and we came across an old farmer. I asked for directions, but I couldn't understand anything he said. Fred said, "I thought you understood French." I told him there really was no way I could understand someone with a strong dialect and no teeth.

It was challenging for Fred to adjust to the cultural differences we encountered in Spain, since his life and studies didn't focus on culture at all, while mine did. One morning he was beside himself.

Fred's default anxiety was ratcheted up by being in a place with rules and assumptions he didn't know. He thought we needed to be at a meeting to look at property at 9 a.m. because that would be true in New York. I kept telling him the office wouldn't be open then, which was indeed the case when we got there. But there was no way I could calm his anxiety.

We met some interesting people in Spain. One was a small man wearing funny shoes with broken flaps instead of laces, who showed up when we were waiting to look at property. He was one of the first famous golf course architects, the British-American Robert Trent Jones, and he was interested in designing the Colgate-Palmolive golf course. He told us he never knew where he was going until he got to the airport and could see where the first flight out was headed; that's the flight he would take. Funny man.

One day Fred and I, along with his business partner, met with a Spanish aristocrat: he showed us property that Colgate Palmolive might be interested in. He later took us on a tour of the Alhambra, the Islamic palace and fortress complex in Grenada. I translated on that tour. Later we went to his office to negotiate about the property.

Fred and his business partner's style while doing business was direct and blunt, not at all conversational, and I had to understand both sides and both cultures to translate effectively and not offend either side. In Spanish culture, business deals are discussed in the context of interesting conversation that helps build personal connections. Translating in that context gave me a huge headache, partly because it was disheartening to see the contrast between the man who was helping us, who was tall, elegant, and refined, and the brashness exhibited by Fred and his partner.

We ended up being invited to our new Spanish friend's home, where we could look out the windows at the caves beyond, home to the gypsies. We could see their lights flickering amidst the rocky projections. It was beautiful! We ate giant prawns dipped in rock salt and then barbecued. They were so delicious I remember them still. It was an amazing trip.

Italy

Soon after my mother and Walter arrived in Italy, my mother bought a new house in a little fishing village, Porto Santo Stefano, north and west of Rome. It was on a cliff overlooking the water and the island of Giglio where the Costa Concordia cruise ship crashed many years later, in 2012.

During our trip to Spain we also traveled to Italy and enjoyed our first visit with my mother and Walter there. She and Walter were married by then. Their house came with a swimming pool, and Walter had the great idea to skydive onto the pool deck to honor my 30th birthday. I was appalled and told him if he did, I would leave and never come back. So he didn't. The house and pool deck were about 100 feet above the Mediterranean Sea: if he missed the pool deck, well, I didn't want to contemplate that. He was the skydiving champion in Germany, but still…

This house my mother bought was new, and it needed some finishing touches. But its quirks made life interesting for us all during our visit. When we arrived, I was tired and wanted to clean up after our long trip, so I went to take a shower. I turned the water on, heard it flowing and felt the steam, but there was no water on me—it was all pouring against the bathroom door. I put my clothes back on and went to look for Walter. He fixed it. I was the first person to use that shower.

Then a couple days later, my mother and I were eating breakfast on the deck by the pool when we heard Walter shrieking, "Alicien, Alicien (his nickname for my mother), we're on fire. Come quick, it's a 220-volt circuit on fire!!!!!" My mother called back to him, "I'm almost finished with my breakfast. I'll come when I'm finished."

And unperturbed, she continued eating. My mother's reaction was typical. Walter called the fire department, and the firemen came on their bicycles. They got the fire out.

A huge metal sign on the hill above their house was driving my mother and Walter crazy. One night Walter climbed up to it, put a big chain around it, attached the chain to their Range Rover, pulled the sign down and threw it over the cliff. He was a man of action.

After settling in, we had a tour of the area: Walter, who had been a foreign legionnaire and thoroughly enjoyed taking risks, drove us around, including to the edges of the cliffs so we could get a good look at this beautiful mountainous terrain. My one phobia is a fear of heights, so I wanted to get down on the floor of the Range Rover and hope nothing was falling, especially us.

All in all, we had a good first visit there with my mother and Walter. We met delightful people, and the food was incredible. Because it was all so fresh, with no trace of chemicals, we ate a lot and never gained a pound.

My mother loved the luxurious life Bill Levitt introduced her to almost as much as he did. She bought a couple of yachts while she and Walter were in Europe: first a 65-foot Bagliatto, and next a 100-foot Benetti. When she and Walter were coming back to the US to live, she sold the Benetti, and the man buying it gave her a first payment of $700,000, but then civil unrest broke out in Portugal, his home country, and he suddenly backed out of the sale. He told my mother to keep both the money and the yacht. She then sold it a second time for over $1,000,000.

My mother and Walter leaving the Bagliatto, 1970s.

The Benetti, 1970s

My Mother's New Husband

Before he met my mother, Walter led an interesting life. He was in the French Foreign Legion and went AWOL in 1955 during the battle at Dien Bien Phu in Vietnam. I remember a later time, after Fred and I were back in the US, when my mother sent us a postcard with a picture of a man standing on a cliff with his hands tied behind him, and she wrote that Walter was in jail in Paris. The police forgot that President de Gaulle had pardoned all those who went AWOL in Vietnam.

My mother and Walter moved back to the US in 1981; it's interesting to note that 20 years later, within hours of the 9/11 terrorist attack, the FBI was at his door, wanting to interview him. Even though he lived here peacefully all those years and was by then an old man, they knew he was in demolitions in North Africa and Corsica in the '50s. They wanted to know if he was still in contact with any of the people he was involved with in those operations, even though that was long before, and they came back a second time as well. The FBI can be amazingly thorough. Even so, this seemed extreme. He was never in contact with anyone from those years. But he was scared.

This is another story about Walter that helped me understand him better. I was playing handball one August in the parking garage in New York City I used for 50 years with a friend of mine, the chauffeur for the building's owner. Years before, he was in Germany and witnessed a discussion among men there at a skydiving competition. They were considering whether to compete that day for the championship, given the weather. Most of them decided it was too windy, and they didn't want to risk it. Walter was there as an observer, but he said he would do it if he could borrow a parachute. Someone gave him one, and he went up and successfully parachuted to win the championship. That's how he became the skydiving champion of Germany. Walter was always very much in shape and always a daredevil.

Austria

After a few years at this house in Italy, my mother and Walter moved to Kitzbühel, a small alpine town east of Innsbruck, in the western Austrian province of Tyrol. It was and still is a fashionable ski resort with incredible charm. They lived in a large Alpine house: Fred and I visited them with Katie and Pam several times, and we often stayed for quite a while.

I loved our trips to Austria. It was beautiful, peaceful, and full of skiing adventures. Katie and Pam shared my enthusiasm, and Fred liked everything but the skiing.

We were there on our first visit long enough to take skiing lessons. We enrolled in The Red Devils ski school, founded in 1925 by an Olympian gold medalist. As the oldest ski school in Kitzbühel, it was famous, and it was also excellent. Because I was athletic and had been a water ski instructor, they put me in the intermediate group with four others, even though this would be my first experience skiing downhill.

Now remember, I'm afraid of heights. My first time out on the slopes, I stood on the top of the run looking down, and it looked like I was going to go straight down...down, down, down. At the bottom was barbed wire. But I did it. I went down that run and made it. Out of the five of us, two didn't make it. After that, things began to pick up, and I did well. Then we went down an avalanche run, which takes skiers through a maze of snow and ice mounds left by an avalanche, and I took a wrong turn and landed upside down. Everyone laughed and took my picture.

I'm picturing Fred on that day: with his ski cap on, he looked seven feet tall. He started out on the bunny hill. Skiing wasn't an ideal sport for him because his balance was bad. The instructor was teaching him how to get started, but then he had to leave Fred so he could take me to that spot looking straight down the run. After

I went down, the instructor took Fred, me, Katie, Pam, and Walter to get on the chair lifts, but Fred was a tight fit. This was the last straw: he was definitely out of sorts.

A bit later we all went to lunch, including the girls, and after we finished, the instructor said, "Let's go back out there." Fred said, "Not me. The only thing I liked was lunch, and I shouldn't have to go through all that to get lunch." It was understandable: Fred was not at all coordinated and when he was anxious, his shoulders would go up to his ears. To compensate for these traits, he used to have a great sense of humor and could be quite funny. Unfortunately, later in his life, the anxiety won.

During our first trip to Kitzbühel, Katie was old enough to use a T-bar herself, but I needed to share a bar with Pam. When an adult uses a T-bar with a child, they stand side-by-side on their skis in front of the horizontal bar, holding on to the pulling cable. The bar pulls them up the hill. Pam and I did that; when we were close to the top, I glanced over, but she wasn't there. She was hanging by her hands on the horizontal bar with her feet in the air—she was such a little thing. I told her to just let go, and we both did. It wasn't a big drop. But we couldn't get out of the way before those behind plowed into us, and it created a huge pile-up. One woman was incensed because it tore her ski suit. We walked the rest of the way to the top.

During that visit, we had a Philippine couple, Pilar and Manuel, cooking for us. One of their favorite dishes was Lumpia, which resembles spring rolls. Their lumpia was full of garlic. One morning I went out for an early morning ski, and an Italian woman, no stranger to garlic herself, asked me if I had eaten it for breakfast. I guess I'd eaten so much of it the night before, the aroma was coming out of my pores.

During this visit, we also skied cross country through the woods to steamy little restaurants in beautiful surroundings—snow, evergreen trees, clear skies, crisp clean air—with the windows always steamed up from the warm bodies and good food inside. Everyone in those restaurants was wearing ski clothes, and there was always schnaps to warm you up.

I remember our first Christmas there: it was beautiful. It was rather temperate, but as we headed out to dinner, walking into town, snow fell gently, the church bells rang and echoed back from the mountains—even now the memory thrills me. Coming out from dinner at another steamy little restaurant, we heard traditional Christmas music, and the man who owned the chalet where my mother and Walter lived came around with his steam iron and incense to drive off evil spirits. It was hard to find a Christmas tree in Kitzbühel: we had to go to Salzburg to get one. Everything about Christmas there was traditional, spiritual, and understated—I loved it.

In Kitzbühel there were wonderful après ski places varying from small and cozy to larger beer or dance halls. My mother and Walter lived in an apartment above the Red Bull Restaurant in town for a short time before they moved to Ascona, Switzerland. While they were living there, Walter would often go down to the restaurant or to another nearby bar for the evening. When it was time for him to come home, my mother would send their German shepherd to get him, because he'd often get "detained" there. One night Walter went missing. It turns out he got drunk and was swinging a Dutch man over his head when he tripped and shredded his ankle. They finally brought him home in an ambulance.

* * *

During these trips with Fred either for our consulting work or to visit my mother and Walter, I focused on my day-to-day experiences as a mother to our growing girls and being a wife in a marriage that was faltering. Fred seemed increasingly tangled up with himself since he was no longer supported by strong work and extended family structures. Our consulting jobs were interesting, but they weren't taking me anywhere. They almost felt like an aside in my life.

My parents were slipping down from the high point of their lives: my father's marriage to Simone was a nightmare, and my mother and Walter were skimming the surface. They continually avoided all conflict in their relationship by moving to a new house, apartment, or country whenever they had a disagreement, and Walter was obviously an alcoholic—charming, but a drinker. None of them found fulfillment in work. Bill Levitt's attempts to build developments were thwarted each time. Walter never worked, and my mother's "job" seemed to be living a life of luxury.

Fred and I got serious about buying a larger home to meet the needs of our family, and I was ready to find a new direction and focus for my life.

At this point, the girls were not yet near the age when they would go away to school, and Fred was still rambling around in his life. I found myself feeling a restless desire to create a home that could pull us all together as a real family. I wanted a home that could give us—me, my husband, and children—a beautiful, peaceful environment we would all feel attached to, that would wrap its arms around us and let us know we belonged there. A place with the allure of Albidale, but on a smaller scale. This was part of my search for the whole elephant.

Chapter 10:

Build It, Love It, Leave It

"Good houses take work."
–Michael S. Smith

"A home is never finished, it's only saved from decay."
–Victor LaValle, Lone Women

Humans need shelter; over thousands of years, we've crawled out from our caves and learned to build houses and remodel them as time takes its toll. Animals living in the wild have no such need. The shell of a turtle, the thick skin of an elephant, the oiled feathers of a cormorant keep them warm or cool enough and shed the rain. They wear their homes, but if we decide to move from a location, we have to seek or build a new home.

Since I lost everything in 1955, home became an incredibly important and stabilizing part of my life, as you'll come to see. Each of my homes was a labor of love.

Our Memorable Home on Cove Road, Huntington, LI

Seeking a new home is what Fred and I did in 1970. We looked at a lot of different options: we needed something that would be beautiful, affordable, and large but not too large. I wanted to recreate for my family the beauty and warmth I experienced at Albidale, but smaller. What we ended up buying was an estate on Cove Road in Huntington, Long Island, designed by Stanford White and built in 1907. It needed major work, but it was my dream home. During WWII, it was owned by Air Force General Benny Meyers, who was known to have the "poshest pads" all over the world. But he used his position to cook the books in a company he owned and was eventually convicted of felonies, stripped of all awards and benefits from his war service, and sent to prison.

Our home on Cove Road, 1973

We knew about the house from Chase Manhattan Bank. It's interesting that during WWII Fred's uncle Nick had been adjutant to General Meyers. After the general was convicted, the estate was sold to Mrs. Sade Elizabeth Osborne, whose husband, Dr. Dean Clay Osborne, was an internationally known dentist. She became an important donor of the Brooklyn Botanic Garden and dedicated a newly acquired parcel there in memory of her husband, which is now known as the Osborne Garden. When she died, Chase Manhattan Bank became trustee of the estate. The sale was contingent on the condition that there be a single owner and the property would not be developed. Sealed bids were required; a friend at Chase Manhattan told us what to bid.

Springtime at Cove Road, 1973

It was June 1970 when we moved in, and it was raining like hell. Katie was seven and Pam was four; they grew up there the next ten years. The house was empty and boarded up for ten years after Mrs. Osborne died, and the lawn and gardens were overgrown. The interior of the house had not been changed since WWII. However, Mrs. Osborne, through her affiliation with the Brooklyn Botanic

Garden, hired the top landscape architects to design the gardens on Cove Road, and they resembled those in the Osborne Garden. The beauty of the landscaping was one of the reasons Mrs. Osborne didn't want the property to be divided, since that would destroy her creation. The gardens' latent possibilities were obvious, and there was even a redwood tree. Four of the seven acres of land were grass, but the entire lawn was kaput because there were chinch bugs everywhere. Despite the obvious shortcomings, I was madly in love with the place. It was like a fairy tale. All I could see was its potential. I could finally make my kind of magic for my own family.

Rebuilding

Before offering our sealed bid to buy the estate, I sat with a legal pad and wrote down all the things I wanted to do and the cost. I needed the right man to work with me full time as superintendent on this project. An Argentinian woman, Nina, worked for me; she recommended her son, Jorge, who was still in Argentina. For the short term, until we finalized the sale, he would have to share a room at the Windmill Drive house with his mother. So I sponsored Jorge to immigrate from Argentina.

Nina was born in Russia and immigrated to Argentina, where Jorge was born. I brought Nina into the US under the Russian quota instead of Argentina's, which was much easier. The story about Jorge and Nina is part of a time in my life from 1965 at least through the 1970s when I helped Argentinians get visas and green cards. I allowed my contact information to be shared among immigrants, and people would show up at all hours asking for help. I got them well dressed, took them to the immigration center at Rockefeller Center, and did whatever was needed to help them. My empathy for these immigrants was borne out of my own experience as a member of an immigrant family, though at the time I wasn't aware of that reason for wanting to help them.

At our new house, I first attacked was the roses, thinking I could clean up those beds in a day, but it took three, and I got scratched all over. Then Jorge and I ripped out three floors of carpeting, which was still in good shape, so we donated it to the local elementary school. Simultaneously with plastering and painting the walls, I also got electrical estimates. This huge house had only a 75-amp electric service, and we wanted to upgrade it to 400-amps.

The remodeling job was enormous both indoors and out—challenging but also exciting. The large library was paneled in cherry, now old and dingy: we kept the wood but stained it a rich, dark color. In the kitchen we found two ancient ice boxes with those little windmill-like fans on top. The ceiling and floors were peeling, the cabinets dilapidated; it was clear we had to gut the room, a job for contractors.

Fred's bathroom was an interesting project. He was 6'3" and weighed 200 lbs. This bathroom was designed for someone half his size: he wouldn't be able to stand up in the tub, and it had no shower. In his typical manner, he had a fit about spending any money on this. He always screamed about things because of his anxiety. I didn't talk with him any more about it, but when he went on his first business trip after we bought the house, I told the construction guys to level it.

When he came home, I told him, "We need to talk about your bathroom," and he said he didn't want to. I said, "Come with me. You may want to reconsider that." When he saw it, what could he say? I showed him my design for the remodel, with sink and toilet at appropriate heights, a floor-to-ceiling glassed-in shower tiled red and black, floor finished with black ceramic tiles, and Wall Street tickertape wallpaper. When it was finished, he loved it.

My favorite part of the Cove Road project was bringing order out of chaos outdoors by addressing the lawn problems, adding a swimming pool and in each corner, a flower bed with a wisteria tree, and installing a sprinkler system. As I write this, I realize that bringing order out of the chaos surrounding me is an important part of my life's journey. Jorge and I thatched the entire lawn, and I designed a Grecian-style pool in one of the gardens off to the side of the house. The window in Pam's room on the third floor was the perfect spot for me to oversee its construction. The big challenge was the sprinkler system.

The four of us at Cove Road, 1973

Jorge and I designed and installed a golf-course-quality sprinkler system using Buckner sprinkler heads. (William Buckner pioneered the hose-less golf course irrigation system at the Pebble Beach course.) I had a working relationship with the German plumbers down the hill. The house was so old we needed customized parts to connect the sprinkler system plumbing to the water supply coming into the house. When I told them what I was doing, they offered to give me whatever parts we needed at their cost. Then, to compare, I went out to the Levitt job on eastern Long Island to see what those suppliers would give me. Their prices were even lower. So I connected the German plumbers to the suppliers at the Levitt job so they could get parts at lower prices.

The water main coming off the main road into the property was 36" in diameter—huge! When we finally had all the sprinkler heads in place and the system was ready to be tested, the German plumbers made the hookup. At this point, Fred, with his usual pessimism, said, "What are you going to do if it doesn't work?" I said, "We'll keep at it until it does." We turned on the system, and the entire property looked like a golf course. We celebrated with champaign for everybody.

Our Life at Cove Road

The neighbors across the street were Chuck and Shirley Riker. Chuck told me later he said to Shirley, "Bill Levitt's daughter bought that house. I don't think we need to know her." One day when I was out mowing the lawn, he saw me and thought, "Maybe I need to reconsider." So he called and told me he was making wine and he'd bring us some.

He had wiry hair, spectacles, and a delightful personality, and we hit it off fantastically. I wanted to try making wine also, so we used our garage that had a sink in it, and we began to make wine there with Chuck. Next door on the other side was the Segona family:

Gina Segona and her father, Gino Gambarelli, of Gambarelli and DeVito wines—importers. He found out what we were doing and was intrigued. He came over to taste the fruit of our labor, and he thought it was good!

While we lived at Cove Road, our cook was Valentina, who owned a restaurant in Seville, Spain. She was trying to get a green card when she worked for us. She was extraordinary. I would think there wasn't a thing in the kitchen, and she would come up with something delicious. If anyone was in the kitchen, she would talk non-stop. But if people spoke English to her, it was as if they weren't speaking.

Unfortunately, she couldn't take feedback—a big problem. She couldn't resist giving leftovers to our two German Shepherds even though we asked her not to: she couldn't help herself. There would be diarrhea and vomit all over the place. I told her, "You can't hear me when I ask you to please not do this." I had to let her go.

Once when my mother was visiting us on Cove Road, it was a truly hot day, and she was feeling the heat. I remember this little voice, coming from the dryer in the basement of all places, saying, "For Christ's sake, Nanny, take your clothes off!" It was Pam.

In 1970, when we were buying the house on Cove Road, I was taking a course at Adelphi University on psychological testing and statistics because I wanted to apply to a Ph.D. program there. I talked to the director and explained that I wanted to do a doctoral dissertation on building cities designed to meet the needs of people rather than those of corporations and industry. It was the beginning of my focus on putting people first rather than money, an interest clearly inspired by Bill Levitt, whose housing was built to meet the specific needs of his post-war customers.

The head of that program was fascinated by my proposal, especially since he knew of my father. He wanted to support what I was proposing because it would add something new and different to his program. However, for it to be approved, it needed the unanimous support of his entire 14-member faculty.

Twelve of the faculty members were clinicians. They were on board, but the two experimental psychologists were dubious: one was a man and the other a woman. I was able to meet with the man, who, until I explained it to him, didn't completely understand what I wanted to do. But the woman refused to meet with me. She ran down the hall, locked herself in her office, and wouldn't come out. I wonder how my life would have turned out if my proposal had been accepted—maybe less interesting.

Moving to Lighthouse Road, Sands Point, LI

After living in our special Cove Road home for 10 years, we left Huntington because our girls were older, and we had no more ties to the eastern end of Long Island. In 1980, we found a beautiful house on the water in Sands Point, LI, 30 minutes from Manhattan by train. It was quite contemporary, with views of the sun setting over midtown Manhattan. It cost us $450,000, which seemed exorbitant, but four years later we sold it for $950,000. This house was almost all glass: when the sun set over the city, it glowed orange. When workmen were there, they'd stand still in the living room transfixed by the view as the sun went down. We lived there four years.

By this point in our lives, Fred was clearly not doing well. He missed working for my father; he still needed someone to fill the role of father figure. But after Fred and I did consulting work for several years, my father formed a new company called Levitt Industries, and he asked Fred to be its president. Fred happily agreed.

I was worried about Fred working for my father again because of what I observed about each of them. The sale to ITT deeply affected them: Fred started drinking more heavily, and my father seemed to be losing his grip. But Fred took that job.

He worked there for a while until he came home one evening and told me my father was running from creditors, and at one point he even crawled out the second-floor window onto the fire escape to get down to the parking lot, find his car, and leave. Then a short time later, Fred said, "Your father is taking out a lot of bank loans he'll never be able to pay back, and I have to front for him. What do you want me to do?" I told him to go to work the next day and quit. I knew if my father's activities were discovered, the legal authorities might exempt him from jail time because of his age, but they wouldn't hesitate to throw Fred in jail. So Fred did that, and my father didn't speak to either of us for quite a while.

Then Fred was hired to consult for the Seabrook Island development in South Carolina, where the only thing on the beach was a lonely bait shop. From working on the Seabrook development to the golf course caper in Spain, finances were relatively good in our family.

The Seabrook work was fun because of the people working there. One guy, Jack, the marketing/advertising person, had a wacky sense of humor. Before this job, he was a salesman who used to travel with a skunk in a cage. Who's going to bother you if your sidekick is a skunk?

While Fred was working at Seabrook, he turned 40, but he didn't want anyone to know. Jack found out, and the pranks began. First, he hired a well-known 100-piece high school all-Black marching band to march and sing happy birthday outside the company offices. Then, when Fred traveled by plane on business, the pilots would congratulate him on his birthday. When he rented a car, the rental agent would slap a happy birthday sticker on the car. The business always arranged these trips, so they were able to pull it off. Jack even gave Fred a Happy 40th Birthday tee shirt, which he kept and delighted in wearing in later years.

* * *

The Itch

As for me, I got the itch to do something entirely different. I was still plagued by questions about why it was so hard for me to grow up in my family. "Why was my mother so distant; why didn't she act like a mother? Why was my sister so crazy? What's wrong with us? Why couldn't we be like everyone else?" All those earlier questions were still bothering me.

Pederson-Krag Clinic

This was the time, in the late 70s, for me to figure out my new direction. The girls were older and were attending Friends Academy, where I went. I was looking for a way to be more useful to people, as per my promise to God when I thought I had leukemia, and an opportunity came my way to volunteer at the Pederson-Krag Clinic in Huntington, which offered counseling for both children and adults.

That experience made me realize I wanted to become a therapist, which would give me the chance to help others while also continuing to figure out my own complex family. Little did I know when I was young my difficult family was in good company, and that group would only grow.

As a volunteer, I was supervised as I counseled my patients. My first case was a beautiful 35-year-old woman with a seven-year-old son. She was sexually abused by her father and battered by her husband, and now her son was starting to be abusive. This is what I've never forgotten about her: she looked at me one day and said, "This may sound crazy to you, but when I'm being abused, I know exactly how everything goes—when it's good, when it's getting bad, and when it's horrible. If I'm not being abused, I don't know anything." Her insight was terribly important; we sometimes try to prevent abuse without understanding how and why the victims may be participating in it.

Ackerman Institute for Family Therapy

The next year, a friend on the staff at the Ackerman Institute for Family Therapy in NYC, one of the original clinics to train therapists in family therapy, invited me to be a video volunteer. Video volunteering was a way to prepare me for coursework at the NYU School of Social Work, where I decided to get my degree. My job at Ackerman was to work behind the one-way mirror video-taping therapy sessions in the company of a team of trainees who were watching. The problem was, I got so involved in the case material I'd forget to turn on the recorder. Fortunately no one ever seemed to mind.

Ackerman made me determined to specialize in family therapy. It was the most effective, all-encompassing kind of treatment I knew of. Individual therapy generally deals with the individual and looks for pathology in the person and then works with them to get rid of it. I thought that was incredibly disrespectful. Pin the diagnosis on the patient and then treat the diagnosis—instead of the patient. I suspect that feels secure for the therapist, but it may not be the best therapy. In contrast, family therapy looks for the meaning of the behavior. All behaviors make sense in the context in which they occur. The case of the Good Mother/ Loyal Daughter comes to mind, which I'll tell you about shortly.

At this point, while I was working at Ackerman, we decided to send the girls away to board at the Kent School in Connecticut. Pam instigated it because she was having a miserable time at Friends Academy, and she wanted to go away to school. I talked to the principal in her middle school, and he told me she was in a terrible class. So they went to Kent, and that was when we moved to Sands Point. A lot of changes were happening all at once.

* * *

My focus during the middle years of my life was on meeting my family's practical needs. My girls were growing through late childhood into adolescence, and my husband needed some propping up. My mother was traveling around with Walter, moving every time they couldn't agree on something. Finding a new spot, packing, unpacking, settling in, and getting to know the new area—all these distractions, along with Walter's favorite, alcohol, kept them on the safe surface of their relationship. My father was disintegrating, slowly—but surely. As usual, I was the organizer, the arranger, the connector of all the pieces. That's always been my role. And all that practice was helpful in my newly chosen profession as a family therapist.

Pederson-Krag and the Ackerman Institute for Family Therapy guided me and affirmed that I was on the right path, the next step of which would be the New York University School of Social Work. Those three educational experiences would land me in my first position as an extern at the Morrisania Neighborhood Family Care Center, where I would jump off the diving board into the messiest of family problems, and where I would learn what I needed to know about how chaos and complexity drive family dynamics. There I would meet Myrtle Parnell, my future therapy partner and best friend. She and I would leave Morrisania at the same time, when it became clear that systemic forces were driving a knife through the heart of our extraordinarily successful program for making family therapy accessible to families in dire need. And we would figure out, finally, why this was happening: that discovery was like finding a part of the elephant we never, ever imagined was there.

Chapter 11:

Becoming a Therapist—
The Path to Answers

I am just a girl chasing her dreams and having an amazing adventure.
–Madeline Stuart

Human progress has always been driven by a sense
of adventure and unconventional thinking.
–Andre Geim

A career as a family therapist seemed like the perfect next step for me. So much was changing in my life, and this seemed the right time to start helping people outside my family. Family therapy was emerging as a promising new method, and my questions about my own family pushed me in that direction. I knew no one person was responsible for all the turmoil I grew up with: everyone had a role in it. Becoming a clinical licensed social worker trained in family therapy would be my next adventure, and I hoped it would help me understand the craziness of my childhood.

New York University School of Social Work

When I entered NYU, my work at Ackerman ended and I was completely immersed in my studies. I drove every week from Sands Point into the city, a commute of almost two hours each way. I loved the coursework, and the two required internships, one per year, let me put this training into practice. During the internships we spent only a short period of time with the patients we were assigned to treat. Here's a glimpse into some of those experiences.

First-Year Internship

Interactions with my first patients in this internship made it obvious that often people needing therapy exhibit unusual behaviors. As we move through life in our own small groups of people, we get used to behaviors that constitute the "norm" for us. When you're a therapist, you meet people doing things that seem totally off the wall. But as I've mentioned, one of the important things I learned from my career is that human behavior makes sense in the context in which it occurs.

Mr. P.

My first-year internship for the NYU program was at Hillside Long Island Jewish Hospital in Great Neck. Each week I worked one day in central intake and two days in the outpatient department (OPD). In OPD I was assigned a patient called Mr. P. Mr. P. came every week for his appointment but said nothing: he just sat there. Because I grew up with an aversion to speaking, this made me want to run away. For four or five sessions, I kept trying to engage with Mr. P. in every way I could imagine. It was torturous.

At the end of my last session with him, he jumped up, grabbed me in a bear hug, and said, "I think I'm cured!" And then he ran out. I was completely taken aback. That was the end of his treatment.

Good Mother/Loyal Daughter

One day when I worked in the central intake department, a mother called to request that we hospitalize her 26-year-old daughter: this would be the eighth time in ten years. This case was assigned to me: the girl was diagnosed as borderline and an alcoholic and treated there for aggressive behavior and alcohol abuse all those times, but that didn't change her behavior at all. I call this the case of "the Good Mother/Loyal Daughter."

After talking with the mother on the phone, I knew Hillside was the family's preferred hospital. I suspected the hospitalizations were to give her some respite from caregiving. One piece of information that stood out for me was that the mother was clearly from Italy and seemed rather isolated, both personally and culturally. She had a thick Italian accent and a speech impediment.

Then I went to look up the daughter's records and found they filled an entire cabinet drawer. I have never seen so many files on a patient. I talked with my supervisor about denying hospitalization unless the family agreed to come in together for a meeting. This was a compelling intervention because the mother didn't want to send her daughter to any other hospital. My supervisor let me do this since she knew I'd been at Ackerman.

The family came in, and after dialoguing with them for 45 minutes, my supervisor and I left the room to consult. I asked her, "Who do you think is the identified patient?" and she responded, "Not the one we've been hospitalizing all these years." The daughter was attractive and articulate. She vacillated between anger and depression. The mother and daughter interacted almost exclusively with each other. The father appeared to have some sort of organic brain problem. He worked the night shift at a bakery and slept much of the day.

The daughter spent most of her time with her mother, verbally abusing her at times. She also drank alone in her room. Her mother brought her meals four times a day. We realized that the mother had no social interactions except with her daughter, so subconsciously she didn't want to disturb the status quo.

It seemed clear to me that the daughter's behavior was a reaction to being trapped. To break this logjam, we connected the mother to a group of Italian women and encouraged her husband to do things with her several times a week. This created space for their daughter to further her education.

Through many twists and turns, within 18 months, the daughter moved two hours away and was employed as a drug and alcohol counselor. At the end of my time working with the family, I drove the parents to the airport to go home to Italy for the first time in 35 years.

Widening the Lens

This case is an example of the benefits of expanding the therapeutic lens from focusing on an individual to including the whole family, and it illustrates the difference between individual therapy and family therapy. In the prior treatment evaluations of the daughter, therapists fastened on the conclusion that was obvious when looking only at the young woman who was brought in as the patient. She was abusive and had an alcohol problem; therefore she was mentally ill and needed treatment.

My supervisor and I broadened our area of exploration and looked at all the relationships in this family system—at the dynamics of the entire family in their cultural and social environment—in other words, the context. We probed there for the causes of the problematic behaviors. Only by doing so could we realize that the young woman was responding in an understandable way to the limitations imposed on her.

When we broadened the focus, we saw that the mother and father needed stronger bonds and the mother needed friends and activities in the Italian community outside the family. When these family needs were met, the daughter was released from her bondage.

When an individual has small issues they want to deal with, individual, analytic therapy can be helpful, but it is no match for complex problems in family situations like this one.

Second-Year Internship

My second-year internship was at a child guidance agency in Manhasset, LI. This agency was in such demand it could take a family two to three months to get accepted for therapy. My supervisor was a tyrant, and NYU was monitoring her. If I had trouble with her, they wouldn't keep her in that role. She and I had some lively discussions; yelling could be heard coming out of her office. She would ask me how I felt about this, that, or the other thing. And I would respond, "What do you mean, how do I *feel* about it? The question is, 'What am I going to do about it?'" Her culture was all about feelings, and mine was British, all about action.

The Irish Family

A case I remember well from this internship at the child guidance agency involved an Irish family of eight, two parents and six boys. During their sessions they sat on folding chairs with one parent on either end like bookends and with the six boys lined up between them. That separation of the parents was telling. One of their presenting problems was that some of the boys were enuretic and encopretic (they soiled their clothing with urine and feces). Again, this family wasn't going to tell me anything. I paced, wishing I could run away.

Then I knew what to do with them: I had the idea to just see the parents together without their boys. During that meeting I gave them a homework task: to go somewhere, sit down, have coffee, and then each one talk for a half hour without interruption about anything except their children. Anything. They were to flip a coin to see who went first and set a timer for the half hour. I knew the half hour might feel like three days to each of them, and I also knew something would happen that would reveal what was going on.

They came into their next session all smiles and asked, "Did you expect us to do that?" I said I didn't know, but either way, they'd learn something. I asked what they learned, and the husband said, "Well, I finally got back in bed after sleeping on the floor for 18 years." His wife smiled. And so ended that case.

When I first started working with that family, I had no idea what would work, but I knew the Irish culture prohibited conversations about difficult problems. I was confident they would have a meaningful interaction doing that assignment.

There is no doubt in my mind about what happened with them at the start of their problem: the wife was mad about something and wouldn't tell her husband what it was, but she told him he wasn't sleeping in the bed. Rather than deal with the issues, the husband stayed on the floor for 18 years. That's a powerful cultural edict! With this assignment, they could agree not to revisit the problems but to just go forward, so after the conversation, he got back in bed and his wife had a big smile!

* * *

During our internships, we were required to write "process recordings" each week, which were thorough reports of our treatment sessions with patients. Each report included what we and our patients said, and in the margins, notes about what happened and our analysis. For our first-year internship, five process recordings per week were required. For the second year, that number was reduced to two per week.

However, this second-year supervisor required me to complete five per week, just as I did during my first year. I tried to suggest that this was more than the school required, but that went nowhere. I knew she would need to review and write comments on every page for the NYU faculty advisors and supervisors. So for my first process recording, I gave her 35 pages. I was providing her with what I call "a worser alternative." At this point, she decided one per week would be fine. After she finished supervising me, she retired.

I was frustrated by my placement in this child guidance agency because the patients were the "worried well." People in serious need can't wait months for their first appointment. I was training for running marathons then, and one day as I was running, I started laughing so hard I had to stop and sit down beside the road. I realized you don't call out the fire department to water your lawn. I felt more attuned to the families the agency was screening out than to the ones they accepted.

* * *

The time came for my graduation from NYU. Washington Square in Manhattan was the site for the ceremony. Trumpeters played from the famous arch overlooking the nine-mile square: Stanford White built it; he was the architect who designed our house on Cove Road. No one walked across a stage because so many students were graduating: the university recognized those in each school as a cohort to stand and be applauded.

Homeless people lived in the park then as now, but the university bussed them all out except for the one person they missed, who "graduated" next to me. Afterwards my classmates joked about that. My mother and father amazed me by coming to see me graduate. My mother didn't speak to me for a year after I entered graduate school. We reconnected after my nephew, Mac's son, Scottie, was killed. It took a trauma like that to get my mother to break her silent treatment. When I persisted in my plans to become a therapist, which I think threatened her, she realized she couldn't control me any longer, and that was hard for her to tolerate.

After my graduation, with the certainty of a career as a clinical social worker in the offing, my mother's attention turned from attempts to control me to other aspects of her life. I think she finally accepted that I was an adult.

As for me, right around the corner was a whole new way of life. I was about to dive into a community more different from my past experiences than I could imagine.

Chapter 12:

The Failure of Success

"If you must break a rule, break it on purpose."
– Josh Steimle

*"Sometimes we have to step out of our comfort
zones. We have to break the rules."*
–Kyra Davis

What Happened at Morrisania

My training in therapy began on a small scale at the Pederson-Krag
clinic, broadened with my introduction to family therapy at the
Ackerman Institute, came into full flower with my studies at NYU,
and culminated when I became licensed to practice. What followed
was my work at Morrisania.

My work there nourished me, and my friendships with Myrtle
and Elsie were among the deepest I ever had. We meshed because of
our shared values, but also because we were in the trenches together
experiencing how incredibly challenging life was for the families
who came to our crisis room.

* * *

At one point during my third year working at Morrisania, Myrtle asked me to lead a seminar for the staff on our families of origin as a way of building community. I agreed. I knew it had to be planned by consensus: it was decided that each of us would present a three-generational perspective on our families to the whole group. If there were problems in the family, we could ask for suggestions and advice.

When it was my turn, I described my sister's role as the identified patient and mine as the fixer. In a rigid, complex family, the members are prescribed roles. I couldn't recognize that my attempts to fix things were part of the problem. The services of the fixer are endlessly required, but the fixer can never succeed. If I could succeed with my family, I could leave, but it would destabilize the system. My presence protected the homeostatic balance in my family, which is why my mother tried so hard to control me.

I posed this dilemma to the staff at the seminar, and I asked if they could see any way, short of leaving, for me to extricate myself from my role. Twenty therapists there from all the disciplines led me to understand that I needed to stop being the fixer in my family, which we knew would lead to some disastrous consequences.

* * *

Growing up in my family was good preparation for my work at Morrisania, but even my family's behavior didn't come close to the kind of crazy things going on in that clinic on any given day. Later I'll describe some of the cases I worked on there.

It's hard for anyone who wasn't working in our clinic to comprehend just how chaotic life was in the South Bronx. That's why I want to share a list describing the patients I personally saw one day in the crisis room. I wrote it down so I could be sure to recount it accurately later.

1. A 21-year-old who sexually molested his 10-year-old sister.

2. A PCP abuser who thought he killed his mother. He dove out of his apartment but was "saved by the telephone cord." I could never figure out how he managed to do that.

3. A Jamaican who was beaten by police in Penn Station. He was depressed, paranoid, and suicidal.

4. An eight-member family with a presenting problem of incest. The mother had an ataque (a seizure resulting from psychological and emotional causes that resembles an epileptic seizure.)

5. A homeless, psychotic patient who was raped and spent the late afternoon in the welfare center. She was partially clothed and totally disoriented.

6. An old patient who stripped and was flashing in the offices on the second floor. (Myrtle said, "You better come see what's happening. You won't believe it." The woman took the trench coat belonging to Velma, and that's how she was flashing.)

This was just one day, and these were just my patients.

Our approach worked for these patients. Even with their extreme problems, we were able to help them function in their daily lives. We helped them understand how to manage and heal their problems. I thought that was amazing. So did our patients. They flocked to us. Sometimes we had to close the door to the crisis room because we couldn't take any more patients that day, or sometimes for a month.

Our treatment protocols were different from those anywhere else. They were designed to meet the complex needs of this group of people living in this particular community. What worked for suburban parents and Wall Street brokers was useless here. We couldn't treat people using individual therapy when their problems and all aspects of their lives were interwoven with the brokenness of their community and the dysfunction of the agencies they dealt with. Individual therapy might help to figure out why a person has an obsessive-compulsive disorder or problems with a roommate, but it's going nowhere when you're trying to help someone handle a big tangle of interrelated problems in a war zone.

There is no way to dispute it: our program was an incredible success, and that was because it defied the norms in so many ways—norms that were suited to a different type of situation than the one that existed in the South Bronx. Here's what characterized our approach. First, in an overwhelmingly White profession, our staff diversity reflected that of its primarily African American and Puerto Rican community. Later other groups moved there: Cape Verdeans and people from the Caribbean, San Salvador, Guyana, and the Dominican Republic. The clinic program started purposely with one-third Black, one-third Latino, and one-third White talented professional and non-professional staff.

Second, we flattened the implicit hierarchy that was, and largely still is, endemic in the mental health profession. Those who are most highly trained or well-known sit at the top and earn the most: that would be the psychiatrists, who are medical doctors also trained in mental health. Psychologists, who typically have Ph.D.'s, are in the next tier down, and social workers are in the third tier. Nurses, and then our community organizers, come next.

Our practice of working in teams softened the mental health hierarchy. Each staff member, no matter their level of education, contributed to our effectiveness to the best of their abilities and from their different perspectives. We were keenly aware that nobody had all the answers, but we knew we could keep fine-tuning our approach if we worked as a team and shared what we were doing with each other. We also had a lot of ongoing staff training. In our treatment sessions, we paid attention to cultural traits and perceptions, and we tried to be accessible to anyone in need of help.

*The cover of the "Family Therapy Networker" issue
that included the article about our clinic*

Third, in everything we did, we considered racial and class differences and the way they functioned in our society, even beyond our commitment to staff diversity. Racism was layered on top of the dangers people faced in the South Bronx. The dereliction in that community attracted desperate people who could be violent, but police and fire department responses could also be unreliable, increasing the danger. Most of our patients, who were Black and Latino, had to deal with racial discrimination all the time, in addition to the violence. Racism was sometimes an aspect of our patients' mental health issues, whether directly or indirectly, and we had to be ready to help them handle that. Our staff diversity helped us meet that need, and our willingness to address these issues openly contributed to our success.

The unusual approach we took with our patients earned us attention, even on a national scale. An article about the clinic was published in 1986 in a nationally distributed magazine for practitioners of family therapy, the *Family Therapy Networker*. It described the type of therapy we offered. But that article also created a problem for us.

After he wrote the first draft, the author, Richard Simon, gave it to everybody at the clinic to read. They all had the same reaction: they thought the article gave the credit for our success to me and one of the psychiatrists, a White doctor named Paul DeBell. They were up in arms and angry: at a big meeting in the largest room, people stood on chairs yelling or paced around muttering. I reminded everyone that the author talked to each of us, same as to me, and then he wrote the article based on what he heard.

I understood the intensity of everyone's reaction, and I was annoyed that this whole avoidable situation was happening. I also thought everyone was right to be upset. After all, the program was founded primarily by Black and Latino practitioners. The author's problem was that he could hear White people, but he couldn't factor in the people of color. It was to me a clear case of racism among the well-intentioned. His brain was trained that way, and his filters were strong. He was not intending to discriminate. What he needed was someone to explain the issues to him.

We called Simon back, and we told him the way he wrote the article was unacceptable. We explained the issues; it was another instance, among so many in US history, of Blacks and Latinos doing most of the work and White people getting the credit.

When Simon came back, he talked to everyone again, and this time the article was better. He described our work at the clinic this way.

"No one at MNFCC believes that family therapy represents a secret passageway out of poverty. Their clients have to contend with problems in too many social systems besides their families to lull anyone into believing that just straightening out family relationships presents the ultimate answer. However, one of the Center's basic principles is that treating a Black or Hispanic person without taking into account their family is less tenable in a community like Morrisania. Jo Vanderkloot believes the bonds of family loyalty are crucial to understanding the people she sees at MNFCC. 'Here the family is number one. If you do something that jeopardizes your loyalty to the family, there is usually trouble...'

"'This is a very crisis-oriented community,' says Myrtle Parnell. 'That means that much of the time you are forced to respond to situations that your training did not especially prepare you for. In that kind of situation, most therapists reach for some intellectual stuff, some neatly guiding principle. Here you've got to hang out. It's a raw happening and you've got to be there.'" (Jan. and Feb. 1986)

That article brought us positive attention, but it wasn't enough to protect us.

When Your Success Breaks All the Rules

Our clinic was helping people in the community, but breaking the rules of a system will cause no end of trouble.

This is what was true about our program.

- Our clinic's reputation spread throughout the city, and sometimes so many people would try to enter on a given day the doors had to be closed.

- People from outside the catchment area and from all five boroughs would sometimes try to be treated using fake identification.

- Our program worked where everything else had failed.

- Our approach brought us national attention.

The reward for this success was that our clinic's program was incrementally dismantled.

The crisis room was closed, and the team approach was replaced by a return to the old model—the standard individual-centered therapy typical of middle-class communities. A trip to Morrisania a few years later found its halls empty, phones silent, and staff decimated. Those who remained were demoralized. It was a ghost town.

We Quit

Myrtle and I stayed long enough to witness this dismantling process. It was truly heartbreaking. We kept trying to understand why it was happening. After a while there was clearly no reason for us to stay at Morrisania. I was the first to decide to quit. I told Myrtle, and she said, "You're not leaving me behind. I'm going, too." So we both left. But four years before that decision, first Myrtle and her husband, Peter, and then Fred and I moved to an area an hour and a half outside the city: Warwick, NY. Myrtle and I commuted to Morrisania our last three years there.

What to do after Morrisania? First, we set up offices in our homes where we could see patients, and we began to establish private practices. After some months we decided to form a professional partnership called, "Parnell & Vanderkloot."

We were already teaching at my alma mater, NYU School of Social Work. I started teaching there alone: at the end of my first semester, I made the case for Myrtle to join me. We were the only inter-racial teaching team in the whole university for approximately 15 years, which was the length of time we taught there. As part of our new partnership, we added more teaching, consulted with corporations and non-profits, and wrote articles and book chapters. Warwick was the perfect setting for our new ventures.

Chapter 13:

Ex-Urbanites

"What was stolen by the city, nature restores."
–Michael Bassey Johnson, Night of a Thousand Thoughts

"Every person is defined by the communities she belongs to."
–Orson Scott Card

Bucolic Warwick

It was in 1983 that Myrtle and Peter moved to Warwick; Fred and I followed in 1984. The Parnells bought a house on a pond with some acreage. Fred and I found a barn renovated into a large home 15 minutes from Myrtle and Peter. Katie and Pam were home during school vacations and summers. Myrtle and I began to get inklings about the coming annihilation of our program early in 1987.

This was an important time in my life: I was comfortably distant from my mother and Walter, my father and Simone, and my sister, Mac. Of those, my mother and Walter were doing fine and enjoying their lives, but my father and Simone, as well as my sister, were not doing well.

Warwick was a small town in the middle of a sprawling rural community, like a spider in the center of its web. This farming area was beautiful: it was a valley bordered by low mountains to the east with winter ski resorts. We lived amid apple orchards, cattle and horse farms, and large onion farms: Warwick included a hamlet called Pine Island, a mecca for growing onions because of its "black dirt." (When I left Warwick many years later, hemp plants were moving into the onion fields.) We could pick up fresh eggs just down the road, drive around and admire the rolling farmland; watch horses, cows, and donkeys grazing; or drive part way up one of the mountains for gourmet freshly made ice cream. Wonderful restaurants were in and near the town. People who worked in New York City were moving there, so newer stores and amenities appealing to city folks opened alongside the feed stores. It was a "farming-plus" community.

After we left Morrisania, Myrtle and I got busy building our professional lives and getting involved with activities and projects in the community.

It was like joining a new elephant herd and finding acceptance. Our lives were less intense in Warwick for the most part, but sometimes it felt as if Myrtle and I were climbing mountains together as we struck out on our own. Our work focused on helping patients and organizations solve their problems, and that led us to figuring out how our whole society works.

After we left Morrisania, we felt a pressing need to understand what caused our successful program to fail. Myrtle and I gave ourselves an assignment. We were going to keep working at trying to figure this out until we succeeded. That failure didn't make any sense—until we figured it out—and then it did.

We had a sense that what happened to our clinic was not unique to it. Figuring out why our program's support dried up would provide information and insights useful to others. We sat together for many hours brainstorming and doing research. We started with a focus just on Morrisania, but we quickly found ourselves thinking about the larger context. More about this later.

While we worked to find the answer to this question, we thought about how we benefitted from working at Morrisania. There we learned what types of treatment worked—and didn't—in settings of all-out chaos. We also learned about complexity, since the South Bronx was a highly complex community in which everything was constantly influencing everything else. In the years that followed, we learned that complex situations are marked by the dynamic interaction of all their elements.

There was no one reason why our program was killed off. We looked at the context, which was the health system it was part of. That system was composed of many agencies interacting with each other according to multiple policies and regulations. Our program broke the rules defining the way these forces operated together, and the synergy in the system had the strength to overpower our success. Our program was snuffed out because it violated the accepted ways of doing things.

We figured this out gradually, so there were no crashing symbols or bolts of lightening when we finally got it. We were blinded by our program's success at first, and we naively thought something that good had to be rewarded. In spite of our background in systems thinking, in spite of the fact that we knew the importance of context, we struggled to turn our thinking in that direction. We didn't think it was all that important that our program broke the rules, since breaking them was the key to our success. How could that matter? But that was the most important factor. That's what did us in. And this information has important implications for many ventures in our society that succeed by moving beyond established protocols and regulations.

* * *

Warwick was a comfortable setting for Myrtle and me to wrestle with the question of how our successful program could be killed off. The natural setting, with woods and fields and domesticated and wild animals, calmed us as we struggled to figure that out and to establish our professional lives in a community very different from the one we left.

The Barn

The barn was an interesting home. Before we moved, a psychic lived in its in-law apartment, the barn's only completely livable area. At first the rest of the structure was dark at night because all the light bulbs were missing. Although we didn't know it until after we moved in, legions of mice made their home there; a whole army lived in the basement. And over 100 bats "hung out" in the attic, which we didn't discover until later. The morning of the day the realtor showed us the barn, the psychic told her that the people coming to see it that day would buy it.

Given that we were now living in a renovated barn, it might have seemed to some of my father's friends that our financial circumstances were headed downhill. But it was large and beautifully unique, despite being less of a show place than the Cove Road or Sands Point houses. I was glad Myrtle discovered Warwick.

I thought it was a practical move: Myrtle and I could commute to Morrisania, and the taxes in Warwick were significantly lower than they were on Long Island. But the girls thought the barn was scary, in part because it was still rustic. Moving to Warwick was intense, but it was time for a non-emotional, practical assessment of our situation, so that's how I made my decisions.

Sometimes it felt as if we were camping out there. Once we went on a trip and our new friend, Suzie Emmerich, came to stay with Teddy, our German Shepherd. She felt cold in the living room and kept turning up the thermostat, but it didn't do anything. And then she wanted to scramble some eggs, but she couldn't manage the computerized stove, so she put them in the toaster oven. She was sleeping in the master bedroom during her stay and woke up the next morning feeling a heavy body lying next to her. After screwing up her courage to look, she saw Teddy lying there with his head on the pillow. Somehow all this didn't scare her away.

As I said, the barn was huge. There were three floors above the basement: on the first floor were the kitchen, dining and living rooms, the in-law apartment that became my office, and at the far end, a two-story office for Fred. The living room was a 40' cube, and a huge fan with lights hung 10' below the roof in the middle of it. On the living room wall towards the kitchen, stairs rose to the second floor, opening into a loft space which was the library overlooking the living room, and then to a hall leading to the master suite and other bedrooms and baths at the front end of the barn. One bedroom had a beautiful mosaic fireplace in it. On the third floor a few bedrooms opened onto a lounge area, and stairs went up to a small cupola where you could sit and look out in all directions.

The back of our barn, a view from the pond, mid-1980s

We improved the property by building a large deck in the back and putting in a one-acre pond. The trunks of two tall trees protruded through openings in the deck and towered above it. Sitting out there you looked down over the lawn to the pond, which became a welcoming oasis for wild birds and the local watering hole for deer, black bears, and other wildlife.

Our pond, mid 1980s

Flowers I planted at the barn before the deer ate them all, mid-1980s

We made amazing friends in Warwick. Living across the road from us were Richard and Patricia Kiley. Richard was the actor/singer who played the role of Don Quixote in *The Man of La Mancha*, a well-known Broadway musical. His version of "The Impossible Dream," the hit song from the show, still sends shivers up my spine. Richard has since died, but I'm still close to Patricia. She was instrumental in my writing this memoir.

Our living room was a large open space, perfect for entertaining. We had all sorts of events there: my favorites were the sing-alongs with Richard and other well-known singers who lived in Warwick, like Shirley Verette, the Black operatic mezzo-soprano. Richard Kimball would often accompany at our piano: he was a Julliard-trained composer and pianist who won the Alexandre Gretchanninov Memorial Prize in composition for his *String Quartet*. When these talented musicians performed, with everyone sitting close to them, our guests were utterly mesmerized.

I remember my grandsons, Nick and Alex, sitting on the couches, feet not yet hitting the floor, just agog with that music. When Shirley Verette sang *O' Holy Night* there, the rafters trembled.

We also hosted fund-raisers for Planned Parenthood and political candidates, and we held wedding and funeral receptions as well. Pam was on the Connecticut College sailing team: she invited the team to the barn one weekend, and they parked their large sailboats in our parking area. People must have thought it was strange to see those large boats parked near our little pond.

I fondly remember the huge birthday party we held for Myrtle there, with a local pianist serenading us all. He died a few years later and we opened the barn for his funeral reception.

An event in the living room at the barn, mid-1980s

* * *

Part of a Pattern

While we lived there, my mother and Walter went from being millionaires to depending on Social Security payments—and me. They spent all their married life together traveling around the world from one place to another, both while they lived in Europe and then back here in the US.

Because Walter was an alcoholic, wherever they went, he found a couple of favorite bars. About 13 years after we moved to Warwick and when my marriage was failing, they lived in Napa, California. At one of his favorite bars there, he met the son of a high-ranking Air Force general who encouraged Walter to invest with him. Walter convinced my mother they could make a great return on their money (her money) by doing this, and so they invested everything. I tried to tell my mother something was off about the guy making this offer, and I tried to persuade her to diversify her investments. She wouldn't listen. I even told her I suspected he was a drug addict, but by then it was too late. The deed was done. Turns out it was a Ponzi scheme and they lost it all. Every last cent of five million dollars (roughly 40 million dollars today) gone in a flash. Non-reclaimable. This was beginning to feel familiar. What could I do? Clearly, it was up to me to pick up the pieces.

I had to start supporting my mother and Walter. I offered to build an apartment onto the barn for them. But Warwick wasn't a resort community where people would hang out in bars day and night, which was what Walter loved. And—he often expressed interest in me, so having them next door was not a viable option. They settled on Arizona, so I went there and looked at houses for them. I found them two choices in Sedona, bought the house they chose, and supported them the rest of their lives. That was the most settled they ever were. This was difficult for me. Finding that extra money meant increasing my workload, resulting in little time to go anywhere or do anything for myself.

Walter planted a small vineyard in their back yard. He studied winegrowing years before, and he planted a one- to two-acre vineyard in California when they lived in Napa. They had a beautiful home there, and after a couple of years Walter bottled their wine. He wouldn't sell it. He was averse to making money: perhaps it was beneath his dignity.

My mother and Walter were happy in Sedona until a brown recluse spider bit my mother's leg. That wound never healed, and it was ultimately what killed her. After her death I continued to support Walter until he died years later. I paid for almost everything: because he never wanted to hold down a job, he had little income.

* * *

But back to Warwick: as well as making wonderful friends with our neighbors and other residents, we also got to know some of the wildlife a little too well. Squirrels loved to run up the tree trunks to the deck, and then they'd zip around and peer in through the floor-to-ceiling glass windows and doors. We didn't dare leave those doors open a crack, or the squirrels would move right in. In fact that happened sometimes.

Our deck overlooking the pond, with the trees growing up through it, late 1980s

I remember walking into the kitchen from the dining room one day feeling as if someone was behind me. I turned around and saw a squirrel following right after me. "Is lunch ready?" Once a squirrel was intent on joining us inside the barn when my friend Judy was visiting; after we trapped it, Judy drove it more than 20 miles away to release it in the woods.

And then there was that other problem. We had a few friends over one evening; we were all sitting around the coffee table in the living room drinking wine and nibbling, and I kept hearing, "ping, ping, ping, ping." The huge fan, hanging down from the lofted ceiling above us, was on. A confused bat hung above the fan, letting loose. It really brought to life that familiar saying, "…when the shit hits the fan." I just quietly told our guests to cover their glasses.

One time Fred was wildly running after a bat, doing his usual yelling. I was going through the kitchen to my office, and Fred lost sight of the bat and didn't see it when it crashed into the wall near me, knocking itself out. I got a glass and scooped it up and put a paper over the top of it. When I showed it to him, he said, "How did you do that? I've been going crazy trying to catch it." I told him I scooped it into the glass. I may have omitted the fact that the bat had a little accident.

Our two cleaning ladies came as a team once a week to clean the barn: Ann and her friend. They were there one day, the friend in the living room and Ann in the kitchen. Suddenly the friend started screaming. I ran to the living room and saw two bats clinging to the cushions on the sofa. Ann hurried upstairs to the loft overlooking the living room with a plan to scare her friend even more: she was going to drop a paper towel down near her. But then Ann started screaming because there was a bat on the carpet in the loft. I got some pots, scooped up the bats, and carried them outside. The next time these ladies came to clean, they arrived ready to work—wearing bicycle helmets, swinging tennis racquets and buckets, proclaiming they were ready for action. It was hysterical. We had quite a reputation in Warwick.

Toward the end of my time in the barn, I hired someone to find the bats' entrance. The guy came and waited until dark when they were all out to dine on the insects (we never had any problems with insects when we lived there), and using a flashlight he found their hole into the attic. He boarded that up, and I hoped that was the final closing of the bat hotel. Wishful thinking.

* * *

Living in the barn was enjoyable in so many ways. I loved being immersed in nature the way I was at Albidale. But of course there were aspects of my life at the time that were less than ideal. There's always a balance, isn't there? We all experience ups and downs, births and deaths. High times are followed by winding-down times, and then we rise back up again. Fred and my father were both winding down during this period, and nobody could help either one of them. It was painful to watch.

Chapter 14:

Father and Husband—Gone

"Death is not the greatest loss in life. The greatest
loss is what dies inside us while we live."
−Norman Cousins

Fred

As we made our transition to Warwick, I could see Fred deteriorating.
His heavier drinking after my father sold Levitt & Sons worsened. I
didn't realize it before because I was focused on other things. Partly
because of his drinking, Fred had difficulty finding work, and as the
work dried up, his drinking escalated—he was in a self-reinforcing
loop. He always had a cocktail before dinner; he told me when we
first married that everybody had cocktail hour, and they enjoyed that
ritual at Yale where he was a Deke. A favorite spot at his fraternity
house was a long bar where Jane Fonda used to sit at one end, so a
lot of drinking went on there.

When we lived at the barn, we had that $500,000 from the sale
of our house on Sands Point; I was seeing patients in the city in
the apartment-office we rented; Myrtle and I were teaching, and I
had a small private practice in Warwick: all together that provided
enough for us to live on, but it kept me so busy I wasn't watching
what Fred was doing. He had some small jobs on and off, and then
Jimmy Vanderkloot, Fred's cousin, appeared.

Jimmy had a deal to build a railroad in China, and he wanted Fred to partner with him. The hard thing about that was the time difference: Fred and Jimmy had phone meetings with their Chinese partners when it was morning in China, which was when Fred was drinking heavily because it was evening in Warwick. After I began to figure out the extent of his problem, I sat on the floor outside his office to see if he made sense on the calls. But even so, I had no idea he was also drinking during the day. I didn't come from an alcoholic family, so I was clueless. Here's what tipped me off.

Fred was good at giving people directions. He could tell me exactly when he'd get home from his trips to China. One morning I went to his office (we both worked from home) to ask him for directions to our house to give to a patient, and I found him drinking straight scotch. He tried to hide it. Seeing him with that drink, I got a terrible sinking feeling in my stomach as I realized, "Oh my God, this is a point of no return." That was the end of our relationship. You can't do what I do and be in a relationship with someone with that problem. There is no way to get away from that.

It was a few more years before we separated. While we lived in the barn, if we were going out to dinner with friends, he had to have drinks at home before we left. Increasingly he resisted going to anybody's house for drinks and dinner because he wanted to be next to his own stock. There was nothing I could do to change these behaviors. I think Fred never really had a chance, just like my sister. Fear and anxiety drove him every waking moment. He'd wake up and think the day was out to get him.

* * *

My Father

While Fred was spiraling down, so was my father. During the late 1970s and 1980s, my father tried to make a comeback, but his two attempted developments in Florida failed. He had to refund prospective home buyers their deposits because he never built their homes. He also failed at completing developments under contract in Iran, Venezuela, and Nigeria. His financial debacle was of his own making. To avoid paying taxes on the ITT shares he received in payment for Levitt & Sons, he didn't convert them to cash—his eye was always on securing more and more money. He borrowed against them, and then when ITT's value crashed during the 1970s' bear market, his stake was down to about 10 percent of its original value. (These details are from *The Dream Builder*, by Charlie Zehren, online). He was flailing around, and he was eventually barred from building in New York where he was once so successful.

In 1981 my father was charged with misappropriation of money from the Levitt Foundation and was forced to pay back $5 million. He stayed married to Simone, but the marriage also deteriorated. As his finances dwindled, he began to sell his belongings, including his art collection and La Colline. He and Simone eventually moved in with a woman who was a friend of hers. It turned out they were more than friends: my father was tolerated as an afterthought to Simone's relationship with that woman. And all this while, he was becoming more and more vacant.

My brother, Bill Levitt, Jr., followed in his father's footsteps in one regard. He, too, was enamored of wealth, and when he had bills he couldn't pay, he "borrowed" money from the family foundation. This was discovered and he was sentenced to a short prison term. Although he lived in California at the time, he was remanded to New York to be sent to Rikers' Island, and he came to spend a little time with me before reporting for his sentence. The night before he was to go to prison, I asked him what his favorite meal was, and I made him linguini with white clam sauce as per his wish.

Then began a very interesting time. I drove him to Rikers the next morning, where they strip-search you and give you prison garb. He was in for three months before they gave him a "work release," which meant he left each morning carrying his clothes for his work assignment; then he went to the penthouse apartment at 56th and First Avenue owned by my friend, Dorothy, where he changed his clothes before he went to his work release at the Brooklyn Navy Yard. Later in the day, he reversed the whole process. He did this for three more months.

Before he went to prison, he and I went to see our father: Bill Levitt Sr. was in North Shore hospital in the wing he donated, but by this time he was penniless, and the hospital cared for him gratis. His friend, Roy Alpert, made the arrangements with the hospital; my father was too out of it to handle such affairs. He was terribly confused during our visit, not sure who we were and thinking we were married to each other.

When my father was dying, I went to the hospital at 5:30 a.m. to see him. I somehow knew he was about to die, and I didn't want to go when Simone would be there. He was semi-conscious. I said my goodbye to him and left. I think it was the day before he died, which was Jan. 28, 1994.

A footnote: My brother and his wife died together right before Obama's first presidential election. I was sorry to lose him. I was closer to him than to any of my other siblings, and it was yet another important loss.

Fred Again

In the late 1990s, when Fred and I were living largely separate lives in the barn, he inherited a sizable amount of money from his uncle. This inheritance was the good fortune he needed then, since he was losing the ability to find consulting jobs. The Chinese railroad project he and Jimmy Vanderkloot worked on ended, and nothing sizeable was in sight. He was dependent on me, and I think he hated that.

When this inheritance was finally his, Fred decided to move to the city. We divorced. There wasn't much left of this man by then. He married a woman his daughters detested; they were miserable together but stayed married until Fred dropped dead May 1, 2015. I didn't marry again: by this time I was laser-focused on helping other people and continuing to unearth an understanding of my family's problems. Marriage would be a distraction.

After Fred left for the city, I stayed in the barn for a while before selling it and moving to a house on Onderdonk Road. Interestingly, it had the same house number as the barn—83. It was just a couple of miles away.

Chapter 15:

True Commitment—a Challenge

"A friend is what the heart needs all the time."
–Henry Van Dyke

"The bird a nest, the spider a web, man friendship."
–William Blake

Myrtle

Myrtle and I became close friends at Morrisania, but our friendship deepened after we left. It was not always harmonious, but it was beneficial for us both. My relationship with her was pivotal. Even though we were close in age, I think she was in some ways another of the matriarchs in my life. I learned so much through our relationship, and she learned from me as well.

When Myrtle and I left Morrisania together to embark on a new phase of our lives, we made a commitment to each other. We were both fully aware that our different racial and class identities, as well as our personalities and personal histories, could get in the way of our continuing to remain close friends. And if none of that derailed us, the larger society would do what it could to finish the job. We knew that. But we had the highest esteem for each other and great mutual respect. We each also had a deep, undying need to understand racial issues before we even knew each other. Our friendship and professional partnership were hugely important to both of us.

Myrtle at Katie's wedding, 1988

Neither of us was in a good marriage. Fred's alcoholism and insecurity were taking their toll, and Peter was his own kind of disaster. There were a lot of reasons Myrtle ended up with this particular White man as her husband, but there she was. On the other hand, our friendship gave each of us a kind of fulfilling relationship that our marriages couldn't. We enjoyed each other's company. We were there for each other, we were true friends, and our differences were often complimentary in our role as business partners.

Our commitment was to stay the course in our friendship no matter what came along to threaten it. It was a serious undertaking, almost formal. There were times when we didn't know if we could keep it, but we did. Along the way, we had some great adventures—and some tremendous fights.

* * *

New York Office

I lived in the barn until 2000. While Fred, as well as my relationship with him, fell apart, my father's life dwindled to a close. Meanwhile my relationship with Myrtle became the crucible for my personal and professional growth.

When Myrtle and I moved with our husbands to Warwick, we each kept the apartments we had in the city. Myrtle and Peter owned a brownstone house on the West Side they converted into three apartments, and before their move to Warwick, they lived in one of them. I rented an apartment on the East Side where Fred or I could stay overnight when we needed to. Myrtle and I both continued to do business in the city, and we loved shopping there. Fred and I gave up our apartment when Myrtle and I secured another one to use as an office.

When we decided to rent a different apartment for shared office space, we went searching and found a beautiful one at 89th and Third. It was recently remodeled and even had marble floors. However, the rental agency told us we couldn't have a professional mental health business in that building. I was suspicious, so I looked at the register to see what kinds of businesses were there, and it turned out there were a lot of private mental health offices. Then we contacted the Equal Employment Opportunity Commission (EEOC) in Harlem, told them the problem we were having and made an appointment to meet with them. When we walked in, they were all smiles as soon as they saw us. They could tell this was going to be a no-brainer.

We told them the rental agency obviously didn't like Black people, and if they thought we were lesbians, they didn't like that either. The rental agency was one of the largest in NYC, so the EEOC filed a complaint. As a result, the agency offered us a deal. We could have the apartment, and they would allow us to do an anti-racism workshop with their 400 agents for one-to-two hours, but we could not ask or answer any questions during that session. Plus, they offered us any amount of money we asked for. We said, "Tell them they can take that offer and stick it where the sun don't shine. We're not about to compromise on such an important issue."

We got the apartment. We had our beautiful office and we continued to see patients there even after we moved to Warwick, until we became more settled. I stayed at the apartment a few nights a week when we were teaching.

* * *

The transition for both of us from the city to Warwick was incremental in that we kept one foot there while we settled into our new homes in the country. While Myrtle and I were teaching at NYU and consulting at times with organizations in the city, we were each seeing private patients from Warwick, and we were getting more involved in the community there in various ways.

* * *

Parnell and Vanderkloot

In addition to our private practices, Myrtle and I formed a professional partnership we called Parnell & Vanderkloot. Together we wrote and published papers and book chapters, and we consulted with corporations and non-profits about chaotic systems and about innovative treatment of the urban poor. We did couples and family therapy together and singly, and we provided systems assessment, policy planning, and cross-cultural team building for corporations and non-profits.

We also did training sessions in race relations and systems thinking and taught graduate courses at the Smith School for Social Work and the Seton Hall psychology doctoral program in addition to our NYU classes. We held workshops across the country at mental health conferences and consulted closer to home at places like Connecticut College, MTV Nickelodeon, New York City Health and Hospitals Corporation, Lincoln Savings Banks in New York, Long Wharf Theater in CT, the New Jersey court system, and other hospitals and agencies.

Soon after we left Morrisania, Myrtle and I found James Gleick's book, *Chaos,* and Thomas Kuhn's book, *The Structure of Scientific Revolutions,* in a favorite city bookstore. These books gave us the language we needed to describe what we were intuitively doing in our therapy at the clinic. They vaulted us into a more in-depth understanding of chaos theory and paradigm shifts and helped us see how our therapeutic practice fit into a larger scientific framework. We found M. Mitchell Waldrop's book, *Complexity,* later, along with Margaret Wheatley's *Leadership and the New Sciences.* These books form the cornerstone in my understanding of how our world and society operate. I highly recommend them to anyone who wants to learn to see the world through different lenses.

In all our professional engagements, we brought an atypical approach. We helped our clients learn how to see their situations differently: we taught them how complex, dynamical systems work, which helped them solve their problems on their own more effectively. At Seton Hall, we asked the following question on the final exam at the end of the first semester: "Was the battle in the campus program between individual therapy and family therapy a philosophical debate, or was something larger at play?" Several students wrote that systems thinking would reveal raw capitalism in all its ugliness. People don't know this but often sense it.

We were definitely busy. As we worked so hard together in the professional arena, we were also determined to figure out how to have a personal friendship across our many differences—how to look around the blinders placed on our vision by our own experiences to try to see the world through each other's very different eyes.

Our Deep Commitment put to the Test

The relationship we forged, Myrtle and I, operated on several different levels simultaneously in addition to our work together. We were always friends, and we were always close but not always in agreement. One doctor we met thought we must have grown up together because of the way we interacted and the way we knew each other so well. And surprisingly, more than once people thought we might be sisters.

My wealthy family was complex in many ways. Myrtle grew up in a lower middle-class family that was complex in different ways. So we were primed to run headlong, blindly, into each other's world view and issues. But we each felt as if we were soul sisters, and we held the utmost respect and loyalty for each other. After all, we hung together in a war zone. We always had each other's back, but staying true to our commitment was one of the hardest things we each did.

Our closeness came from our understanding of the enormity of our commitment. We were two people turning ourselves upside down, leaving behind some of who we were and how we understood the world so we could bridge an incredibly difficult gap. To do this, you have to suspend everything you know in order to know what you need to know, and not many people are willing to do that. It requires courage because other "friends" will abandon you, you'll face professional attacks, and even your family will question what you're doing. In the midst of all that, you must trust this other person who is so different from yourself. Even ahead of time, you know the going WILL get tough.

Particular experiences from our work together stand out for me. Myrtle had connections in Harlem, and we were asked by the head of a Black radio station to come to the famous Apollo Theater there to talk about bridging the racial divide at a time when race riots were happening in Harlem. Was I a little apprehensive about doing this? You could say so. Me, a very White person, with frosted hair and large green eyes on stage in front of a Black audience—me, with stage fright and shyness from my childhood lurking in the back of my consciousness—apprehensive? Yes, I was! But I wasn't afraid, if you understand the difference. I was willing to die for this cause. And I wasn't the only one to feel some apprehension. Myrtle said to me, "For the first time, I'm afraid to be with you."

The auditorium was nearly full, people were walking in and out, and the show was broadcast on the radio. We gave the talk somehow, sharing our own personal experiences working together at Morrisania and how we learned from each other. Myrtle wanted to go first, and that was smart. At the beginning someone asked us a question, and a long pause followed. But then she started, and we were ok for the rest of the program. Afterwards, we jumped in a cab, and the cabbie turned around and said, "You ladies were great!"

We also did grand rounds in hospitals, which are meetings of all concerned to discuss difficult cases. Typically psychiatrists, medical doctors, and nurses attended. We told them beforehand, "See if you can come up with the toughest cases you have, and we'll help you brainstorm."

People in other hospitals heard about what we were doing and invited us. It was gutsy for sure, as outsiders, to come in and advise the insiders who were aware of nuances we had no way of knowing about. We did ten or more of these, in the Bronx, in Harlem, at Lincoln Hospital and at St. Luke's. When you're doing something so different, and you're an interracial team, word gets out.

An example of one of the cases we heard: the head of the Harlem Mental Health Clinic had us talk to the lead therapist on a case in which each of the five members of a family had their own therapist, and the therapists didn't talk to one another. We revealed the secret hidden by this multi-therapist structure—that this was an incest family. The traditional policy against disclosing a patient's information was inadvertently keeping the family's secrets, and it was system-maintaining. It was necessary to break the medical code of silence to help this family.

We taught interns for several years as adjunct professors at Smith and Seton Hall, and at NYU we were adjunct *associate* professors, even though neither of us had a Ph.D. For the most part, our students were overwhelmingly engaged with what we were helping them understand.

What we were teaching wasn't to be learned in any of their other courses because we weren't discussing the model of therapy used for middle class patients. Our students were shocked when we shared our experiences in the South Bronx with them. For the first time they could see what it was like for families stressed and vulnerable on every level because of poverty, racism, and past generations of abuse and relentless challenges. We showed them how to help such patients manage their lives. No one else taught that as far as we knew. I can tell you that no one fell asleep in our classes. What we taught was literally an eye-opener.

The Connecticut College Medal

The most excruciating and critical moment in Myrtle's and my relationship centered on my being awarded the Connecticut College medal at my college reunion in June of 1993. That medal is the highest alumni honor, and I was selected partly because I supported the college, financially and otherwise, and partly based on the work I was doing with Myrtle—diversity was an important issue and goal for the college. I continued to be extensively involved with my alma mater in many different capacities after I graduated.

Shortly before I learned of this award, I met Judy Kirmmse, the affirmative action officer at Connecticut College and assistant to the president at that time. The president, Claire Gaudiani, asked Judy to invite me and Myrtle to the college to review their diversity programs. We made that trip and hit it off with Judy, who then became our friend and began to work with us consulting with organizations and trying to design an institute we could launch.

Judy suggested to the president that the college offer me the medal, and she was instrumental in getting that to happen. She also negotiated the citation's wording with Claire, which I'll tell you about in a minute.

When the alumni office called to tell me about the award, my immediate reaction was surprise and happiness. But that call came when Myrtle and I were angry with each other. Myrtle didn't hesitate to show her anger, but I was afraid to even acknowledge it. She kept asking me if I was angry, and I kept telling her, "No, everything's fine."

When I called Myrtle to tell her about the award, she at first seemed pleased, and then she was anxious to get off the phone.

Within five minutes after we hung up, she called me back, and she was boiling! Here is how she expressed her feelings in a conversation we taped later.

Myrtle: "I was angry because the award was being given for work that we had each done on the issue of race. You were being awarded, and I had participated as fully as I could possibly do on an issue that was equally important to me, and I felt that I was not being acknowledged. And I was furious because I felt that this is really very much the way society in general treats subjects of this kind. A Black person cannot be awarded for anything that even suggests that they have an influence on anyone who is White. And therefore to acknowledge that I had made some contribution to improving relations between the races was just not doable.

"I mean I was so angry I could hardly talk, as I do recall. The college could very readily see that Jo had made a contribution and I had no problem with that part of it. But over the years, I had probably made at least as much of a contribution through my experience of having been subjected to tokenism since I was in junior high school, and that, too, is a real contribution to integration. It is not fine. It was an absolute misery for me most of the time." This is a reference to Myrtle's experience as a member of small groups of Black students selected to integrate schools from when she was in junior high all the way through college. Even in graduate school, she was one of few Black students.

She went on. "And there is absolutely no acknowledgment. It's as though I went to school invisibly. I agree that the need to integrate the schools was a very high priority and a high need in urban centers, such as New York. So I felt that Jo ought to do something to acknowledge the fact that this was happening, that it was time for her to say that she didn't do this alone and that it would be unfair if her partner were not acknowledged. I just felt so strongly about that issue that even though we had made this commitment probably

12 – 14 years earlier, that we would stay the course, I really felt, but I don't think I said this to Jo at that point, but she probably picked it up, that I could not continue in a partnership where my part of it was going to be ignored. So we had some very difficult times right after that phone call."

As you can see, our relationship was imperiled despite our commitment, when the toxic forces in our society were also pushing us apart. We didn't just have a conversation—it was a *shouting match*. I realize now Myrtle heard only part of what I was saying, and I heard only part of what she was saying. My investment in my college was deep: I was still actively engaged with that institution, both my daughters and my son-in-law were graduates, and I gave the college a significant amount of money. So I was seeing the award as a recognition of my involvement and financial support more than for the work I did with Myrtle, although that was certainly an important part of it.

Both our husbands heard each of us during that loud phone conversation, and I think both wondered if this would be the last one. Our friend from Morrisania, Elsie, told us we probably needed couples therapy, and I think she was right.

One of the sticking points for me was that I learned in my culture growing up how important it is to be right—it could even mean survival at times. And now, when I heard Myrtle questioning my assumptions about this medal, I started feeling as if I wasn't right, and I feared this was the last blow to our relationship.

I felt despair. The larger issues, larger than Myrtle and me, seemed to be doing us in. My fear was that these social forces don't let even those people with a tremendous investment in one another and many years of painful struggle together succeed in their commitment to each other.

The one thing that stood out for me in our conversation was what Myrtle said about the larger systems issues. When I thought about that, my anger dissipated, and I could see how important it was for me to demonstrate that none of us succeeds on our own; we are always part of a larger supporting team. In my case, the immediate team included Myrtle and Elsie. This would be important not only for them, but for all the other alums at the award ceremony.

I called the college to see if the award plaque citation could be rewritten to express this important fact, and I asked if Myrtle and Elsie could each have a copy of it. They were very obliging. So we got through this gut-wrenching time, and if anything, it strengthened our relationship.

Here is the text of the citation:

The Connecticut College Medal

The Connecticut College Medal, created in 1969 to mark the 50th anniversary of the first graduating class, is the highest honor the college can confer on those whose accomplishments and services have enhanced its reputation and nourished its growth.

I take great pleasure in awarding the Connecticut College Medal to Joanne Levitt Vanderkloot, class of 1962.

At Connecticut College, you majored in economics and minored in Spanish. In 1982 you obtained your Master of Social Work at New York University's School of Social Work. That same year, you and Myrtle Parnell founded the interracial and bilingual partnership of Parnell and Vanderkloot at the Morrisania Neighborhood Family Care Center in the South Bronx, specializing in institutional systems assessment, policy planning and cross-cultural team building. You currently teach at NYU's School of Social Work, and you have previously taught at Smith College's School of Social Work, where you and Myrtle Parnell were named as the 1992 Distinguished Lydia Rapaport Professors for your work with dysfunctional systems. You have balanced these responsibilities with those of being a parent. Your two daughters, Kathryn and Pamela, followed you to Connecticut College, graduating in classes of 1985 and 1988.

You and Myrtle are breaking new ground in the treatment of the most difficult of situations characterized by chaos—in dysfunctional families, the workplace, and communities, particularly where race and poverty are factors. You share your insights by training professionals to deal with these situations. Your work has taken you to a myriad of settings, from hospitals, banks, mental health organizations, schools, courts and even to MTV. You have sought the worst problems in the toughest communities and have succeeded. Always, your focus is on people. Because of this, you are able to see to the heart of large-scale problems. You have learned to look at entire systems, rather than at isolated symptoms, thereby arriving at far-reaching solutions. You and your partner are currently at work on a book entitled *Chaos, A Survivor's Manual*, which will summarize the understandings growing out of your work.

Your work carries into communities beyond our campus the values espoused by Connecticut College, which is committed to preparing students to live and work in a world rapidly growing smaller, where people of all backgrounds must learn to understand each other and themselves. Because people cause the world's problems, your focus on helping people function effectively contributes at a most basic level to finding important solutions.

Joanne Levitt Vanderkloot, you have benefitted our society by allowing your sensitivity to people and instinct for getting to the root of problems shape your life's work. You have shown others that the most difficult problems can be solved if they are perceived from new perspectives. You are making the world a better place for all of us and the graduates of this college in the years to come. Therefore, it is with deepest affection and esteem that I award you the 1993 CONNECTICUT COLLEGE MEDAL.

Claire Gaudiani '66
President of the College

My battle with Myrtle over the college medal taught me that when there are race and class issues in a relationship and this kind of anger builds, if there isn't a deep and abiding respect for the other person, the chances of getting past the disagreement are slim. Myrtle and I had that for each other. I respected Myrtle to an extraordinary degree, which made me able, after my first reactive anger, to stop and say, "Wait a minute, what am I not hearing? She's not unreasonable. She doesn't begrudge me awards from my school. What is she trying to tell me that I'm not getting?" And that's when I called her four or five days later and asked her that question.

The second time around, I heard. We were both so angry, and then she said to me, "Look, this is not easy what we have agreed to do. You have an obligation. Even though they only give the medal to you because you're the alumna, you have an obligation. You have an audience in front of you that's predominantly White, and you can make a statement to them. That's all I'm asking. I don't begrudge you the medal or anything else, but you need to use the award ceremony to advance what we're fighting for and believe in, and not just do what most Whites do, which is to stand up and say, 'Thank you very much! Aren't I wonderful?'"

At the event, I was surprised by the responses. The feedback I got for accepting the award in that way was overwhelming. There was a murmur—people all around in the audience were murmuring about it. I didn't accept in a cute and clever way, which I think is what is generally expected at such events. I got up and talked briefly. I accepted it on behalf of the three of us: Myrtle, Elsie, and myself, and on behalf of all those who worked at Morrisania without any fanfare, who like many others toiled and never got credit for their work. I accepted it fast. There wasn't much else to be said. I felt in a way kind of funny doing it, because I was violating the expectations I was taught as part of my culture. But one woman came up to me afterwards and said, "I just want you to know, I am so glad to be a graduate of a college that would give an award to somebody like you."

Racism

Throughout our friendship and work together, Myrtle and I dove deep into the issue of racism, which has always been important to me, partly because my father couldn't sell to Jews or Blacks in the early days of the Levittowns. He was also concerned when he was planning to adopt Mac and me that I wouldn't want to have a Jewish last name, making me a potential target for anti-Semitism.

When I was little, I had a friend who was Portuguese, and I noticed even then that people talked differently about her, and they didn't want me to play with her. They thought I could get germs from her, and since I was sick a lot, they were worried. But I didn't care: I played with her anyway. As my father always said, nobody could tell me what to do.

When I found out my father wouldn't sell to Jews and Blacks, I was furious. But he said, "Listen, if I sell to Jews and Blacks here, I don't have any business. I can't make a living. That's why I don't do it. Everybody else who's building is doing the same thing, so I won't be able to do business." He knew a federal law was needed to force everybody to stop discriminating at the same time.

When the first Black family moved to Levittown, PA, in 1957 on a resale, I saw a flaming cross on the lawn of a house there. I was 17 at the time. That Levittown was a community composed mostly of Bethlehem, PA, steel workers. It was terrifying. When it hit the newspapers, we had to unplug our phones because we were being bombarded.

In 1968 when Reverend Martin Luther King, Jr. was murdered, my father took out a full-page ad in the New York Times saying that Levittowns, in a tribute to Martin Luther King, Jr., would open every one of its communities and every housing job to Blacks from then on. I was very proud of him.

Our Personal Styles, Shaped by Race and Class

These experiences were my baptism into racism, which was part of Myrtle's experience her whole life and an ever-present challenge to us when we worked together. Race and class are almost always intertwined; when one is foregrounded, the other is often in the background. Race and class affect people's personalities and style; when we gave presentations together, we found our styles were noticeably different.

All that private-school, upper-class training taught me to put on a well-organized performance: tell the people what you're going to tell them, then tell them, and then tell them what you told them. Start with some humor and keep it lively. It's not interactive: you're the expert and you're there to connect, entertain, and educate. Myrtle's style was not like this at all. She was much more conversational, talking to people more naturally.

But there was more to it than that. I was an institutional kid, and in that kind of setting, you don't make it if you can't connect. It's like being a foster child, only families with money call it boarding school. You go there and your whole life is your ability to connect.

There is no safe home to go to. The ability to go out into the world and connect powerfully is the way to survive and to thrive. That's what was drilled into me, right into my DNA, and that's why I was so passionate about succeeding.

But Myrtle got different messages growing up in a Black lower-middle-class family where any kind of middle-class status was uncertain and easily lost in a White world, and in a family that lost four sons, one right after another, before Myrtle was born. Myrtle's parents were so fearful for her they wouldn't allow her to visit friends or to date: she couldn't have those connections. Only her family was considered safe.

The messages she received were to be cautious and at times to disconnect. And always to be wary and on the alert, because not only were there the family losses, but there was always the background music of societal racism, of Myrtle growing up Black in a White culture that was hostile to Blacks. All of that was amplified by her experiences as a token Black student integrating previously all-White schools.

The messages I received prompted me to be assertive, while Myrtle was taught to be on the defense, to always watchfully analyze the situation to see if it was safe, and sometimes to disappear. This was another family systems situation which could easily look like a "one-up," and society lets it be that. This was what was painful: it was the exacerbation of our personal issues, shaped by race and class, that threatened our effort to work together while keeping our differences intact and without having to give up our crucial personal identities that were key to our survival.

Myrtle and I worked mostly in the White world, except for the presentation we gave at the Apollo Theater and the mixed-race groups we worked with. That put her in the position of trying to figure out her place in that world most of the time, which can be exhausting and rob you of initiative. It's hard to take initiative when you feel like an outsider.

For me there was pressure, too, working in the dominant culture. If it's my group we're working with and I mess it up, Myrtle wouldn't be in trouble, I would. But if we're working with Myrtle's group, I could feel relief. I could come along for the ride, and I didn't have to worry.

Also, I honestly think Blacks aren't on the spot to perform in their own group the way Whites are in theirs. The White subordination of Blacks reinforced Black cultural norms which teach everyone in their group to be there for one another no matter what, while Whites, some of whom assume the world is theirs for the taking, are in competition to rise to the top individually, at the expense of whoever gets in their way. Not all Whites, certainly, but that's an important aspect of the culture, particularly White male culture—individualism and competition. That's why Myrtle had a hard time understanding my anxiety about potentially failing in front of my group: it was unthinkable in her culture.

When we presented together, she insisted on being true to her natural style. But from my perspective, that put us in a paradoxical bind. If we did not follow the dictates of "White style," people in our White audiences would look at me and think, "What do you expect? She's a jerk; she picked a Black partner, and now she's off violating the rules." But if we followed those rules, Myrtle would be negated.

I also knew the farther up you went on the socio-economic ladder, the more you had to be seen as participating in White culture. It took us a while to figure this out, but when we did, we used it as a teaching tool. In the classroom the expectations were different, and we were not teaching the dominant model. We found we could each be ourselves there; some students would gravitate to Myrtle and some to me. When we stayed after class to answer questions, two lines of students formed, one waiting to talk to me, and one for Myrtle.

In the beginning of our partnership, we thought we'd have to do "dog and pony shows" since that's what corporate America wanted, and we wanted to share our message. We decided we needed help to get it right. We knew we had to dress the part and speak in a certain way, so we hired an expensive woman to teach us how to do that, with all the nuances—to teach us how to perform in public and on TV. She was a New York corporate woman—tough and smart—who was helpful in one way. She told Myrtle to look at the person she was talking to so she wouldn't lose the words. That was worth the $10,000 we paid her, which was a lot even though she gave us a break because she wanted us to succeed.

She started by having us memorize scripts and learn gestures until we felt like trained seals. Then she had us walking around the chairs in a certain way. We started to giggle because Myrtle was tripping over the chairs, intentionally or not. It got silly. Finally we looked at each other and we said, "You know something? This is not what we're about. This is not about relationships. This is about, 'Let's pretend.' We're out of here." We thanked her and left.

One thing this trainer taught us was to make sure there was never any dead air. Never silence. But we decided that if there's going to be room for all people to come together and have a conversation, dead air is part of it. Not being perfect is part of it. Being human is an essential ingredient. And that means you'll "Ummm," and you'll hem and you'll haw, and you'll say whatever you'll say, and it's all part of what has to happen.

Hiring the trainer was expensive, but it was necessary because it made us articulate to ourselves what we weren't and who we were. We agreed to go out there as a team, and we talked about the temptation to get sucked in for the money, which meant we had to play by their rules. We weren't going to do that. Period. We weren't going to be part of the problem.

But I have to say, my fears about Myrtle's presentation style were often unfounded. They were rooted in early experiences when we either presented separately at the same events or together, when she was so terrified she could barely mumble a few sentences. But later when we presented together, if I sat back and she had free rein, while I was drowning in anxiety rooted in my perfectionism, she'd be fantastic. When I got anxious, I over-functioned to make sure everything that had to happen *would* happen. To stop doing that and let Myrtle do things her way was extremely hard.

Myrtle's family messages played into mine in a negative way. She was taught she wasn't supposed to do anything but sit quietly and not draw attention to herself. If she did that and I over functioned and kept talking, she thought I was giving her that same family message, which made her furious with me, just livid. Then I felt terrible. So to present together, we had a lot to overcome. But if you saw us do it, you wouldn't think we were struggling.

When we first started working together, trying to get beyond the race issues, she would try to be White, and in some limited fashion, I'd try to be Black. Of course it didn't work, and we knew that almost immediately. There we were, caught in this same horrible bind. We had a message to bring, and people felt it and wanted it, and they wanted more. But I hated doing it: I felt tortured every time. I wanted to crawl in a hole and die, and so did Myrtle. We came away exhausted. We had every kind of plan, and we tried every kind of thing. And it just didn't work internally for us. People thought we were fantastic; but they couldn't see what we were going through.

We finally hit a turning point. We decided our style together was to be blunt as we laid out the way we saw the organization's situation. We were organized but also spontaneous. When a workshop is interactive, and the people in the room have an opportunity to say things and ask questions, the structure you start out with, the posing of the initial understanding of the problems, for example, evolves into something everyone in the room shapes and molds, which means everyone owns it. The leaders stop being experts and become experienced facilitators who have dealt with these issues and learned from them and who are there to ask the questions that lead the discussion.

We figured out an effective approach: we told our clients what we could do and what we couldn't, and we let them know we weren't there to step on their toes, that we believed in a no-blame approach. Everyone's part of the problem, and everyone's needed to solve it. That helped defuse the situation, because participants are afraid of being blamed and humiliated for things they did or said that had unintentional consequences. We discovered most of our audiences did not understand how systems worked, even if they said they did. That was something valuable we could teach them.

One of our projects was doing a weeklong workshop during the long winter break at Connecticut College, as part of a program called "Dean's Term." We did this for four years running. Judy partnered with us in planning and holding these sessions—8:30 to 5:00 for five days. She was a good friend by then and visited us often in Warwick. We called our sessions "Team Building in a Multicultural Society," and they were hugely successful.

As you can see, while Myrtle and I did all this work together— the writing, the teaching, the consulting, and training—the most important thing we did was build our relationship through thick and thin. We kept trying to figure it out, to understand all the different strands and how they wove in and out with each other: who we were as individuals and how our family backgrounds, our social class, and our race and ethnicity influenced us. We thought about how one of these strands would amplify others and how they all affected our friendship and professional partnership.

Another Devastating Loss

Some years into this stage of our lives, it became clear to me that Myrtle was losing ground. She was becoming confused. There were little signs at first that I tried to ignore or explain away.

When it started, if we were presenting, Myrtle lost things. Or her papers weren't in order, and she couldn't find her place. When we did a presentation at EACUBO (the Eastern Association of College and University Business Officers) with Judy and another staff member from Connecticut College, Myrtle got lost in the hotel building where the meeting was held, and we couldn't find her until just before we were to start. ANXIETY! When it was her turn to speak, she went on a tangent and didn't make a lot of sense. She knew something was wrong and apologized.

One day I dropped Myrtle off at the bank in NYC where she had an account and needed to make a withdrawal. I circled the block and when I came back, she came to the car without the money because she couldn't remember her pin. Another time, I left her in the car in the city when I went in to see a patient on Park Avenue. She was supposed to wait for me in the car. I came out to find the car gone; I had no idea where she was. She started driving aimlessly around in a circle and finally came back.

Another time when we were at the checkout in the small grocery store in the city where we often shopped and I wasn't paying attention, Myrtle took the groceries out of the cart of the person behind us and put them in our cart. In Warwick, I got calls at all hours because Myrtle was wandering around town and didn't know where her car was. Each time I went to rescue her.

Teaching at NYU the last year was hair-raising. She couldn't remember anyone's name and was so confused I had to listen to what students were saying to both of us. At the end of the year I told her, "I can't do this anymore." She was upset and she asked me,

"Are you going to do it without me?" But I couldn't do that to her, so our teaching career was over.

Alzheimer's ran in Myrtle's family: her father once went out in the street scantily clothed and got lost. But more than that, Myrtle's marriage was suffocating her, and she couldn't leave it. Not with all the loss issues in her family and the importance of her finally marrying, especially marrying a White man with a Yale degree, after all the restrictions she lived with. Dementia was her way out.

At one point during her deterioration, a year after Fred and I separated, I invited her to come and stay with me, and she did, for almost a month. I wanted her to get away from Peter, who was a thoroughly frustrating and manipulative person. His graduation from Yale implied he was intelligent, but emotionally he was geared for failure, and he was jealous of Myrtle whenever she seemed to be succeeding. He was even jealous of her friendship with me. He always found ways to put barriers in her path.

Once she and I were going to meet at the airport to go somewhere to do a presentation. When I arrived, there was no Myrtle, and she hadn't called me. This was before cell phones. Finally Peter drove in with her, and she looked half put together. When she got in her car in the morning, it wouldn't start. It was stone cold dead. She finally woke Peter up to drive her.

We later found out he took the battery out of her car the night before. This is what I mean when I say that Peter was an infuriating kind of person. I used to say he always steered for the rocks. That's because Fred and I went canoeing with Myrtle and Peter, and he steered straight for the rocks on purpose. He didn't know I earned a vanguard classification in canoeing at camp: I saw what he was doing and dug deep to block him, gritting my teeth the whole while.

When Myrtle came to stay with me, she went through a dramatic transformation. She started looking a lot younger, she was relaxed, her thinking became clearer, and she seemed happy. We had good times together, just talking, watching some TV, relaxing. The improvement was amazing. Judy came to visit, and she couldn't believe the changes in Myrtle: she looked and sounded so happy. That's why I was sure the dementia was partly in response to her feeling trapped in her marriage. Then came Thanksgiving, her favorite holiday, and she decided to go back home. She did, and that was that. She was back with Peter, back to the downward spiral.

Finally Myrtle was in such bad shape she couldn't leave home on her own, and her niece, Beryl, tried to help her. Then Peter became ill with liver failure and called me Thanksgiving Day from the hospital to say he was dying and had no will. Judy was visiting again at the time. We went to the hospital to help him write a will, a difficult process because Peter couldn't stop hiccoughing. No one in the hospital could notarize the will, so I called a lawyer friend down the road from me, and she did it. Peter at first wanted to leave most of his assets to his brother. I said to him, "Peter, that's not fair. Over half of that money is Myrtle's. And Beryl is the one who will take care of her when you're gone. She'll need money to do that." He listened. By that time, even though Myrtle could visit Peter, she seemed to be in a daze and wasn't processing what was happening. He died shortly after that.

Beryl was there for Myrtle during the rest of her life. She arranged for caregivers to come to Myrtle's house and take care of her around the clock, and she also stayed with her as much as she could. This lasted several years. It was utterly heartbreaking for me. Another huge loss. I'd visit, and sometimes she didn't know who I was. I realize this is a familiar story for many. It became harder and harder for me to go. It tore me to shreds each time.

One time when I was there and she wasn't talking—hadn't talked for some time—as I was having a conversation with her caregiver, she leaned her head around to face me and smiled and said, "You're fabulous!" Those were her last words to me. Her death a few years later was the end of one of the most important chapters in my life. I cried for the next two years. I shut down for a while; I didn't see people socially for quite a while, and I lost interest in a lot of things. Fortunately, I had my patients and a few close friends during that time.

After Myrtle

After Myrtle was no longer able to work, I continued with my private practice. Along the way, rather early on, she and I stopped renting the apartment in the city where we each saw patients, and my private practice continued in my home office in Warwick. A few years after Fred and I separated and then divorced, I sold the barn and moved to another beautiful house in Warwick on Onderdonk Road, the first house I bought myself. My Onderdonk home was beautifully situated; in the springtime it was a fairyland. The driveway to this house went down a hill from the road and branched to my house and my neighbor's. All around us were woods inhabited by deer and other wildlife, even black bears. I used to walk up and down the driveway picking up sticks on my lawn as exercise. I usually carried my bear bells. It was beautiful and peaceful there. An in-law apartment was perfect for my office, and my practice thrived; word-of-mouth brought me patients. I was part of a community of friends who often shared dinners together.

The view from my front door on Onderdonk
in the spring. Notice the deer? (2005)

My dog, Fritzi, in my front yard on Onderdonk, 2012

After moving to Onderdonk, I began sharing my home with a friend who became unhoused when her landlady died of cancer. Helga was a German immigrant who lived in the US her entire adult life and at 80 years of age lost her lease of 35 years. She and I were good friends for years. In her earlier years, she worked for Vogue designing women's clothing, and later she was a designer/seamstress for local Warwick clients. Since she lived only on Social Security after she retired, she was in a bad situation.

Helga lived with me on Onderdonk and in the other house I later moved to in Warwick. It was a reciprocating relationship. I provided her with a home and companionship, and later caregiving. Until her last few years with me, she cooked dinner and helped around the house. With her background of courses at the Culinary Institute of America in the Hudson Valley and her delicious German recipes, we ate well!

Offering Helga a home was not something I thought twice about. It seemed the natural thing to do—it was a win/win situation. I had the room, and we could help each other. It worked out well for us both.

After 15 years at Onderdonk, I moved with Helga to Horizon Farms, another beautiful but smaller home, this time in a suburban development, albeit in the semi-rural community that Warwick is.

Judy's and my friendship and working relationship continued through Myrtle's waning years, and it is she and I who have now partnered in building the Chaos Institute—finally figuring out how to do what we hoped to do years earlier, partly because technology makes it so much easier now. Our website, www.chaosinstitute.org, along with this memoir, is our way of trying to share with the world the knowledge and resources sorely needed to enable humans to solve the problems threatening our country and this planet. (I'll enlarge on this in the last chapter.)

At this point in my life, after so many experiences—wonderful, exciting, fulfilling successes counterbalanced by all the losses, I knew it was again time to take stock. The world was becoming more chaotic all the time, and I kept thinking, "If only more people knew what I know about chaos and complexity!" As the pressure to find ways to share my knowledge grew, Judy and I talked endlessly about it and tried various things, like building a website from scratch, even though neither of us is trained in web design.

After Helga and I moved to Horizon Farms and Judy retired from Connecticut College, the way seemed to open, and we thought we were poised to accomplish our dreams. Of course life is always throwing monkey wrenches into the best of plans, and while Judy and I were old enough to know that, we were still optimistic about finding a way. At this point, there was no matriarch to guide us, but our growing knowledge and experience kept pushing us forward. Maybe together we could find a way to take on that matriarch role for others. We were surely on to something. The elephant was beginning to take shape.

Chapter 16:

Too Much to Bear

"Everything changes as you get older - your mind,
your body, the way you view the world."
—Antonio Bandaras

"One of the defining characteristics of all extant elephants is their
longevity. Wild savanna and forest elephants, and zoo and semi-cap-
tive Asian elephants, are known to live into their 7th decade of life
(Lee et al., 2012; Keele, 2014; Lahdenperä et al., 2014; Chapman et
al., 2019), with some Asian elephants documented to live into their
80s (Lahdenperä et al., 2014). Wild elephants have been living to
advanced ages for millennia, without the aid of science or medicine.
Such longevity is rare in any terrestrial mammal, which suggests
that elephants have evolved mechanisms to protect against aging
diseases." (Frontiers in Aging. "Aging: What We Can Learn From
Elephants," 26 August, 2021, online)

Surgery

Elephants seem to age more healthfully than we humans do. By the
year 2018, when I was 78 years old, my tennis and marathon-running
days caught up with me. For years I favored one hip when I walked,
and when the pain became insistent, I went to a wonderful orthopedic doctor in Warwick. The diagnosis was unwelcome but not a

surprise: my hip bones were rubbing together, and a hip-replacement was in order. I'm glad for elephants that they don't play tennis or run marathons. They seem to carry their heavy bodies around, walking through each of their days without the orthopedic problems we humans suffer from. However, my bone-on-bone condition was the wallpaper in my life while other things were grabbing my attention during that time.

I did have the surgery. Pam arrived to be there for the operation and stayed about a week. When it was time for her to leave, Judy came for another week, and other people took care of things around the house I couldn't handle.

Having weathered so many losses in my life, I was toughened by this time, which was a good thing because I was entering another hard period. Mother Nature was about to score a triple hitter at my expense. I've read that elephants sometimes have bumps on their hides where bullets hit them without penetrating. I've grown a thick hide as well.

First there was Helga; then there was my patient, Saul; and finally there was Katie. Those were the people who have now passed out of sight. But ultimately, I also faced the need to leave Warwick, my home for 36 years.

When Helga and I moved to Horizon Farms, my last home in Warwick, she was already beginning to slip. We lived there for about three years before I needed hip surgery. At the age of 91, she was able to help a little, but she was experiencing worsening dementia, and my sudden physical incapacities were upsetting and threatening to her. She was as dependent on me as a child. It was a difficult time.

Because of my childhood bout with osteomyelitis, after the surgery my surgeon wanted me on an infusion of antibiotics for six weeks: they implanted a port in my arm, and a nurse came to help me with the first few infusions. Doctors have been extremely wary about a recurrence of osteomyelitis throughout my entire life, a good reason for the lengthy course of antibiotics. A physical therapist also came to help me retrain my muscles.

Meanwhile, Helga's dementia was continuing to worsen and she experienced some paranoia. She decided to visit her sister, Mumi, in Germany, but she didn't want me to know. She told the person I hired as a companion for her, who fortunately clued me in. I let Helga know that I was aware of her desire to visit Mumi, and I offered to help her plan the trip. Eventually, she was able to go, in spite of her mental condition.

Saul

Then things began to crumble on other fronts. A new patient, Saul, a referral from someone in the North Bronx, started therapy with me, and shortly thereafter Katie was diagnosed with stage four metastasized breast cancer. Katie's diagnosis was not a complete surprise, but it certainly got my attention. First let me tell you about Saul. (His name and those of his family members are changed to protect their privacy.)

Saul was diagnosed with stage four melanoma late in 2018. He began seeing me that October, soon after his diagnosis, and Katie was diagnosed the following March. Saul overcame cancer twice before by using alternative treatments, but this time the melanoma was disrupting everything in his life, and he needed help with the turmoil the illness was causing.

With my daughter and a patient both suffering from an advanced form of cancer, I hit the warpath. For years I intuited that serious diseases like cancer get an upper hand when a person's immune system is battered by enough emotional trauma during their lifetime to weaken it. Now I suspected that if a good therapist could help a patient heal their emotional wounds, their immune system could regain enough strength to defeat the physical disease in partnership with advanced medical treatment, such as immunotherapy. I now had two important incentives pushing me to show how this could work.

Saul's case is one of the most important family therapy cases I've ever been involved with. I describe it here in some detail because for me it was both personally and professionally important. This case unearths deep understandings about how families work and about how patterns in family relationships across generations can determine what happens in the current generation. Saul and his family agreed to become a case study for me early on, and I am grateful. I think you'll see how intense their struggle was, and mine as well, as I tried to figure out how to help Saul access information that could save his life. I hoped by working with Saul I would gain knowledge that could help Katie as well.

Saul's cancer was aggressive; he and I needed to engage in intensive work together to uncover emotional triggers that might exacerbate this new onset of cancer.

Saul and his wife, Rosa, sought my help because the illness was affecting their marriage, his relationships with his children, and his job. I knew that Saul, Rosa, and I would need to look at the patterns running through past generations in both their families to discover unconscious issues playing into their current situation. For many years I've been certain that chronic illness is more than just its physical manifestations.

My questions for Saul were, "Why did you get sick when you did, and what in you is resisting your healing?" He and I spent hours talking about his family, since the family of a chronically ill person is typically riddled with all sorts of major problems over recent generations: that's one reason I believe life's stresses impact chronic illness. I believe the reverse is also true, that illness can play a role in family dynamics: sometimes it helps stabilize them, as surprising as that may sound.

* * *

Some behavioral patterns in a family threaten to tear it apart, and chronic illness can protect the family by minimizing that behavior. A therapist can intervene by helping a family find those patterns of behavior so they can see what's throwing everyone off course. The therapist can then stabilize the family in healthier ways, releasing the illness from that role, and freeing the patient to be open to cures or remedies.

Often, chronic illness protects a family from conflict, which can make an ill patient worse, so it's avoided. When a therapist teaches family members how to handle conflict constructively, the chronic illness often diminishes or fades away. Of course, patients are also usually being treated by physicians, but at times, physical interventions don't work if emotional issues aren't also addressed.

I first became aware of this function of chronic illness in a family I treated at Morrisania. Two other therapists and I were working with three families: each family had a chronically physically ill member as well as one with a presenting problem in mental health. In these families, when our patients' mental health issues went into remission, to our great surprise and concern, the members of their families who had chronic physical illness dropped dead! My colleagues and I were so struck by these "coincidences," we asked ourselves a question that isn't usually asked in mental health practice: "Are these mental and physical conditions in different family members related?" The answer is yes, and I went to talk to doctors… I went to talk to doctors on the medical side of the hospital to see if they would be interested in forming a team with the three of us in mental health to explore the mind/body connection with their chronically ill patients.

Three of the doctors were excited at this prospect. They described their patients as walking time bombs who were non-compliant with taking their medications. A week later the three doctors met with us: they were disheartened. They couldn't get any of their patients to participate in our study. I asked them, "What were you saying to them?" They told us they were telling their patients they were working with a team to help cure their illnesses. We told these doctors, "You can't say that! You have to tell them you're working with a team to help them *manage* their illness better." When the doctors went back and used this different approach, they got all the patients they could handle. The patients were unconsciously concerned that curing their illness would threaten their families' cohesion.

In a troubled family in which chronic illness is playing such a role, if only physical remedies are used, without family therapy, it's like Russian roulette. If the family can't let go of the illness because it's holding everything together, even if the physical intervention would normally be strong enough to make a difference, the patient may die anyway.

In my practice, I put families into three groups. Type One families are simple. All the members are mostly healthy, and so are their relationships with one another. Healthy communication within the family predominates. Of course family members have problems, as we all do, but they have the skills to resolve them. Type One families have smooth sailing for the most part.

Type Two families have a certain amount of dysfunction and experience problems such as alcohol and drug abuse, divorce, and depression, but they have some level of cohesion and mutual support. These families are beginning to sail in troubled waters.

Saul came from what I call a Type Three family, which is the most complex. Its complexity is expressed as the same issues facing Type Two families, but Type Three's will have in addition other more serious problems such as chronic physical and mental illness, verbal and physical abuse, suicides, and the death of children, and they lack family cohesion. These families are navigating through white water rapids.

All the most difficult families, the Type Three's, are the same in that they are extremely rigid in response to any change that could threaten the family's homeostatic balance. Homeostasis is the balance created when the members' interactions hold the family together as a unit, whether in healthy or unhealthy ways.

* * *

Saul was so scared by this latest diagnosis of melanoma he quit his job to spend all his time researching alternative treatments, even though Rosa wasn't employed. He also talked about having their older son, Ben, transfer from his college to a state university. Marco, their younger son, was just ten years old. Financial worries were escalating, and both boys were confused and upset.

As Saul and I talked about his family, we found significant structural patterns in different generations, like adopted siblings and deep mother/son bonding. Remarkably, some aspects of these special relationships in complex families can determine the time when a family member will die of illness, and this was true in Saul's family.

In Saul's recent family history, he and I identified two important relationship patterns: 1) fathers dying when their children were young, and 2) people dying close to the time of a significant family occasion. These patterns were expressed in Saul's own life as well, in serious measure. When he was twelve years old, his father, at age 50, disappeared on Christmas Eve. Three weeks later they found his body floating in the river: he drowned himself.

Saul's medical history revealed a critically important pattern. In his late twenties, he was diagnosed with testicular cancer; it went into remission following alternative treatments. The current cancer, melanoma, appeared when he was about 52 years old, when Marco was ten, and it seemed to go into remission. But then it returned with a vengeance. So the pattern predicted that Saul would die two years later if the disease were not disrupted—when Marco was 12, the age Saul himself was when his father died.

Furthermore, before Saul's father killed himself, he started crying incessantly and called his best friend to ask for help. His friend told him to go to a therapist, but Saul's father refused. Now Saul was crying a lot and Rosa told him he needed to seek more aggressive cancer treatment, but he refused.

There are always behavioral patterns in families. It's important for a therapist to help a patient identify them. Some will be unrelated to the patient's situation, but others could make all the difference.

Saul's disease expressed itself in an enlarged lymph node under his left arm and another on the right side of his neck. His gestures and what happened to him physically during therapy sessions were rather remarkable. As he talked about his parents, without thinking about it, he pointed to parts of his body that unconsciously represented the disease and the loss of his mother and father. When he talked about his mother having a heart attack, his hand went to a point just below his heart, marking the site of her heart attack, certainly, but it was also precisely where his melanoma was first discovered. He was also registering the lung cancer she had five years following her heart attack. His mother had three rounds of disease before she died, and Saul was now on his third.

When Saul told me about the last night he spent with his father, he touched the nodule on the right side of his neck. That nodule unconsciously represented his father to him. They were sitting on the sofa watching TV, and his father's arm was around him, cradling him as he fell asleep, his hand touching the spot where this nodule was on his neck. When Saul told me about this, he began to cry uncontrollably, saying that was the last time he saw his dad before he disappeared, and it was the only time his dad ever hugged him. By the end of this therapy session, the nodule was smaller, cooler, and more pliable, rather than hard and hot as it was when we started.

Both nodules visibly responded in many of our sessions when Saul talked about his relationship with his parents.

At the start of one session, the nodule below Saul's left armpit hurt as he was talking, and then he started describing his dad's funeral. He remembered crying hysterically and feeling as if he were in the coffin, too. He told me that at Jewish funerals people close to the deceased person place a ripped cloth on a part of their own bodies in remembrance. Saul placed the cloth on the spot under his armpit where he now had a nodule.

Patients often find a way to act out what they don't know consciously, and Saul's pointing to relevant parts of his body as he talked about his family relationships was striking and dramatic. He was showing me the way his body expressed his bottled-up grief.

Saul found other patterns as well, as he thoughtfully explored his history. His family members got sick and died during certain months of the year—from October through January, when Jewish holy days occur. As we worked through all this material, Saul cried a lot, which wasn't like him at all. He told me he always said he wouldn't be like his father. I told him his unconscious mind doesn't register negative statements, so when he said he wouldn't be like his father, his unconscious mind heard, "I will be like my father."

It's always rewarding for me as a therapist when patients have "Eureka" moments, when they finally see what's going on beneath the surface. When Saul's conscious mind accessed awareness of the patterns of disease and death in his family's intergenerational dynamics, he told me his mind was blown open. He got it—those dynamics were encouraging him to follow patterns of behavior that could lead to his own death in two years.

Unconscious programming happens to everyone: it's as if an unwritten rule is imprinted in our unconscious mind compelling us to repeat family traditions (patterns). It tells us what to do. Saul's unconscious mind knew he was following his family pathway into tragedy, while his conscious mind frantically tried to find solutions to his problems. His conscious mind wouldn't be able to find solutions that could prevent the tragedy unless it could access these new understandings in time.

This tug of war between our conscious and unconscious minds can create confusion, stress, and anxiety, threatening our immune system. Unconscious knowledge derives its power of compulsion from its hidden nature: what we don't know (consciously) *can* hurt us. But when that knowledge becomes conscious, exposure diminishes its power. When knowledge resides in the conscious mind, we can interact with it, negotiate with it, appreciate it, and make peace with it until it no longer holds sway over us.

For Saul, accepting that the excruciating memories of physical contact with his father related to the sites of his melanoma nodules allowed him to consciously express the grief embodied in those sites for the first time, draining away emotional toxins. His intense crying spells washed the grief out of his mind. That helped his body use alternative medical treatments to drain away the physical toxins that were locked in by emotional barricades.

Another hindrance to recovery for a chronically ill person, or someone with any serious condition, is that it gives them power. Other family members often give the ill person top priority. As I've mentioned, illness can also suppress conflict in the family because it can upset the patient, and who wants to do that? Saul had to become aware of these dangers. He received too little attention as a child, so having people show him they cared gave him comfort and made him feel important. These are the secondary gains illness can provide. It's natural for people to respond to illness that way, and the patient isn't to blame for it.

Saul came to understand another way suppression was a part of his condition. He discovered he learned to deal with difficult situations by shutting down and "people pleasing," which meant stuffing every angry thought and feeling into his unconscious mind. He did this his whole life. Like anaerobic bacteria, anger and toxic feelings fester and grow when they don't see the light of day.

Because their problems were so urgent, I saw Saul and sometimes Rosa intensively several times a week for some months, with texting and phone calls in between sessions. Then Saul came to a crossroads that involved his career. Before the melanoma was diagnosed, he increasingly felt he needed to leave the business he co-owned with a partner, and after the diagnosis, he began to see that his business represented death. That's why he told his partner and Rosa he had to stop working or he would die.

I told Saul a battle was being waged in his armpit: it was repressed grief versus new awareness. The repressed grief stemmed from inadequate love and care when he was a child along with the feelings he hadn't expressed after his father's suicide. Now he was newly aware that as a child he repressed those negative emotions. This conscious awareness of what had been unconscious was trying to make it possible for him to let go of those emotions. If he completely opened himself to the old grief and felt it now, he could release it. It would then lose power, allowing the medications and treatments to possibly heal the cellular damage caused by the cancer.

He told me he was finding new energy from this discovery process and was experiencing a rush of ideas. He texted me, "The illness was created to move me forward in work and in my relationships. Now I'm moving, moving, moving! Things are moving and flowing, and I can now connect with the flow and move with life like healthy people do."

Saul continued to open to the possibility of healing. He undertook treatments at an immuno-oncology center, and made excellent progress, watching his tumors drain away. Rosa went with him to support him. He thought that without the family therapy, his outcomes there might have been different.

Unfortunately, that positive outcome wasn't enough. His illness soon regained the upper hand, and he was hospitalized. He and his family knew he was dying. Saul told me he was on the right path in his therapy, but he waited too long and the cancer became too established. I asked him if he thought we could have saved his life if he started therapy earlier, but he said he wasn't ready to do it then. And there were two other factors as well that may have played into his failure to conquer his third bout of cancer.

The first factor was Saul's determination to do everything himself. After his father's death, his mother had to work hard to keep the family together, and at the age of 12, he was largely on his own. Lacking the usual support system for children his age, he had to trust and rely on himself alone. He also assumed adult responsibilities. For example, a week after he got his driver's license, his mother had him drive her into New York City. Because he was self-reliant as an adolescent, he thought he should be in charge of his healing at this later time.

As Saul got older, his self-reliance kept him from taking advantage of resources outside himself. His medical research was always scattered: he jumped from one alternative to another. In fact, he had a scattershot approach to life in general. He would flit from one thing to another, both in his work and in cancer treatment. He searched endlessly for he knew not what. As his disease progressed, he became insecure about future work. At times he'd be fired up, and at other times he was less energized. He knew he couldn't go back to his former partnership because he was changing. Periodically I checked in with him to ask, "Are you sure you want to keep living?" He would say, "Yes," but he sometimes looked like he wasn't so sure.

The second factor was his deep distrust of Western medicine. His cousin had melanoma and was treated using chemotherapy treatments: they were painful; they left him seriously disfigured; and he died anyway. His cousin's experience was partly what caused Saul's distrust of the American medical system, pushing him toward alternative practices.

There are some people who steer clear of alternative medicine, trusting only Western medicine, and others who rely almost entirely on the alternatives. I've seen a lot of success in people over the years using alternative medicine. In some situations, it's the only remedy that works. In fact, there are pros and cons with both systems. When patients are in as threatening a situation as Saul's, they need to be open to trying appropriate and promising treatments from both schools. Sometimes it's a combination of alternative AND Western medical treatments that brings relief.

Was Saul's work in family therapy in vain? His wife, Rosa, answered that question. With her permission, I'm including her text message to me following Saul's funeral, which I attended by Zoom. I made a few edits to protect her privacy.

"Good morning, Jo. Were you able to Zoom the funeral? If not, I can send a recording.

How are you?

We're hanging in there. Very sad. We are crying and walking around without focus and forgetting to eat, etc. Friends and local family are there for us. Saul's out of town family members left yesterday.

Boys and I are crying and talking every day. I'm so focused on their well-being and processing the whole thing—want to avoid what happened to Saul. Ben is extra sad because [his girlfriend] flew back to school (she's really special!) …Marco comes out with amazing comments and insights daily…so far we're in decent shape.

I think I'd like to keep talking to you as we go along.

Even though we lost Saul, you gave our family a year and a half of much-improved relationships and were instrumental in Saul's being able to sign a DNR in the end and leave us all with loving connection.

I hope Saul is feeling the impact he made and the inspiration he provided—I think he would've been surprised."

Saul's death was a big loss for me. I was more than usually invested in his outcome because of Katie's concurrent case of stage four metastasized breast cancer. In fact, I was so hyper-focused on my work with him and my attempts to find a cure I kept banging my hip on the metal hinge in the door of my car without realizing what I was doing, and I ended up with a serious hematoma that wouldn't stop draining. It may be hard to believe that someone could keep hitting themselves so often it would cause the severe, oozing bruise called a hematoma without even realizing it. But that's how I am: I was focused SO intensely on trying to figure out how to save Saul and Katie I was completely oblivious to this thing until one day I saw it in the mirror.

Katie

Throughout her early adulthood and while she was raising her children, Katie relied on me heavily as a sounding board. We spoke on the phone several times a day, and I always took her calls, day or night. My concerns about my older daughter started early because Katie never seemed entirely happy. One night after Pam was born, I went in to sing Edelweiss to her, as I did every night. She threw her arms around my neck and sobbed, "Mommy, you don't love me anymore." Of course I held her and reassured her, and I made efforts to pay special attention to her. I knew first children typically felt this way, but with Katie, those feelings seemed to fit into a larger scheme of negative perceptions.

When I look back at photos of Katie from throughout her lifetime, there's a reluctance in her expression, as if she's trying hard to smile or wishing she wasn't there. It's a holding back—it's as if she's sad and trying not to show it.

As early as Katie's teenage years, I was aware of my family's history of mothers losing a child going back at least three generations, and I was driven not to let that happen again. I had a ring-side seat when my grandmother lost her oldest daughter, my aunt Kitty. And then my sister, Mac, lost her son, Scottie, and next, my mother lost Mac. Knowing that legacy, I worried that of my two daughters, Katie would be the one to die in my lifetime, and that drove me. She was unhappy when she was a baby, depressed when she was a teenager, and unrooted as an adult. Katie's tentative nature and her intense dependence on me made me fearful that she and I would reenact the family pattern, although I was determined to short-circuit it.

Katie was a successful professional. She was always artistic and attended the New York School of Interior Design. After she spent time as the associate buyer for all of Ralph Lauren at Bloomingdale's in NYC, she blossomed into an interior designer for wealthy clients. She never advertised; they found her. She was exquisitely talented, with an unerring sense of design, proportion, and color. And she really enjoyed her work.

Nick and Alex

Katie married Richard when Fred and I lived in the barn. We held her beautiful wedding there. Her first child, Nicholas, was born in 1990, and her second, Alexander, in 1993. When Katie was about to give birth to Nick in a hospital in Greenwich, CT, I got the call to come there. I was nervous and jerky as I went to the reception desk and asked for Katie Vanderkloot—but they didn't have a patient by that name. I walked away in total confusion, and then I suddenly turned around, went back, and asked for her under her married name. Yes! They sent me up to her.

Katie's two boys were totally different from each other. When Alex came along, that difference was clear. He was an unmade bed. As lean, lanky, and neat as Nick was, Alex was chubby with everything coming undone. Nick would be dressed up for an event, shirt tucked in, tie in place, shoes shined, hair combed, and Alex's shirt would be hanging out, tie askew, hair going in all directions, smiles all around. Nick looks like my side of the family, like his mother in fact. And Alex looks like my birth father, Bill Habermehl.

When Nick was about one and a half years old, Katie called me in a panic. She said she needed me to come and help. She was interviewing a woman who spoke only Spanish to help care for Nicky and she knew I'd had experience with that. She wanted to do for her children what I did for her and Pam—raise them to be bi-lingual. So I went.

A little white car pulled up where we were meeting the woman, and it was like those clown cars where a whole bunch of clowns gets out of a little car. About seven adults emerged, one after the other. Katie said to me, "I'm so glad you're here. I wouldn't have known what to do." So Katie talked to the woman who was interested in the job, and I talked with all the other members of the family who came to make sure their mother/grandmother would be in a good place if she took this job. It all worked out.

At age two Alex went into anaphylactic shock from an antibiotic. After that he began to gain weight and became a fat child, which mortified Nick. Katie and her boys visited with us often. They lived in the Westport/Greenwich, CT area. A spike in child abductions was happening there—in one instance, a mother shopping in a big store turned away from her cart for a few moments, turned back again, and her toddler was gone. She alerted the store management; they locked all the doors and found a couple with the missing child in a restroom, dying his hair and changing his clothes.

This prompted Katie and Richard to move to Tuxedo Park, which was closer to Warwick, and then they saw us more often. Katie completely restored a beautiful old mansion there to its original grandeur and took on other clients. At their neighborhood pool, Alex, ever the extrovert, would walk around talking to every group of people. When they came to visit us in Warwick, he was fascinated by the fish in our pond. He and Richard came to visit with their fishing poles and stood by the pond fishing for hours. Alex now owns a profitable fishing boat.

Unfortunately, Katie's marriage to Richard ended in divorce after nine years. Subsequently, she proved to be an excellent single parent, taking care of the boys and relentlessly seeking the causes for Alex's digestive ailments and learning disabilities. She solved those problems; Alex lost the excess weight and eventually grew to be over 6 '3", lean and muscular, a rowing champion who won every event worldwide up to the Olympics.

At my house on Onderdonk, when I had a birthday party to celebrate my 60th with about 30 guests, Katie helped a lot. Pam and Bill were there, Pam pregnant with Zoe. Myrtle and Peter were there as well of course. At one point I wondered where Alex was. We found him under the dining room table poking through the bottoms of the chocolate candies.

When I lived on Onderdonk Road, my German shepherd, Polo, had his bed on one side of my bed. When Alex visited, he wanted to sleep on the floor on the other side. He would often ask me to wake him up when I got up in the morning so he could snuggle with Polo when I did. That's something I did every morning.

Nick liked to take walks with me. When he was nine and we were walking one day, I noticed he was crying. When I asked what was bothering him, he said, "Nanny, do you think my daddy doesn't love me? Since the divorce, it seems like he's not interested in me at all." He told me his father wasn't home much. He was playing a lot of golf. I told him that when people are going through a divorce, it isn't just difficult for the children; it's also hard for them. This was the beginning of my close relationship with Nick, which grew organically through the years. Katie's interior design business and Alex's medical issues took a lot of her time, so if Nick had problems, she'd tell him to talk to his grandmother. And he did that.

Alex; Katie; Nick; my dog, Polo; me, Pam, and Bill at
my 60th birthday party on Onderdonk, 2000

Over the years, he called me if he wanted to talk through issues. After
he was able to drive, he came to visit me on his own, in addition to
family visits. My relationship with him evolved in a way that was
reminiscent of my relationship with my grandmother, coming full
circle. It wasn't that Katie wasn't good with Nick: she was good with
both boys, as Pam is with her two children. But with Katie being
so involved with Alex, first because of his medical issues, and later
because of all his rowing events, and because Nick's father wasn't
available, I became his last best choice.

Katie and me at about this point in our lives, 2018 perhaps

When the boys reached high school age, Nick went to Exeter and Alex went to the Kent School in Connecticut, following in his mother's and Pam's footsteps. While there, Alex broke the 100-year rowing record. He then went to the University of Washington, which has one of the best university rowing programs in the country. He was the stroke, and the team was the national champion all four years. After graduation he was hired as the rowing coach at Boston University and is now head coach at Northeastern, in addition to being a fisherman on his own boat four months of the year. In January 2023 he married a lovely young woman, Grace, in New Zealand.

January 12, 2023: Alex and Grace

Nick excelled at St. Andrews University in Scotland majoring in international politics. He had some extraordinary experiences there. He was hired for a summer internship with NBC that led to his being the only American asked to work during the royal wedding, when Prince William married Kate. He had to sleep in the street guarding the cameras. He was also the head of the International Political Association at St. Andrews, responsible for hosting speakers, many of them important people in the world, such as leaders from the International Monetary Fund and the World Bank, and diplomats, military personnel, and security specialists. He hosted the Israeli ambassador, who had to be protected by full security because his life was threatened.

Following graduation, Nick worked for two years doing investment research at Fidelity Investments in London. Then he returned to the US and spent a year and a half exploring the wilderness before he went to law school.

Katie's tentative nature took a back seat when she became a mother. She was involved with both boys and obviously loved them very much. But there were loose ends in her approach to adulthood. Early on, Katie was interested in spirituality, alternative medicine, and past lives: these interests were all related to what lies beyond our material existence. The pull to exit this life on Earth gave her a half-hearted attitude toward adult responsibilities (except for parenting) and was responsible for her continual reliance on me. As an adult she went into anaphylactic shock when she got bug bites or bee stings, and she reacted strongly to certain antibiotics. There was no family history of this. I kept saying to Katie, "I'm sure there's a serum for bug bites that would increase your tolerance." She said, "No, there's nothing. They've told me." Of course that wasn't true. I knew someone who used those serums during that time.

When she suffered from Hashimoto's disease and then melanoma in her late twenties, she didn't want to go the route of Western medicine but looked for alternatives. With the melanoma, I knew in my heart we were headed for trouble, and I vacillated between hope and dread. But she healed from both using alternative medicine. She even attended sessions with John of God before he was arrested for sexual crimes, and whatever he did seemed to work for her. These illnesses of hers intensified my concerns about the possibility she would die early. I don't remember when I wasn't worried about her.

As early as 30 years ago, I realized that while our bodies are non-linear, Western medicine is steeped in linear thinking. I wanted to find out more about non-linear innovations in medicine because of Katie's melanoma at that time, and I found the contact information for a chaologist who taught at West Point. I called him to tell him I was researching recent medical advancements for the treatment of melanoma, and he told me to look at non-linear, dynamical systems in medicine, which I did. You may be wondering what non-linear medicine is. Here is a descriptive quote, the abstract from a paper by John Higgins, called "Nonlinear systems in medicine," published online in the Yale Journal of Biological Medicine in their 2002, September to December issue. You may find it helpful.

"Many achievements in medicine have come from applying linear theory to problems. Most current methods of data analysis use linear models, which are based on proportionality between two variables and/or relationships described by linear differential equations. However, nonlinear behavior commonly occurs within human systems due to their complex dynamic nature; this cannot be described adequately by linear models. Nonlinear thinking has grown among physiologists and physicians over the past century, and non-linear system theories are beginning to be applied to assist in interpreting, explaining, and predicting biological phenomena. Chaos theory describes elements manifesting behavior that is extremely sensitive to initial conditions, does not repeat itself and yet is deterministic. Complexity theory goes one step beyond chaos and is attempting to explain complex behavior that emerges within dynamic nonlinear systems. Nonlinear modeling still has not been able to explain all of the complexity present in human systems, and further models still need to be refined and developed. However, nonlinear modeling is helping to explain some system behaviors that linear systems cannot and thus will augment our understanding of the nature of complex dynamic systems within the human body in health and in disease states."

I followed this new way of thinking about medicine until it became immunotherapy and then watched for immunotherapy articles online. I did this so I could stay up on the latest thinking as part of my effort to protect Katie and keep her here on the planet.

In trying to save Katie, I was tapping into my role as fixer in my family. We never totally outgrow those roles we have from early in life. When I long ago presented my family dilemma to the staff at Morrisania during the Family of Origins seminar, they told me, and I agreed, that I had to step out of my role of fixer in my family. And I did after that, with the exception of Katie. I had to keep trying to help her because I was afraid she would die, perhaps by suicide, and that was unthinkable. By the time she was diagnosed with cancer, I knew my efforts were futile. Maybe my work with her kept her alive for many years, but at this point I knew a curtain had been drawn in her life. So I stopped trying to find remedies and tried to simply be there for her during this last part of her life. She did die, but she didn't commit suicide, which I believe is extremely important for the generations that may follow her.

Katie lived her entire unrooted adult life with emotional intensity. After her divorce, she didn't buy a house; she preferred renting. Her business as an interior designer thrived as her reputation spread by word of mouth, but she would never advertise or hire anyone to look after the financial aspects. In some ways she floated around in her life. She always looked for someone to take care of her. For 58 years, I struggled to keep her going. She had relationships with some men, most of them older, but was not committed to any of them. At least, not until she met Freddie.

With Freddie, Katie seemed happier than I'd ever seen her. But they didn't marry. He was also involved in rowing, so her life seemed to be coming together nicely until Freddie was diagnosed with kidney cancer. I think that was in 2017. When Freddie was diagnosed, I believed Katie would take that as her cue to leave. He was success- fully treated, but I knew his illness would knock Katie off course, especially since he was older. I was sure her loose connection with life on this planet would reassert itself, and I worried there would be a resurgence of melanoma. More recently, late in 2018, I sensed she was sick, and she did as well: she finally told me she was throwing up her coffee every morning. I urged her to go to the doctor.

Katie went to the doctor in March of 2019, and she was diagnosed with stage four metastasized breast cancer. When she told me about the diagnosis, she said, "I'm so glad you aren't hysterical." This time she was open to using Western medicine. She went through a program using a trial drug, which was effective at first, and everyone was hopeful. But then when her disease progressed, they stopped the trial, and she simply followed her doctor's advice from then on.

This cancer was more seriously threatening than Katie's melanoma, and my mother-bear reaction was to start searching for treatments. I also continued doing as much research as possible to figure out, based on my understandings of the way our emotional problems can affect our physical maladies, how I could add something meaningful to the medical help she was receiving, in the same way I did research relating to Saul's melanoma.

One day Katie called me and told me her oncologist asked if she were an alcoholic. I asked her why. She said, "Because my liver is damaged. The bile duct is blocked." I asked her, "What is all the bile about?" She didn't tell me, but 10 days later, her liver was clear. The doctor was shocked. Then I knew she was able to use what she'd learned from John of God to heal herself. I was hopeful, but shortly thereafter I realized that while she could do something about this cancer, she wasn't going to, and she went downhill after that. I think she wanted me to know this was a choice, and she knew I understood. That was her definitive statement to me that she'd had enough.

From her infancy, when I brought her home from the hospital, I worried about Katie. When she was 28, the melanoma amplified my worries. When the melanoma went into remission I thought she was OK, but I didn't trust it. My worries resurfaced with the anaphylactic shock from bug bites and her sensitivity to antibiotics about 15 years later. At the time, she was living in part of a converted barn in Connecticut that had bees. But when she was tentatively battling this latest cancer, I knew all my trying was futile. I failed as a fixer. That role ended for me in my family forever.

Alex, Katie, and Nick before cancer struck, 2011

At that point a fog descended on my brain. I persevered until then, but with this new understanding, I had to let go. I couldn't do it anymore. At first, I felt despair, and then I realized it was her choice always, not mine.

Katie ultimately succumbed to her disease, as I intuited. I realized there was nothing I could have done to change this outcome. I visited her a few weeks before she died. She told me she was worried people would think she didn't try hard enough to stay alive. Now there were two more losses added to my list. Each time, as I unpack those experiences to try to understand them, I grow stronger in the aftermath of the grief. Unlike Saul, and in opposition to British tradition, I allow myself to feel that grief.

Following Katie's death I felt totally apart from everyone. No one knew that my struggle to support her lasted for over 50 years. After both Saul and Katie died, I stopped tracking immunotherapy advances. However, I do believe that line of inquiry holds great promise for the future of medical interventions.

There is some degree of closure for me now, since I went with Pam and her husband, Bill; their children, Zoe and Zach; along with Nick, Alex, and Alex's wife, Grace, to scatter Katie's ashes into the ocean from Alex's fishing boat and plant a tree in her memory at the Kent School. Nick and Alex are both doing well: they have also processed their mother's death in healthy ways. Nick said he'd been front-loading a lot of grief over the previous two-and-a-half years.

To honor my daughter, I include her obituary here, written by Nick. I removed the surnames of Katie's living relatives.

Kathryn Van Der Kloot Obituary

Kathryn Alicia "Katie" Van der Kloot

Cambridge, MA — Kathryn Alicia "Katie" Van der Kloot, 57, of Cambridge, Mass., died peacefully on July 11, 2021 in Boston, more than two years after receiving a metastatic breast cancer diagnosis that she met with characteristic grace, strength, and good humor.

Katie was born November 1, 1963 in Philadelphia to Joanne L. Vanderkloot and Frederic J. Vanderkloot. Raised in Huntington, N.Y., Katie attended Friends Academy in Locust Valley, N.Y., before graduating from Kent School in Kent, Conn. in 1981, and Connecticut College in New London, Conn. in 1985, with a degree in Art History and Spanish. She excelled in tennis and field hockey, and discovered a lifelong love of travel at a young age.

Katie began her career in New York, where she worked as a womenswear buyer at Bloomingdale's, and met Richard___, whom she married in 1988. They had two sons – R. Nicholas ___ and Alexander V. ___ – and settled in Tuxedo Park, N.Y. After their marriage ended in divorce, Katie raised her sons in New York and Westport, Conn. She spent her later years in Cambridge, Mass. and Hanover, N.H. with her beloved partner, Frederick V. ___.

Katie channeled tremendous creative energy into her interior design firm, Van der Kloot Interiors, Ltd. She inherited a love of design from her grandmother, Alicia von Kees, an early member of the American Society of Interior Designers. Katie's work took her across the United States and Europe, often with her adored Yorkshire Terrier, Weezie, in tow. For nearly 25 years, clients entrusted Katie to create the settings for their lives. In that intimate endeavor, Katie became a dear friend and confidante to many, and made the world a more beautiful place.

Family meant everything to Katie. She was a loving and devoted daughter, sister, aunt, and partner, and, above all, a wonderful mother to her sons. She found great joy in supporting her boys' academic, athletic, and professional pursuits, and enjoyed an exceptionally close bond with both of them. Katie's greatest satisfaction came from raising her sons, who loved her dearly. She was enormously proud of the men they became.

Katie was a well-known presence on the rowing circuit through her son Alex's athletic career at Kent School and the University of Washington, and her partner Fred's involvement with the Head Of The Charles Regatta. Katie's glowing smile, joyful laugh, and mischievous sense of humor will be missed on riverbanks from Henley-on-Thames, U.K. to Seattle.

Katie is survived by her partner, Frederick V. ___, of Hanover, N.H.; sons, R. Nicholas ___ of Boston and Alexander V. ___ (Grace C. ___) of Jamestown, R.I.; and mother, Joanne L. Vanderkloot; sister, Pamela V. ____ (William G. ____,); niece, Zoe E. ____; and nephew, Zachary V. ____, all of Colorado. She is predeceased by her father, Frederic J. Vanderkloot.

Katie was widely beloved, and will be deeply missed. Services will be private. Memorial contributions may be made to the Dr. Gerburg Wulf Research Support Fund at Beth Israel Deaconess Medical Center by visiting www.bidmc.org/giving and specifying an «Other» gift designation of «Dr. Gerburg Wulf Research Support Fund.»

Published by Valley News on Jul. 25, 2021.

Someone sent me a poem when my sister's son, Scottie, died, which I've shared with others on occasion, and which comforts me now when I read it and think of Katie. It's by Edward Guest, and it follows. I must have known this was coming because I saved this poem for 40 years. Note: I've changed the pronouns from masculine to feminine to reflect my experience with Katie.

I'll lend you for a little time, a child of mine, He said.
For you to love while she lives, and mourn when she is dead.
It may be six or seven years, twenty-two or three.
But will you, till I call her back, take care of her for me?
She'll bring her charms to gladden you, and shall her stay be brief,
You'll have her lovely memories as solace for your grief.
I cannot promise she will stay, since all from earth return.
But there are lessons taught down there I want this child to learn.
I've looked the wide world over in my search for teachers true,
And from the throngs that crowd life's lane, I have selected you.
Now will you give her all of your love, nor think the labor vain,
Nor hate me when I come to call, to take her back again?
I fancied that I heard them say, Dear Lord, thy will be done.
For all the joy thy child shall bring, the risk of grief we'll run.
We'll shelter her with tenderness, we'll love her while we may,
And for the happiness we've known, we'll ever grateful stay.
But shall the angels call for her much sooner than we planned,
We'll brave the bitter grief that comes and try to understand.

Our family spreads Katie's ashes, May 21, 2022

Surgery #2 and Helga

As I mentioned, I was so focused on trying to save both Saul and Katie I created a hematoma at the site of my hip replacement by banging that hip on my car door's hinge without the slightest awareness I was doing it. I went to the surgeon repeatedly, and after quite a long time, when it wasn't responding as it should to his treatments, he told me it would be best for him to open up that hip again to make sure there wasn't internal damage.

When I had the second hip surgery, Pam came to be with me for almost a week as she did when I had the first surgery, and the day she left, Judy arrived to spend another week. They were my tag team. I did in fact cause internal damage: the cap of the replacement joint was dented, and there was an open space near it where fluid

242

accumulated before seeping out through the hematoma. The surgeon replaced the cap, repaired all the damage, and set me up for more infusions of antibiotics. This was getting to be a habit.

Before Katie died, and after Helga left for Germany, as I began healing from the second surgery, I realized Pam was right. She told me I needed to come live with them in Colorado. Pam and Bill were looking for a larger house with an in-law apartment, and the whole family was in cahoots trying to get me to move, knowing how stubborn I am. I never imagined I would ever live anywhere but New York, but it was becoming clear that most of my friends were dead or had moved from Warwick and the city. This realization led to another: that Helga could not return.

As soon as this was clear, I wrote a long letter to Mumi to explain things. I knew Helga would need to move into an assisted living facility soon. While suspicious of me at first, thinking I wanted to get my hands on Helga's money, Mumi began to understand where I was coming from, and she and I became good friends. We talked regularly until she died suddenly of a heart attack six months after her sister.

When it became certain that Helga would stay in Germany, I packed her belongings and shipped them to her; next I dealt with lawyers and other officials to arrange for her Social Security funds to be sent to her. I was also involved with the courts to get her inheritance of $150,000, left to her by a friend, released and sent to her. It was an enormous relief when the arrangements for Helga's care were finalized, and another relief when her financial situation was set up. Those funds enabled Helga to live in an assisted living facility in Germany near Mumi, where she was happy despite her dementia. This eased the minds of her family, and they could visit her often until she died.

* * *

Did I mention the Covid 19 pandemic? That was happening, and in response, I isolated. I learned to do therapy sessions on Zoom. This was a challenge on top of all the others. But since Pam and Bill bought a larger home that included an apartment for me in northern Colorado, I put my house on the market and hoped someone in the city, fearful of Covid, would want to buy it to escape to the countryside. Pam and Bill rented an Airstream RV to come pick me up, along with my essential belongings and my dog, Fritzi. This was the only way I could move during the pandemic with Fritzi in tow; he was now an old guy, suffering from some age-related infirmities. Judy came for a week to help me pack, since I was still recovering from hip surgery number two. It was a whirlwind for sure.

Pam and Bill arrived in Warwick on my 80th birthday, May 2020. I ordered a delicious dinner from my favorite restaurant so we could celebrate, but I was so exhausted from everything I have little memory of that week. While I didn't lose my resilience, it was sorely tested. Pam and Bill packed the RV, got Fritzi into his place in the truck that was pulling it, and off we went into the sunset. It took us three days to cross the country to Colorado, and it was four months before the movers came with the rest of my belongings. One fond image stands out in my mind from the blur that is my memory of the trip, and that is of Bill, backing that huge Airstream into a little bitty space at a campground between two other caravans, and then getting out and taking Fritzi for a walk. Such a good family I have.

Colorado

I now live in the West, seeing patients from Warwick and some new Colorado patients via Zoom. Other new patients come to see me in person. When I arrived here in northern Colorado, Zoe and Zach had flowers waiting for me in my room, and Pam planted flowers outside my window before they came to get me. After we got here, they watched me struggling to walk Fritzi outside: I was hurting and clearly in need of a medical consultation. Pam told me it was painful for them to watch the old lady and the old dog walking slowly together. I couldn't drive during my first months here. I didn't know where anything was and my eyes were bothering me, so Bill and Pam took me wherever I needed to go. Fortunately for me, I was still in a daze.

During the first six months after the move, I tried to find myself in this person living in a strange location. In addition to my physical healing process, I was also worried about Katie, who didn't die until after I had been in Colorado for about a year. Also, Pam's job was stressful, and I could sense that. Although she showed me every day, in countless ways, with wonderful meals and flowers and attention, how much she loved me, I had a hard time accepting it all, and if she was on edge, I chose to take that as affirmation of my distrust. Being here in Colorado, living with Pam and Bill, brought to light an emotional legacy from my childhood. I'm glad for the opportunity to deal with it. I realize that within my family, because of the way I was conditioned growing up, I'm always looking for evidence I'm not wanted.

So, while Pam, Bill, Zoe, and Zach go out of their way to make me feel at home—more than welcomed—it's difficult for me to trust that I'm wanted within my family. That's the result of feeling my parents valued me only as a prop when I was growing up. There's evidence to support that, but it probably wasn't the whole story.

When I first arrived here and for months afterwards, I found it hard to accept help, but I wasn't aware of that. Bill schlepped around for me, everyone helped. My childhood experience caused me not to expect it, trust it, or want it. I'm afraid I appeared ungrateful. But there was never an easy day in my life except that time on the chaise longue in my mother's bedroom, which always stands out in my memory as a contrast to what my life was like. And then I picked Fred to marry, which guaranteed that my life wasn't going to get easy in a hurry. So here in Colorado I have to work hard not to discount all my family is doing as my unconscious mind tries to find evidence that they don't want me here.

I've come to realize no parents are perfect. Most parents do their best to raise their children successfully, making sacrifices along the way. Then it's their children's job to try to overcome the deficits they've been raised with so they can grow into decent people who will again do their best to raise their children. And on it goes.

During my last months in Warwick and my first months in Colorado, the pain in my hip continued. Pam and Zoe recommended an orthopedic surgeon nearby, who had many patients suffering from skiing accidents. He determined a third surgery was needed.

When I was anticipating the surgery, it felt as if my apartment in their house was a city block from the kitchen, and it was upstairs as well. I thought, "After this next surgery, how am I going to make it? I may never get out of my room."

Then Fritzi started having diarrhea, and he was crawling around. One night I went to snuggle with him before bed, and he ignored me. Three or four days before my hip surgery, he went into my closet and hardly moved. I called Pam and told her we needed to take him to the vet. She got the car ready, and I had to drag him up the hill to where it was parked. I remember Pam saying, "This is one very large dog." We got him to the vet. It was clearly his time to go. He was my last shepherd, and I was heartbroken to lose him.

For several days before the surgery and following the death of my dog, I felt distracted by thoughts of Katie. I talked with her, and she said, "You better not die before I do. Pammy needs you. You deal straight."

After the surgery, the third on the same hip, my recovery was much easier than when I was living alone in Warwick, when family and friends had to come from near and far to help. Now nested as

I am with Bill, Pam, Zoe, and Zach, and with an excellent surgeon, all went well, and my recovery was faster. That hip is finally fixed, and I'm determined not to mess it up again! Zoe told me as soon as the surgery was done, "You need Nancy."

I followed her advice and as soon as I could, I began to see Nancy, a massage therapist trained in the Rossiter technique. She uses her feet to work the tissues in my back and hips. I've now healed successfully with great help from my family and Nancy, and I can comfortably walk a couple of miles and go up and down 15 flights of stairs as a form of exercise.

I miss a few friends who still lived in Warwick and New York City when I moved. Pat was one friend who lived nearby; she helped with landscaping, gardening, pet care, and anything else that needed doing for 25 years. She came to my house daily, and we often had wonderful conversations. I first met her when I lived in the barn and hired her to walk my dog, Teddy, who was failing. Pat is an artist, a terrific photographer, and a devoted animal lover. She and her husband, John, go on frequent hikes looking for wildlife, and Pat captures them with her camera. She's an excellent photographer and artist! We became lifelong friends over the years. Even today she contacts me almost daily and sends me her most recent photos.

Kitty LaPerriere was a dear friend who lived in New York City, a therapist who was one of the original practitioners of family therapy at the Ackerman Institute and the first female head of the American Family Therapy Academy. She was also a fellow Connecticut College alum. She and I were friends forever. She was devastated about my departure, even though I reassured her we could talk by phone just as we did during my last years in Warwick. Kitty was in her 90s, and she died after I moved; in fact, she died the day after Katie. I called her the day before to tell her about Katie, and she told me she wasn't feeling so good. She said she'd call later. I was waiting for that call when someone else called instead to tell me she died. I was numb.

And I miss living near Bonnie Fine, a friend from college who lives in the city and has a house in upstate New York. We sometimes met in the city to catch lunch and see a Broadway show, or she came to visit me in Warwick. We talked frequently on the phone for many years, and still do, but those casual visits are a thing of the past, and I miss them. Now I'm actively trying to build a social network in Colorado.

Pam

Let me backtrack and tell you about Pam. She was always fiercely independent, and she was my imp. I fondly remember one day when she was three years old. She was all dressed up in her plaid jumper and Mary Janes, eating a banana, and I told her not to leave the kitchen while I was getting ready for us to leave. She stood at the door tapping the toe of her shoe on the other side of the threshold, on the very edge of doing what I told her not to.

While Katie wouldn't put her foot out of bed without permission to get up, Pam was all about doing whatever she intended to do. Even as a baby, she could crawl faster than Katie could walk. And while Katie was fussy and disgruntled when she was a baby, Pam was quite a different experience. She was so happy and quiet I could at times forget to go get her. In the hospital the night she was born, she slept with me all night, peacefully. Our body rhythms were totally in sync. As a toddler, during the day she would call to get my attention. She sat there calling, "Mommy, wook, Mommy, wook," as she swung from the canopy over her crib and then flew across the room, fortunately landing safely.

Pam followed in Katie's footsteps in the schools they attended. Both went to Friends Academy, which I attended, and to the Kent School, and even to Connecticut College, my alma mater. It was at Conn that Pam met Bill, her future and present husband. She and

Bill have a lot in common: they're both athletic, they love to hike, ski, and sail. And their children share those interests.

Following college, Pam and Bill took off for California, while Fred and I stood in the parking lot crying. When they came back, they got married in the barn with a beautiful wedding, just as Katie had done. From there they went to Wayzata, Minnesota, where Bill's parents live and where Pam went to law school.

Pam and Bill were married for years before they began their family, and they did a lot in those years. They spent time skiing and sailing and went on many adventures. When it was time for them to have children, they were ready to settle down into parenthood, into being a whole family. Zoe and Zach, like their grandmother and parents, are true athletes: they excelled in competitive swimming. Zoe not only holds many Colorado state records, but also competed and won a number of international events as a member of the National Junior Team. In 2017 she won the 200 breast stroke event at the FINA World Junior Swimming Championships and was then recruited to swim at Stanford University, where she contributed to two NCAA titles. She was named Colorado athlete of the year in 2018. Zach followed in his sister's footsteps winning multiple Colorado state championships. Covid delayed his collegiate career, as he navigated his way into Harvard University. Both Zoe and Zach were recruited by their universities because of their academic and athletic prowess.

Pam is a lawyer, and Bill is a web designer and manages other aspects of their lives together.

They've been focused on Zoe and Zach since they were born, going to all their swim meets and being there for everything else in their lives. And look at the results…

Pam, Zach, Zoe, and Bill in the Colorado moun-
tains, with Gus, their dog, about 2016

Zoe recently completed her undergraduate degree at Stanford and has an exciting job in Washington, DC. Zoe and Zach are athletic in every way: in addition to their competitive swimming, they're expert hikers and skiers and spend a lot of time outdoors—they're always active. And they're both good photographers; the landscape out here merits it. Best of all, they're close friends, and they are warm, generous, fun human beings.

When Zoe and Zach were growing up, they lived so far away from me I seldom saw them, unlike Nick and Alex, who grew up nearby. Also, while they were growing up, I had to support myself as well as my mother and Walter, so I had limited time to travel. I've been getting to know these grandchildren much better since I moved here, and that's a special treat.

When Zoe was 15, I was out of sorts that year and had no idea why. Now I realize I expected another patterned event to occur. I was 15 when my grandmother died, and I felt as if my whole world collapsed, so I believe I expected that I, or someone else, would die, or some other catastrophe would happen. But the difference between the situation I was in when I was growing up with my distant mother—and the environment Zoe and Zach grew up in—is enough to disrupt that pattern. Pam and Bill are warm, loving, and involved with their children.

A wonderful aspect of my life in Colorado is the opportunity to talk with Pam when the spirit moves us. Having lived so far from her during most of her adulthood, we grew out of touch on a deeper level. Now we can work at understanding our family together, and that brings a rich feeling of fulfillment to me. It's good to have her perspective. For example, she shared her observation that Fred and I were too busy to be fully involved with her and her sister when they were growing up, just as Bill Levitt and my mother were too busy to care for me and Mac. It's a pattern I hadn't seen until she mentioned it. Then I realized that shoring up Fred took an enormous amount of my time and attention, in addition to the consulting work we did together. She also told me that by being the youngest child, she wasn't caught up in all the money and drama in our family, as well as the triangulation that bound Fred, me, and Katie together, so she was able to move on and move away later. One of Pam's strengths is the way she's able to perceive and understand relationships.

As I'm opening up to new understandings about how my childhood predisposed me to doubting my family wants me, I appreciate Pam, Bill, Zoe, Zach, and their dog, Gus, for welcoming me here in Colorado, and for the opportunity to be part of a thriving family.

*Alex, Nick, me, Zach, and Zoe--2019. (I look at
this and laugh. I always thought I was tall!)*

Me with Zoe, Zach, and Pam. I'm taking root in Colorado.

Moving in with Pam and Bill took the load of home ownership off my shoulders. I wasn't aware I carried that burden before it was lifted. Now I have more time, and I've been getting to know people in Colorado. With Judy, the other co-founder of the Chaos Institute, I'm trying to wrap words around what I learned through my family experiences and work as a therapist to share that important knowledge. We think of this memoir as part of that effort, along with our website (www.chaosinstitute.org). The last chapter in this book shows how my therapeutic approach can help solve human relationship problems of any magnitude. But first, I want to introduce you to some of my patients and show you what we learned together.

Chapter 17:

Therapy In Action

"There are no individuals in the world, only fragments of families."
–Carl Whitaker

Elephants' lives are simpler than human lives; that's why they don't need therapists. We humans get ourselves all tangled up with each other, with our perceptions and misperceptions, our emotions and our assumptions—most particularly when they miss the mark. And sometimes others treat us so badly we become traumatized, especially if that abuse happens when we're young. That's why *we* need therapists.

You're Invited into my Office

What I learned over my years as a therapist might be helpful to you, so it's important for me to invite you into some of my therapy sessions. My early focus was solely on helping troubled, complex families, and I was learning how to do that as I went along. Later I realized the scope was much larger. Before we start down that road, though, I want to share with you some of what I learned helping families with Mount Everest-size problems. They taught me about human relationships of all kinds, in different contexts. I've also discovered effective methods for solving relationship problems at every level of magnitude.

The patients I worked with at Morrisania were overwhelmed by their problems, since they were living in a community that was utterly broken. How can a family thrive when everything around it is disintegrating? Nothing I learned in social work school introduced me to such complex individual and family situations. My learning at Morrisania was intense, to say the least. It helped me understand complex human dynamics in a chaotic context. My need to share that knowledge fueled the decision to write this memoir.

But first, let me introduce you to one of my early patients. Then I'll explain how I work before sharing other vignettes from my practice.

The Rapist. This patient, whom I call "The Rapist," came to me during my first weeks at the clinic. Myrtle stopped by my office and said, "I have a convicted rapist who needs therapy, and he's Spanish speaking only. He's afraid that with so many women therapists here nobody will take him." I agreed to try.

He was a small Puerto Rican man clutching a newspaper—I found out later he couldn't read. But he always sat quietly in the waiting room with that newspaper. I walked over to him the first time I saw him to invite him to my office; I reached out to shake hands and spoke to him in Spanish. Now you have to realize that at the clinic, I was an anomaly. I didn't look like anyone else there—nobody resembled me even remotely—and I spoke Spanish fluently. So this patient looked at me and immediately went into a trance: he had no place to put what he was seeing.

He followed me to my office and told me his former therapist at the hospital was nice, but he left. He said, "I was afraid none of the women here would talk to me, because I did rape some girls in the park." He had three daughters at this time, all of them teenagers. He thought God was going to punish him, perhaps by hurting his daughters. Then he told me his story.

When he was eight years old, living in a town in Puerto Rico, there was a guy everyone knew and loved called the "Bird Man." He was often around. One day Bird Man asked my patient to go on a walk in the woods with him, and of course he went. Bird Man raped my patient twice and threatened to kill him with a machete if he told anyone. My patient was broken by this experience; he wouldn't go to school, and he was running wild. His mother didn't know what to do with him. She asked his uncles to take charge of him. They chained him naked to the house and fed him on the ground like a dog. He never told anybody what happened.

While he was telling me this, he was crying like I never heard a man cry. I thought—this man is right now an eight-year-old boy experiencing this trauma all over again. But he's also a rapist. I threw out that last thought, moved my chair closer, and put my arm around him to comfort him. As he was beginning to come out of the trance, I told him he could remember what happened to him or he could just let it go away. He said he wanted to remember. Knowing this man came from a machismo culture, I told him the sexuality of a small boy was more like an itch. Nothing more. After he was out of the trance, he told me he remembered being raped before, but he didn't remember his uncles' brutal treatment of him until the trance.

Most people who suffer severe trauma and can remember it later experience themselves as being alone at the time it happened. When they relive it, there's often no one there to console them as they go through it again. That's the reason I tried to comfort him as he was coming out of the trance. When he emerged, he told me that until I came over to put my arm around him, he thought he was dying as he relived those experiences. But when I did that, he knew he would be OK.

At the end of this session my patient said, "You know I had a very nice man therapist until you came. I asked myself, 'Why did this happen with you?' And I thought, 'It's as if I were out in a canoe in very rough water, and all the people on the shore were yelling instructions, but you dove in and showed me a new way to shore.'"

After he left, I was exhausted and shaking from the emotional intensity and drama of all I just experienced with him.

Later the receptionist said to me, "What happened in there? A different man came out than the one who went in." A week later he came to see me again. He had a sort of ratty legal-size paper with him, which he didn't mention at first. First, he said, "This is the strangest thing. I have some kind of eczema rash on my hands." Then I knew the trance work had taken, and he was not in danger of raping anyone else. His unconscious replaced the urge to rape with an itch to represent what happened. Then he showed me the legal paper and said, "These are the multiplication tables. Ask me any of them in any order and I'll give you the answer. I know them all." The next month he began to read.

Six weeks after my first meeting with this patient his parole officer called me. He said, "I don't know what you did with him, but he's a different man. We're thinking of letting him walk—cancelling his parole. What do you think?" I explained what I did with him and told him I agreed with their decision. This man ultimately became a community organizer.

* * *

Every therapist has a somewhat unique approach to working with patients, partly resulting from their training, and partly based on who they are. My approach is born out of my personal experiences growing up in a mixed-up family, but it's my innate and intense curiosity about how things work that pushes me to help my patients keep digging. That same intensity I felt as a child continued through most of my life. An essential quality of my personality is a drive to succeed beyond expectations, which was instilled in me by the way my parents treated me in relation to my sister. That gets expressed as commitment to my patients. In terms of training, family therapy and hypnotherapy structure my practice, but as I explain below, I rarely set about to hypnotize a patient. When it happens, it just happens naturally.

How Do I Work? When I'm engaged in a session with my patients, a deep part of myself takes over. Without effort or even awareness, I'm keenly observant of the nuances of what my patients are saying and not saying. When I first meet them, I notice everything about them: their gestures, posture, and facial expressions, how they greet me, where their eyes are looking, what they first say to me, and what they're wearing. I also engage with the energy they bring into the room. In these sessions, it's as though I'm on auto pilot. A part of me slips into control, and I'm hyper-focused without trying to make it happen. The rest of me goes along for the ride. After the session, I take a few notes, but I often don't refer to them.

In these sessions, I sort through the details that emerge as we talk, looking for important nuggets of information that link together to form critical patterns. When I say the pieces of information "link together," I mean there's a natural relationship among them. The patterns they form through the patient's life is organic, and it's important to identify them. It's as if a part of that person keeps emerging again and again at different points, which signifies its importance.

I ask questions that lead my patients to discover those patterns. It's only when they make the discoveries themselves that the new information is real for them. If I tell them what I think or know, it'll typically stick to the surface for a while and then fade away.

Certain assumptions guide my interactions with patients. I doubt these are fundamental for all therapists, but I believe they're essential in dealing with chaotic and complex situations. First, I don't start out thinking my patients are mentally ill. That's a pathological approach. Patients can sense that assumption right away and may feel blamed. Instead, my relationship with my patients is grounded in respect for them as individuals trying their best with limited experience solving complex problems. I give them the benefit of the doubt by having what I call "unconditional positive regard" for them. Most people try hard to make life better for their children than they had it, but so many things can derail them. I also believe most people have basic integrity: they are whole individuals and don't need anything added to them or taken away.

The two assumptions above lead naturally to a key component of my practice: that patients can solve their own problems when they're helped to explore all that has made them who they are so they can find the information they need. I'm there to guide them, to ask the necessary questions, to steer them back to the right path when I see them veering off it, perhaps from resistance, fear, or confusion.

Because most of us have not been taught that context is important, I help my patients understand it is absolutely critical, and I help them probe the far reaches of the context of their lives. Together we look at their relationship to everything and everyone relevant in their lives, past and present.

I also deal with resistance in my sessions. People can be resistant in therapy for all sorts of reasons. I think of it as a kind of quagmire they can get stuck in, but it's also a reservoir of information. "Why resistance to this particular thing? What does it mean to you? Why is it important? What would make it OK to explore this thing you are resisting?"

In that moment of hesitation before I put my arm around the patient I call "The Rapist," I chose to view him with compassion instead of fear, and that made all the difference. Without my warm response to him, the outcome would undoubtedly have been different. He was clearly doing his best in his life, but his horrific childhood experiences traumatized him; the rapes he committed expressed that horror as a cry for help. Those experiences took over part of his brain. Because his unconscious mind had a role in causing him to rape, the only way to stop that behavior was to address it while he had direct access to his unconscious mind during the trance. It was in the trance that I could bring him into full recognition of the emotional and experiential context of his early trauma and begin the process of moving beyond it.

Hypnotherapy. If my rapist patient hadn't gone into a trance, I doubt we could have reached the same outcome. In the same way he did, other patients also become hypnotized without any effort on my part. I was trained in the Milton Erickson hypnotherapy method: he was a well-known psychiatrist who taught therapists how to use indirect hypnosis with patients. My supervisor in the case of the Good Mother/Loyal Daughter told me I was using techniques that reminded her of Dr. Erickson. I didn't know about him then: I was just doing what came naturally to me. Her comment prompted me to seek out training in his method.

Erickson's method didn't dwell on the past, but focused on the present, and he specialized in "brief therapy." To effect behavioral changes, he used contradictions, told anecdotes, and made indirectly related statements while the patient was in a trance. You plant the seed, and then the person's mind uses it later as a guide for changing their behaviors.

I don't swing watches in front of people or do anything that suggests popular notions of hypnosis. Patients go into a trance when the totality of our interaction in a session prompts them to do so.

When someone is in a trance, information arises that may not be regularly available to their conscious mind. A therapist has the opportunity, when a patient is in a trance state and recovering from past traumas, to substitute a healthier suggestion to mark the original trauma in place of what happened, and in the case of my rapist patient, the suggestion that the sexuality of a small boy was akin to an itch was effective. During the trance state, the patient is living exactly what the trauma was but is also aware of the voice of the therapist. Milton Erickson said, "My voice will go with you. You can either remember what happened or forget."

* * *

A Few of my Patients

In the following case histories, I hope you'll notice how stuck my patients were, how it must have seemed impossible to them that there was a way out of their terrible entanglements. They were in the grip of intense emotional reactions to their situations. They had no idea which way to turn or how to think constructively about their problems.

I had only a moment in which to assess these patients as soon as I met them so I would know how to initiate our first conversation. I needed to signal right away that I was not judging them, that this was a safe place, and that I was not some voice of authority telling them what they had to do. I had to assess who they were and speak their language immediately, and I don't just mean English or Spanish.

The Bullet Man: One day at Morrisania Myrtle pointed out one of the patients who was yelling and pacing back and forth in the reception area, intimidating everybody. He was hard to miss: he must have been about 6'5", he had an athletic build, and he was probably about 25 years old. He was wearing a leather vest and pants covered with bullets fitted into little slots. Myrtle said, smiling, "It looks like this one's yours."

Nobody else wanted to work with this man; he was scary. He came into my office, threw himself in the chair, and glared at me. He told me Lincoln Hospital threw him out and told him to overdose on Thorazine. I said to him, "Look, I have no idea why you're here, but if you want help, you have to know you're scaring the shit out of everybody." At that, he started sobbing. He said, "I'm going to prison tomorrow, and my 20-year-old girlfriend is dying of cancer."

When I first saw him, from his facial expression, his intimidating attire, and the way he stood and walked, I knew immediately he was in an all-consuming crisis. I knew I had to take charge of him right off the bat, because he was overwhelmed and needed to be with someone who could take care of him. He was in no condition to be in charge of himself. I had to rise above the messages all those bullets were sending and disarm him right away. I had to view him as a man in need, asking for help, rather than as a threat to the safety of the whole clinic.

What was I paying attention to with him? The contradiction between his macho clothing and the pain and confusion on his face told me everything I needed to know. There was a lot going on in that man's life, and he didn't have a clue how to handle it. Prison, his girlfriend's cancer, lack of resources—all these things were inter-twined, swirling around him.

What did I do with him? I calmed him down and listened. His main concern was that he was leaving behind his girlfriend, and she needed help. We planned how she could be cared for. As it turned out, he did go to prison, and I made good on my promise to see that his girlfriend was receiving care. He called me every day, and I continued to reassure him.

* * *

Mrs. Jones' Resistance. Sometimes it's important to get a patient to distance themselves from their situation so they can get past their emotional blocks and face it. One day a White male therapist came out of his office in exasperation after trying to work with a patient. He said to me, "You have to talk to her. I'm too angry! She refuses to believe what's really going on."

Mrs. Jones was a young woman who said she came to our clinic to get her children back. Her boyfriend was getting out of jail. Her two young girls were removed from her home following extensive sexual abuse by this live-in boyfriend: it was medically documented and that's why he was sent to prison. Mrs. Jones thought he was wrongly accused. She was hysterical because the authorities wouldn't let him come back to live with her and her children. She kept insisting the abuse never happened, and she could not understand why no one believed her and why her children were in placement.

It was tempting to argue with her, to brand her as "crazy," or both. Instead, I took her into my office and as we began, I said to her, "Let's assume for one minute it's true he assaulted your children. I'm not saying it is; let's just make that assumption." That proposition honored her integrity and made it clear her input was valued. Immediately, she said, "I'd kill myself. I was sexually abused when I was little." Mrs. Jones later promised herself that when she became a mother, she would protect her children from ever being subjected to that horror. The dilemma was that if she acknowledged the abuse of her children, she would have to acknowledge as well that she failed in her promise. She was also caught in a bind between her need for her boyfriend, with his emotional and financial support, and her desire to have her children back. Being caught between this kind of rock and a hard place is not uncommon.

In this context, what initially looked like resistance now had a different meaning. Mrs. Jones' "resistance" to believing the abuse was protecting her very life.

My job was to help this woman recognize the facts and not kill herself. She needed to understand a new and different way going forward. If she didn't figure out how to accept her boyfriend's guilt, her children would be further damaged.

This is an important example of taking someone's statement that seems ridiculous and dangerous on the surface and exploring the deeper roots that make sense of their position. It's also an example of helping someone find positive behavior to solve their problems instead of the harmful solution they're fixated on. Then the need for the harmful behavior falls away without being forced to. If I were to argue with Mrs. Jones, which would be a simplistic approach, she would be offended and angry. Instead, I was able to engage her in solving the problem. As it was, because I distanced her from her situation, she was able to state the real problem right away, and then we could deal with it. I was able to help her accept that the relationship with this boyfriend needed to end.

*   *   *

A Caring Person Underneath the Psychosis. Marilyn was one of the most problematic cases in all of New York City. She was well known at Morrisania when she came to the crisis room. Her family was involved with psychiatric facilities and treatments from her childhood on. Throughout her life she experienced multiple psychotic episodes; she was hospitalized and treated with a variety of medications numerous times. When she began treatment with me and Myrtle, she was a familiar a patient at our clinic. At that time, she had three children, and two more were born during the more than five years we worked with her and her family.

The two older children, Meurice, 12, and Tammy, 8, were in foster care with relatives, and both were competent students. Marilyn had spells when she thought Meurice was a demon and she would have to kill him. She was often harsh with her children, and she had frequent fugue states in which she would disappear and wander the streets or ride the subways. Despite this, her children were loving toward her. Tammy watched over her mother and reminded her to take her medications.

The two younger children were Kathy, who was a year old when we began to work together, and Tommy, who was born later. Initially a sociable toddler, Kathy developed slowly and functioned with a mild intellectual disability. Tommy's speech was slow in developing, and he, too, required special attention. Her fifth child was born toward the end of our relationship with Marilyn. It was some years into her relationship with us that Marilyn allowed us to work with her children. It took that long for her to appreciate that we would not turn them against her or take them away from her.

In our work with Marilyn, she was our main concern since she was the center of her family—a center of gravity whose holding force sometimes threatened to deteriorate and allow the children to fly off in all directions. Our focus of attention was on her episodes of psychosis and our need to find solutions other than medication and hospitalization.

Typical episodes involved Marilyn's delusion that Meurice was a demon and she must kill him. When she knew she was slipping into psychosis, she would come to the clinic requesting medication. Since it wouldn't help immediately, she developed fugue-like states in which she wandered the streets, not being able to recall where she was or whether she was with anyone. She first fed the children and asked a friend or family member to watch them, and then she went out to ride the subways or walk the streets alone until morning. Hospitalization was not a viable alternative in these situations because Marilyn would not agree to go voluntarily. Whenever she was brought to an emergency room for psychiatric evaluation, she always had the ability to pull herself together to avoid involuntary commitment. Instead, she would walk out with some medication and a referral back to our clinic.

As it became clear that these fugue-like states were precipitated by her fear of loss of control and served to remove Marilyn from a situation in which she could do her children serious harm, or harm herself, we stopped encouraging Marilyn to stay at home for the time being; instead, we crossed our fingers, hoping she would come to no harm while walking the streets.

We even helped Marilyn attend an exorcism at a church to rid her of her demons. Myrtle spent the day with Marilyn while the minister and "sisters" (older female members of the congregation) prayed over her for the entire day. Marilyn was calmed by this and returned for the next day.

We also worked with a psychiatrist to help her; he used hypnosis to prompt her to take her medication and close herself in her room to protect her children. This technique worked for a longer period, and the fugue states all but vanished. She followed the suggestion except for rare occasions when she would resume her wandering.

One day Marilyn, in a paranoid psychotic state, crawled under the desk in my office, where she stayed for the next five hours, whimpering whenever she heard footsteps in the hall. She was so afraid that I didn't allow anyone else to come in the office, and I kept up a soothing flow of conversation as I attempted to write in my charts. Part way through the afternoon, Marilyn seemed much improved and felt she could go home. After she left, I discovered she had somehow absconded with her medical record. She was wearing a loose shift, which made it easy for her to hide the file.

Marilyn could certainly try our nerves. On one occasion, she tried to set the psychiatrist's hair on fire, and one time when she threatened us, we had to go to the police station at the 41st Precinct, which was known as Fort Apache. I was surprised to see how deserted everything was around there. There were no people, no cabs, no nothing: it was deserted except for burned out buildings. It was so dangerous the police had to bring us back to Morrisania. I realized how hard it must be for Marilyn to walk around the South Bronx alone at night and in a fugue state.

As we worked with Marilyn, she began improving in fits and starts. She had another baby after Tommy, and the children still seemed to be doing well, given their circumstances. One day, as it was time to leave the clinic, she and I were sitting on the hood of an abandoned car when she told me she was going to kill herself that night, and I found myself bargaining with her for her life. She said, "Why won't you let me do it?" She really was upset that I was trying to dissuade her from taking her life, and when she asked that question, I said, "You have five little children, and when you kill yourself, they'll be parceled out into different homes and one or more of them will ultimately commit suicide." So I told her, "Please call me at home before you do that." My phone rang somewhere between one and two in the morning and she said, "I've been riding the trains all night, and I think you're right. I wanted you to know I won't kill myself." This was the turning point for her: she finally understood her life had meaning and purpose.

*   *   *

My Patient, the Dog. Another patient was referred to me, and I met with him over an extended period. Myrtle told me that Hal drove everybody crazy because he was so boring, and he always stayed the full hour. He'd been around the clinic for a long time. She said that when you work with him, you just zone out. That's what she did; she fell asleep in one of her sessions with him.

Hal was a Jewish man in his late 50s, and he seemed stuck in his mental illness. He had a lot of phobias: he couldn't cross bridges and he couldn't use public transportation. He was curious about things but couldn't go to the public library. He poked around in trash to find things he could use to make art or put in the little library he created in his apartment. He was the only White male living in that part of the Bronx where people were frequently murdered. When he was a teenager, his father died suddenly, causing Hal to have a full psychotic break, and now he was nearing 60. At the time of the break, the doctors considered him schizophrenic, but by the end of his therapy, he certainly wasn't.

With Hal I learned to take my time, not be in a rush looking for progress, and to meet him on his own terms. He talked about his dog endlessly, a German shepherd mixed breed; our conversations were always only about the dog, about the dog's diet and the dog getting his shots, where the dog went and the dog's experiences. We talked about everything you'd talk about with a man living in a dangerous community who was entirely focused on his dog—but we never talked about Hal himself. He was gradually building trust. After a year and a half, he came in one day and said, "I don't think I need to talk through my dog anymore."

Myrtle and I invited Hal's dog to the country, to Warwick, where we lived, because it was so hot in the city and "we thought it would be good for the dog." Of course, Hal came along. He never left the city before. During the entire drive we talked to him constantly because he was sweating profusely. Once we got there, he enjoyed it, and then we took him home at the end of the weekend.

After a time, we helped him move out of the city to Warwick. That move was an adventure not to be forgotten. I rented a full-size moving van, and Myrtle and I arranged for our former patient, Sherelle, who was a tough city cop, and two other cops we knew, to help us move Hal. He lived in an apartment on one of those narrow little streets in the Bronx.

I drove the van, and I had to back it down the curving street, where cars were parked on both sides, so I could back into the place where we could load it. As I was doing this, with some concern as you can imagine, a muscular man standing on the sidewalk called out to ask if I needed help. He said he worked for a moving company. But knowing what you know about me so far, I'm sure you won't be surprised that I told him I was fine and had this covered. So the guy disappeared.

When I got out of the truck, there was Sherelle, pacing up and down in front of Hal's building muttering, "Fucking shit! Fucking shit! Fucking shit!" Hal lived on the fifth floor, and we discovered the building's elevator broke that morning. So we hiked up the stairs and went into Hal's apartment to find he hadn't packed up anything. More "Fucking shits" from Sherelle, with the other cops joining in.

We all went to work on the mess, but another challenge was that Hal built his "library" out of cardboard, and he was very protective of it. It housed all the treasures he found in his trash rounds: he and his dog went out at four or five in the morning looking through garbage, collecting articles, books, and papers he wanted to read, and he kept them in this personal library. So we had to figure out how to get it down five flights of stairs and safely into the truck, protecting it from getting crushed. We managed it.

Hal was beyond nervous during the trip out of the city to his new life in Warwick. When I look back on that move, I'm amazed it came off successfully. But I decided it needed to be done, and so we did it.

I had an in-law apartment in the barn, which I later I turned into my office, but at the time it was furnished as an apartment. Hal stayed there for about a month while Myrtle and I looked for a place for him to rent. During that time my mother and Walter came to visit. The day after they arrived, my mother was sitting on the couch in the living room when this crazy looking man quietly approached her and said, "Excuse me, can you tell me where Jo is?" She panicked and jumped up as if shot from a cannon. He had long shaggy hair;

he always wore a knitted cap and raggedy clothes, some of which he probably found in the trash. He was not what my mother was expecting in my house.

Hal's portrait of us, 1986

We found Hal an apartment that would take his Section 8 housing subsidy; he also had Social Security Disability income and was able to be self-sufficient. A huge event in his life was that he got his driver's license. He told us, "At 60, that was my first success ever." It was life changing, to say the least, for to him to live away from the dangers of the South Bronx. He was amazed by things he saw in Warwick, especially the way people put out their garbage neatly and held yard sales. He told me, "You know, out here you don't have to go through the trash. You just look for yard sales and you can buy things really cheap!"

He reconnected to his brother, and his dog loved living in the country. To show his appreciation to Myrtle and me for changing his life, Hal painted our portraits on a couple of T-shirts. We gradually lost track of him, and I'm sure he's no longer alive. I've kept my T-shirt to this day.

* * *

Trans Patients. During my time at Morrisania, I worked with twelve trans people, all male to female and from all five boroughs. After the first one, word spread widely, because most trans people were treated badly in the health and mental health systems. When they found someone who treated them well, they went there. I also joined the Harry Benjamin International Gender Dysphoria Association (now called the World Professional Association for Transgender Health), a society for medical professionals working with people transitioning. Treatment for sex transitioning was somewhat primitive at that time, but it worked. Much less was known then about it. Everyone going through this process was mandated to have a year of therapy before they had the surgery to make sure that was what they wanted to do.

When I say the treatments were primitive, I mean the medical establishment didn't yet know very much about this phenomenon. Most doctors didn't want to do castration surgery on these seemingly healthy males. The required year of therapy could turn out to be devastating if the therapist didn't accept the patient's need to transition and engaged in blame. With the right therapist who was in accord with it, it could be helpful.

I looked at the family histories of all my transitioning patients to see if I could find some kind of pattern running through them. Such a pattern would suggest that family history and interactions could be a causative factor. But there was not one common denominator among all these families. Instead there was something inherent in each of these individuals that made them certain about their need to transition. That was amazing and a surprise to me. I, too, was new to this phenomenon. We've been making tremendous strides medically over the years, but now the political situation is taking us back over a hundred years.

What I learned at the time was that to transition from male to female required one to two surgeries, but to transition from female to male took 26 surgeries. All these twelve patients, who were around 30 years old, did sex reassignment surgery. I had to use hypnotherapy with a couple of them because they were so anxiety-ridden they were having a hard time doing anything.

These patients kept coming back to see me so they could be socialized in how to be female. They had to learn things like, if you're wearing a short skirt, you have to keep your legs together when you're sitting. I suggested they watch movies with their favorite female movie stars and study carefully how they move and behave.

My office was down the hall at Morrisania, and these patients had to walk past all the other offices to get to it. When they first started coming to see me, heads were popping out of the offices staring at them as they went down the hall. At the end of my time at Morrisania, the first of my trans patients, who became a beautiful woman, invited me to her wedding. I did couples therapy with her and her fiancé first.

* * *

Not What They Seem. Some of my patients were puzzling to me at first. They came to the clinic acting crazy, but when I assessed them, things didn't add up. I had an older patient, an African American woman about 55 years old, who always functioned extremely well and then began to act psychotic. Her children brought her to the clinic, but there was no obvious cause and no family history of such behavior. I asked the children if she was on any medications. They said yes, but they didn't know what they were. I sent them home to get all her medications. They came back with a shopping bag filled with pill containers. I turned them over to one of the psychiatrists, who identified the problem as an interaction of drugs, and when the prescriptions were changed, she returned to her normal self. This can happen especially to poor people, because it's easier and cheaper to medicate the problem, and often no one checks for harmful interactions.

Another patient was an interesting, good looking, dark Cuban man who was a dancer at one of the clubs. He was acting psychotic. You couldn't make sense of anything he was saying. What he was saying led me to believe he was off the wall, but it didn't resonate. He didn't feel crazy or look crazy, but he did sound crazy. I assess my patients using, in this order, my visual, auditory, and then kinesthetic senses: if they don't line up, I'll go further, because that means there's a good chance something else is going on.

The more I talked to this patient, the more I realized he was not crazy. I looked at him and then said, "Who acts like this?" After a moment's pause, he said, "My mother. I knew she needed help, but I didn't trust she'd get the right help. I tried a few places, and they never asked me about her. So I'm trying to get help here." When he saw I understood, he decided to trust us at Morrisania and brought her in for medication. He pretended to be a patient at various clinics to determine where to bring his mother to be helped.

When people came into the crisis room, therapists would often look to see if they'd been there before, and if there was a diagnosis, they'd treat it. I didn't read the charts until I got to know the person because the charts could be wrong, often due to the pressure of time and the complexity of the issues. I'm thinking of two examples close in time.

The first was a woman bringing in her 13-year-old son; she said he was acting out and behaving badly. They were from another catchment area but moved, and doctors there were medicating the boy. In talking to the mother, she made no sense to me. She didn't look, sound, or feel right to me. So I did the usual. I called the boy in by himself. I looked at him and asked, "How long has your mother been acting like that?" He said, "Since my father and her husband were murdered." In the clinic where she brought the boy previously, the mother was receiving no treatment, but the boy was getting medication, and he was the one trying to hold everybody together.

The second example involved a mother with a rebellious 13- or 14-year-old daughter. She brought the daughter in for treatment. The mother was erratic, and her thoughts didn't hold together. I did the same thing with this girl I did with the boy I just described. I saw her alone. I asked her the same question. She said, "She's always been that crazy." So I said to the daughter, "Was your mother ever getting medication and treatment?" The girl replied angrily, "No, they believed her and medicated me."

I find it upsetting that we so often treat the diagnosis and not the person, which is what was also happening in the case of the Good Mother/Loyal Daughter I described earlier. I taught my students that if there's been a long history of psychiatric involvement, you broaden the context to find out what the function of this problem is in that family.

* * *

The cases I just described were all from my work at Morrisania. The patients I saw in Warwick were much better off financially and were living in a well-functioning, beautiful community, but typically, they were just as stymied by their problems.

Maria. I particularly remember one family I worked with soon after I left Morrisania and began practicing there. The person who came to see me was a young woman, Maria, whose father and sister died earlier. The young woman had a boyfriend who was about 30 years old, and she wanted me to see him too. His parents were aging, and he bought them a house and lived with them there.

Here was the problem. His mother, who was in her 70s, had a heart condition, and she never wanted her son to be away from home, not even for one night. Maria was torn: she loved this man, but she was unwilling to move into that house with his parents because of his controlling mother. He agreed to come and see me, and on the first visit, I told him he could try to establish his independence from his parents, but it might well mean that his mother would have a heart event of some sort.

He wanted to come for another visit, and when he did, he told me he truly was stuck, as his girlfriend had indicated. I told him his mother had lived more than 70 years, and he was young. If he started to live on his own, his mother would probably die, but if he didn't live on his own, he would remain stuck for a long time. I told him he needed to consider the pros and cons.

On his third visit he told me he did some hard thinking, and he decided he needed to live on his own. If his mother had a heart attack because of his decision, he understood she lived a long life, and he was confident he had been a good son. If she died, that would be her choice. He knew she couldn't stay forever. He and Maria married, and his mother died the following week. I think this case demonstrates that we should be careful judging people based on their decisions. There is no way for us to know the context of those decisions.

* * *

What do these patient situations have in common? It is that the issues they presented with are not what turned out to be the crux of the problem. The "Bullet Man" looked to be violent, but violence was not part of his situation. Mrs. Jones was not being ridiculous in refusing to believe her boyfriend had abused her daughters. In Hal's case, the dog was not our patient. In Maria's case, the real patient was her boyfriend. What this means is that a therapist must start where the patient tells them to start, with their story and their perception of what's going on, with what they think is important, and then help them explore their situation further, widening their lens to look at the context, where it's fairly certain they'll find important information.

The Essence of my Practice

If I could name one aspect of my work that is key, it would be that I focus on my patients themselves.

Most of my patients come from families not functioning well at the moment, and people in messy families are intense. I have to match their intensity, and in especially tough situations, I often have only minutes to establish the connection that can make a critical difference.

As I engage my patients in therapy, they are center stage and I am in the wings, directing. The critical point is that I accept everything about them: I notice it, file it away, and accept it. Each patient is whole. They are who they are, and they're in charge of making any changes that need to be made. I am not there to impose my values and preferences on them, not even my morality.

My goal is not to make them perfect or help them have perfect lives; it's merely to help them improve whatever situations they're struggling with, and to make their lives more livable. My first task is to bring some measure of calm and positivity, when often they're telling me that nothing is working either at home or in their community.

So I begin asking them questions. I want to hear their story, just as I did with the rapist. It may be that one person is sitting there with me, or there's a large family in its entirety. What they tell me and show me determines where we go next. If there are multiple family members, I note how their perspectives are similar and different, and I uncover the reasons for that in future sessions. I'm not there to blame anyone. It's not helpful to identify someone as the skunk at the picnic, because as soon as you do, the picnic is over. Blame fuels resistance and creates innumerable barriers to our progress. Also, when people start blaming, it relieves them of responsibility for the role they play.

One thing I look for when I'm working with a family is what I call "third party talking." When someone wants to avoid conflict, it is possible to get close to a family member by talking about another member who is not there. The illusion of closeness is temporary, because this pits family members against one another generating more conflict. This is where so many families get into trouble. This problematic behavior isn't limited to families, however; it's often found in larger settings such as the workplace. Wherever it occurs, it creates havoc and confusion. My mother was particularly good at this tactic.

Instead of blame and negativity, I always look for what's working, for my patients' strengths. I want to help them become more aware of their strengths so they can build on them and expand their use. It's important that what I say to them perfectly resonates with what I'm feeling. There can be no discrepancies. When people are in crisis, they immediately pick those up, and then there will never be trust between us. But this part is fairly simple for me because I truly believe that my patients are doing their very best in their difficult situations with the information available to them.

I also look for patterns among the ways my patients are failing. I had one patient who was unable to be successful in all but one of her activities. Her one success was going to a bingo game each week. That led to a simple explanation. She wasn't crazy—it was that she had reliable transportation to the bingo game and not to any of the other commitments in her life. She was obese, asthmatic, and lived on a steep hill, making it hard for her to get around. But ultimately, those factors weren't causing her problem—it was the lack of transportation.

When a patient's behavior seems completely odd and out of place, I try to discover what its function is. The function of Hal's focus on his dog was to build trust in us over time. Once he could trust us, we could help him. And the function of the rapist's sexual assaults was to express the pain of his childhood trauma.

I believe all behavior makes sense in the context in which it occurs. Think of Marilyn, wandering the streets in the South Bronx alone at night in a fugue-like state. Crazy behavior? That's what it looked like, but it was preventing her from killing her son. That's a pretty good reason for doing something. Or Mrs. Jones, who couldn't accept the fact that her boyfriend was abusing her daughters. She seemed pathologically obstinate, angering one therapist to the point he couldn't work with her. But if she faced that overwhelming truth, she would be compelled to kill herself. So I want to look inside my patients' minds to understand what is making sense in their lives from their perspective, particularly in their role in their current situation(s).

I'm always interested in knowing about an individual patient's or a family's context. What is going on for the children in school and in their relationships with friends, and how do they respond to adversity? How are they getting along with their parents and other family members, and with other adults in their lives? What is a couple's relationship like between the two of them, and for each of them in the outside world? What is their general emotional state in different settings? What's working well, and *where* is it working well—in which segment(s) of their lives?

An important goal for me is to discover where a patient finds love and support. It's a critical question. Sometimes love is there, but it isn't working. Marilyn loved her children: she went to great lengths to protect them, but even so she sometimes thought she had to kill her son.

I always look for anomalies among my patients' behaviors and the words they use. In one case, a female patient didn't tell me about any abuse she was experiencing, but she used expressions like "it strikes me," "that knocks me upside the head," etc. Those expressions stood out for me, so I asked her, "Who's abusing you?" And then she told me. The three other therapists who were observing this session asked me, "How did you know she was being abused?" I told them it was those expressions she was using. They were anomalous in her story.

After working with Hal and Marilyn, I understand how important it is, especially with some patients, to take the time needed and not to give up on them. Allowing the duration of their therapy to meet their need expresses your value for the patient as a person. If you lose patience and close the door on their treatment, it signals you don't really care about them.

I have two graphic tools I find helpful in working with patients. One is a genogram, which is a schematic drawing of the current and past two generations of a family. On the bottom tier are the current children, above them their parents' generation, and at the top, the grandparents' generation. A genogram uses circles to depict females and squares to depict males. Connections between these symbols are shown by solid lines if they are active and lines with hash marks if the connections are broken, as by divorce or death.

Important information about each person in each generation is indicated, such as age, career, illness or disability, addictions, etc. Children are presented in the order of their birth, from oldest to youngest, left to right. This graphic rendering of three generations of a family can illustrate important, but previously unnoticed patterns, such as intergenerational addiction or illness, or the death of a child at a specific age in each generation. It's extremely helpful.

The other tool is an eco-map, which consists of a circle in the middle of the page with lines radiating out to the edges creating segments. The family's name is at the center, and each segment is labeled to depict an area of a family's life, such as "School," "Work," "Recreation," "Hobbies," etc. Details about the family's participation in each area are listed in the segments. By looking at the details listed in all the segments, patterns can be identified, which can focus the work being done in therapy. It was by using an eco-map that we discovered that our patient was succeeding in attending her bingo nights, which led us to the understanding that her problems in all the other areas of her life had to do with transportation rather than mental illness.

A therapist's job is difficult. The problems patients present with are often messy and ugly, which can be off-putting, to put it mildly. The models we were trained in were designed primarily for the White middle class at a time when families in this country were not so fragmented. When a therapist with that training is confronted with chaos and complexity in families and communities, those models fail. That therapist will find that not only their training, but all the resources available to them, are being tested.

At Morrisania we needed a different approach that would be up to the task. In such a devastated, chaotic community, we needed therapists who were familiar with the contexts of our patients' lives. Our wonderful community resource staff members, such as Velma, provided that insight. They knew the community because they were a part of it, and they filled in the gaps in our knowledge of the context.

Moving as I did across the social spectrum, I learned some valuable lessons from Myrtle, not the least of which is what she shared with me my first day in the clinic. She told me, "Do not assume that what is wrong with these people is that they are not like you." Our ability to succeed in our clinic was amplified by the fact that our staff was diverse in all directions: in terms of race and ethnicity, social class, education, breadth of experience, and knowledge about the South Bronx. And we used a team approach, rather than each of us hunkering down in a silo. Each of us had to dig deep inside ourselves to bring to the table our individual and collective abilities to solve the apparently intractable problems we faced.

* * *

Not Just about Families

Through my decades of work with patients and their families, I've learned how to untangle complex human situations, but this understanding doesn't just apply to families. Each of us is born into a family, however small or large, but we also interact with people in other structures. Our schools, workplaces, communities—up to the largest—our country and our region in the world—these are all human structures. And therefore, when you understand how complex families work and how to help them solve their very serious problems, you also know how to solve such problems in workplaces, communities, and even in the largest human structures. The dynamics are basically the same.

I've proven the applicability of my therapy process in these larger settings. In our partnership, while Myrtle and I were seeing families in therapy, we were also consulting with all sorts of organizations. Our skills were just as helpful in these larger settings. And they apply as well to navigating political terrain. When I read or watch the news, I can easily identify incongruence, and I can predict what will happen next based on a situation's context. It's clear to me that the process I use with families works as well in these settings and with increasingly complex situations. As I mentioned, sharing this information is the main motivation for me to write this memoir.

The information I've learned is critical now because we're living in a world in which the commonly shared value system is upside down. Across the globe, material wealth and the lust for power have risen to the top of the hierarchy of values many people subscribe to, displacing the value of life itself. Additionally, the way most people think and try to solve complex societal problems is outmoded, unsuited to meet the challenges we face. We're in a dire situation, so dire it's hard to get some people to face it. The process I use with families and am describing here is often more effective than approaches currently used to solve world problems.

I'm not alone in understanding that we need to reinstate "life" as our top value. It's in everyone's self-interest. I write with the hope that my voice can join with others in prompting an effort to figure out how we humans have forgotten how to live in balance with each other, with other species, and with Nature itself—and how to redirect ourselves back to what humans once knew.

The most important question for me at this time is—how can we make the changes we desperately need to make? Describing how my therapeutic process can be effective with larger groups is my contribution toward the answer to that question. In the next and final chapter, I'll share with you an example of Myrtle's and my work with a university that was at a critical impasse and jump from that experience to lay bare what I see as the life-threatening risks we face and my ideas for confronting them. While I don't claim to have the whole answer to tackling our complex global problems, I do have ideas about how we can bring many people together in a process that has a good chance of figuring out what we need to know.

Chapter 18:

The Whole Elephant at Last

"Complexity prods me to consider how I can participate in the world around me, rather than simply cower with my head down."
–Neil Theise

"When you believe in something that is absolutely right and necessary, you're prepared to die for it."
–Jo Vanderkloot

As I'm about to tell you about Myrtle's and my adventures consulting with organizations, I want to warn you this is where I have to get a bit more technical. I need to do that so you'll understand specifically how my approach works with large groups. If you care about what's happening to our planet and all living beings, you'll want to bear with me, and I hope you do.

Working with Organizations

Myrtle and I instinctively knew that the therapeutic approach we used with families would work with groups of people no matter the size. People are people, and their behaviors are similar in families and organizations. The inability to work out conflicts at home is the same problem wherever we go. We welcomed the chance to prove we were right about this by consulting and leading workshops with corporations and non-profit organizations.

During this time, our research showed how institutions in all social sectors across the country were experiencing breakdown, i.e., enough dysfunction to cause serious trouble. Widespread breakdown across sectors is an intensely critical situation we knew could ultimately threaten everyone's well-being and test all our coping skills. The world seemed to be careening into a disastrous situation. Was it possible our systemic model for working with families could also help solve problems in large groups, even the largest? Would we be able to figure this out? This was only a question: we were too busy with patients, consulting, teaching, and writing to think hard about it.

Before I describe my thoughts about tackling the largest problems we face—those affecting the entire world—I want to show you how Myrtle and I worked with organizations. One case was a particular challenge for us, and it shows how we could use our approach with a large group ensnared in a complex, threatening situation.

* * *

A University in Peril

Myrtle and I were sought out by staff members at a public university. The tensions on their campus were severe enough they believed someone might be murdered or the institution could fold if calm couldn't be restored. Tension was escalating and people were acting out. Employees were stealing each other's mail, spreading rumors, and scapegoating certain people, for example. The university had cause to be worried.

After many phone conversations and an in-person interview with 30 people, we were hired. Recent speakers polarized their campus around race issues, and this group thought we were a good match for their situation because we were an inter-racial team. As it turned out, race was the icing on the cake. The problems at this university were deep and structural, causing fissures running in all directions, but the structural issues were like background music no one linked to the current problems. The racial discord pulled everyone's attention away from things like state cuts to their funding and barriers to communication on campus. Amid escalating polarization, nobody was thinking beyond the immediate crises.

Without being able to identify the underlying problems, various groups and departments on campus blamed each other for their frustration. Everyone was focused on hostility and blame, and no one could see a way out.

We held a two-day workshop for an inclusive group of 200 administrators, faculty, and staff: in our proposal we required that the group be racially diverse and the same people attend both days so they could work through the racial divide. We proposed that day one would look at where the university had been, where it was now, and where it needed to go. Day two would envision how to get there.

This was a tough job for us, but it was a perfect test to see if our systemic model would work with a group this large, which was representative of an even larger institution. The campus was volatile: enough was going on to spark violence. The stakes were high for both the university and our partnership. A misstep could trigger the violence we were there to prevent.

For this project, we were not as strong a team as we could be. Judy joined us because of her background in higher education, but she was new to this type of work. To make matters worse, although I didn't fully acknowledge it, Myrtle was becoming more confused. She took our carefully prepared, individualized scripts and scrambled them. So the onus for our success fell on me, and my knees were quaking as we began the first day.

This workshop was an exercise in reframing. We had the participants name the problems they saw, and then we helped them look at their context as a university dependent on a fiscally strapped state that was imposing new mandates even as it was cutting their funding. We pointed out problems which at first glance didn't seem related, such as the fact that their president was leaving, and no one knew what process would be used to hire his replacement. That part of their context added to their sense of instability.

We put the surface problems they were experiencing—racial polarization and widespread active hostility—into the context of the structural problems destabilizing the campus. We also described for them what breakdown looks like in any organization, and they could see they were experiencing the same symptoms, dispelling the assumption they were unique. We told them the winding down of the industrial era was a hidden cause of the breakdown they and people elsewhere were experiencing: its linear[1] thinking is of no help whatsoever in solving complex problems in chaotic situations.

We were successful in helping the participants realize their blaming was misdirected. As we did so, we were teaching them how systems work and how to approach a chaotic situation like the one they were part of. We showed them how to look for patterns running through their problems to identify structural issues.

We borrowed an excellent learning exercise from Steven Covey's *Seven Habits of Highly Effective People*, which allowed participants to

---

1   **Different ways of thinking.** *Linear thinking* is an analytical process in which you break everything down to its smallest components. *Systems thinking* is a nonlinear process. You increasingly enlarge a problem, expanding your angle of observation to include everything that touches it. You next search for a pattern that connects all the pieces; once you have that, you look for the underlying structure that sustains the pattern. Linear thinking and systems thinking are opposites. Both are useful, but systems thinking is not widely used.

see they had influence over most of their concerns. That left them feeling hopeful and empowered.

We ended the second day by having the group build an action plan to guide them as they took responsibility for changing the way their university operated, using their new knowledge of the underlying problem it faced. I'll describe that more in a moment.

We believed this workshop was successful, and the participants gave us high ratings. We proved to ourselves that our model worked with large, complex systems. But one thing marred it. A small group of people showed up for only part of the first day's work, were angered by that little piece, and left. They then denounced the process, the administration, and Myrtle and me in an article in the local paper. We anticipated this, which is why we stated in bold in our proposal that people attending the workshop must commit to both days. In this type of situation, the same problem you're trying to solve can play out while you're working on it. All of what happens is information about the system.

What this small group did in going to the press happens also in families: often at least one person wants to obstruct the changes needed for the family to go forward. This is normal; it's part of the process, and it needs to be anticipated and ultimately dealt with.

It's my experience that when an individual or small group resists needed change in a family or organization, they tend to end up either being isolated or changing, whereas the others use what they've learned and take the group forward. This happens consistently, and it happened with the university.

That critical newspaper article caused headaches for the university—they had to engage in damage control. But we effectively trained most of the 200 people who signed up for the workshop, and they brought what they learned into their work on campus. In their action plan, they identified ways to accomplish all their goals.

They were able to defuse the scapegoating and blaming and direct efforts on campus toward healing their problems.

When complexity is dealt with, people go forward with new problem-solving skills, and that university is thriving and winning awards many years later. Knowing that gives me great satisfaction.

* * *

Complexity

The problem facing that university was complex, as are the major global problems currently threatening existence on this planet. What do I mean by that? There is a world of difference between that which is merely complicated and that which is complex. A *complicated* situation has many parts; a *complex* situation has many parts that interact with each other and are constantly in flux. The machines, devices, and technological advances configuring our world today make our lives more complex, but complexity itself isn't understood by most people.

Educational systems have failed to prepare the general populace for handling complex situations. We're not used to describing situations as "being non-linear in nature, with parts that are constantly changing and interacting with each other." These are characteristics of complex situations: we're still teaching people to rely on linear thinking and to see situations as if they're fixed in time, like insects pinned to a board. We focus on what the parts of a system are—their identities—rather than primarily on the way they interact. We need to be more like the Japanese, who in their flower arrangements focus on the spaces between and among the flowers more than on the flowers themselves. We're not preparing ourselves to live in this world we're creating.

To survive in my family and the South Bronx, I had to figure out how to live in a confusing, constantly-changing-without-any-warning complex situation. At that time I wouldn't have used the terms "chaotic" and "complex" to describe my environment, but my whole being became attuned to those characteristics. It was extremely difficult, but these experiences were an important gift. Now I'm understanding chaos and complexity in a cognitive way.

Complexity isn't broadly understood, either as a science or when it inserts itself into our lives. You would have to look hard to find courses in chaos and complexity in any high school or college curriculum. Consequently, what I explain in this last chapter of my memoir may be difficult for many readers.

Let me portray complexity this way. Imagine a cartoon octopus. That's what I see when I conceptualize the way it's sometimes structured. It's a rough analogy but imagine a bulbous head with tentacles dangling down. Within the head and the tentacles, the internal parts are in continual interaction. The head represents a major, complex problem usually hidden from sight. The tentacles represent derivative problems, which are the parts we see clearly. These are often complex as well and may themselves have derivative problems. The university's derivative problems were racial discord and people acting out in destructive ways.

Now think of climate change. A network of interacting causes created what we know as climate change. Some of its derivative problems are

1. Climate migrations, not just of people, but also of animals and plants;

2. Climate catastrophes, such as hurricanes, tornadoes, drought, sea rise, and flooding; and

3. Political realignments as countries most at risk
   attempt to build supportive alliances.

These are examples of the problems derived from climate change, each of which is a complex problem in and of itself. There are more, of course. If you try to solve any of these derivative problems by itself, you will amplify others. But what's the ultimate cause of climate change? Using fossil fuels is an immediate cause: what is the ultimate cause? We can't address it effectively until we figure that out. I'll share what I believe it is in a moment.

Complex problems come in all sizes and levels of complexity. They're hard to solve in part because they keep changing. And they have so many parts and details you can easily get lost or distracted.

The ironic thing about complex problems is that they require simple solutions. Oliver Wendell Holmes is quoted as saying,

"I would not give a fig for simplicity on this side of complexity, but I would give my life for simplicity on the other side of complexity."
–(The Simplicity on the Far Side of Complexity - PlanPlus Online)

I agree with him wholeheartedly, and I would add that "Complexity is elegantly simple." Because it is, if you don't get lost in the details. A complex problem's simplicity resides in its structure—that it has an underlying cause (the head of the octopus). Getting past all the derivative problems to identify the underlying cause is a "simple" pathway to solution.

When I think about complexity, I'm reminded of the ancient myth about the Hydra. It was a monstrous coiled beast with nine heads, one of which was immortal. It attacked people with poisonous venom. Trying to kill the Hydra was a supreme challenge: if one head was severed, two grew in its place. The Greek god, Heracles, and his nephew were able to dispatch it together: Heracles would cut off a head while his nephew held a flaming torch to the tendons in the neck, preventing new heads from growing. Perhaps the ancient Greeks understood something about complex problems, which sprout smaller, derivative problems in the way the Hydra grew new heads. To deal with derivative problems, we have to get to the underlying problem, the Hydra itself. Without addressing the underlying problem, if you solve one of its derivatives, you'll typically amplify the others or cause new ones to emerge.

We can't solve complex problems unless we understand them. Legislators can't write effective policies for living in this world unless they understand complexity. When a situation breaks down because of a hidden underlying major problem, as it did in that university, people can't pull everything back together unless they know how to identify the real problem. To get to that point, they have to know how to look for patterns running through all the details. This is one important aspect of successfully working with complexity. The university administrators didn't understand that, which is why they couldn't fix their situation without help.

The university's underlying problem. Wrestling with complex problems without that knowledge usually results in failure and frustration, just as it did in that university. The campus was taken by surprise at first when speakers brought polarizing messages. The administrators didn't know how to stop people from taking sides and blaming others. Faculty, students, and staff reacted emotionally, some aligned with one speaker and some with the other. Everyone was frustrated; the administration tried appealing to different groups, got nowhere, and tried harder, but failed again. Their attempts were superficial—they were dealing only with derivative problems—and they stood no chance of success. They knew they were stuck, which is why they called on us.

The university administrators focused on parts of the problem: the speakers, the groups, the aggressive behavior, etc. They didn't think about structure, process, or how groups on campus related to each other. They used the linear thinking taught to all of us who grew up during the industrial era. It's a fragmentation model—it ignores how things are connected.

As people keep trying harder and harder to solve complex problems without the needed knowledge or skill set, their frustration can lead to aggressive behaviors and sometimes to violence. They also become more rigid in their approach to the problem and more resistant to new ideas. As the rigidity increases, their problem-solving options decrease.

This happened at the university before we started working with that group of 200. But as the workshop participants looked at the patterns running through the derivative problems on campus—the racism, blaming, and aggressive behavior, they noticed one pattern that stood out. Departments and functional groups existed in silos, and communication was severely broken on campus. This is typical in bureaucracies. Structures to connect the groups and facilitate communication didn't exist. When external forces put stress on the university, the groups couldn't collaborate in response, and fragmentation was exacerbated, fueling polarization. The workshop participants realized this was their hidden underlying problem, and because it was structural, no one could see it until then. People often ignore structure until it's exposed by serious collapse. When their action plans changed this structure, the university could move forward.

Let me give you another example of ignoring structure, this time from our work with a different organization in which a small department of three people kept failing. The initial group of three employees left and three new people were hired. The same problems developed. Frustrated, these three people left as well. We intervened and started looking at the structure when the third set of people in those positions experienced the same problems. Here's what the underlying problem was: the way the job descriptions for the three positions were written, if the employees did their jobs well, they would conflict with each other, and the department would implode. It never occurred to the administrators in this organization to look at the structure—they just kept hiring, thinking they somehow couldn't find good employees.

Where are We Now and How Did we Get Here?

In the world today, intersecting complex problems of all sizes resist solution because we collectively lack the skill to address them successfully. Our situation is dire: a set of global problems threatens the existence of all life on the planet, and in the face of that threat, instead of collaboration across the board to solve these problems using an understanding of complexity and systems thinking, we have political polarization and stalemates.

How did we get here?

The university case I described shows on a small scale what's happening globally. It fit nicely into what Myrtle and I learned years earlier when we were doing research to figure out why our program at Morrisania failed. We were reading, discussing what we read, and wracking our brains as we tried to pull the different threads of our research together. It paid off. As you know, we discovered that the program failed because it violated the rules of the system of which it was a part. But much more important information surfaced as we did that research, information that can help us understand our current global situation, as I'm about to share below.

These four areas of our research came together in an unanticipated way to generate exciting insights: 1) organizational and social breakdown, 2) fractals, 3) paradigm shifts, and 4) the way the industrial era shaped our society. I'll briefly describe this synergy, and I think you may agree it helps explain how we got where we are right now.

Breakdown. First, we looked at what was happening in all the different sectors in our society: education, law, medicine, etc., as I mentioned earlier. We were surprised to see how much breakdown there was among institutions and organizations across the board. We knew there must be a common cause—this was too widespread to be coincidental. We had an "aha" moment when we finally saw that the institutions in all the sectors were being undermined by a focus on money and power at the end of the industrial era.

For example, we saw that in education, cutting expenses was more important than children's needs, and that's one of the reasons schools were in trouble. In medicine, with the business model conjoined with insurance companies and pharmaceuticals, patients' health was secondary to finance. And what was endangering our environment? Money interests. So the drive to acquire and save money was a clear pattern across all sectors. It was causing destruction everywhere. We wanted to figure out how this happened.

Fractals. Second, our research introduced us to fractals: we hadn't heard of them before. According to James Gleick, in his book, *Chaos,* a fractal is a way of measuring things that, without that name, don't have a clear definition. A fractal is a depiction of the degree of irregularity or brokenness in an object. In such an object, the degree of irregularity remains constant over different levels of scale. (Gleick: *Chaos,* p. 98)

A fractal displays a kind of pattern: it takes on a visual appearance when relevant iterative equations are rapidly fed into a computer with the solution replacing one of the parameters each time. The computer then prints a beautiful, detailed image in which a basic design element repeats again and again at different levels of scale, from tiny to large.

Fractals appear in nature as clouds, rugged coastlines, and even heads of broccoli. The tiniest element in a head of broccoli looks like a tree no taller than the height of your thumb nail. Many little trees join to form a bigger tree, the floweret, and flowerets join to form the large tree that is the broccoli head. Thus, a head of broccoli is an example of different sizes of the same pattern repeating throughout the whole. You can also see these patterns of similarity in the way tree limbs or blood vessels branch as they get smaller and smaller. Same pattern, different sizes. Similarity across levels of scale.

An image of the Mandelbrot set, one of the first and most familiar images of a computer generated fractal.

We were excited to learn about fractals because we thought the brokenness we saw in our patients (small) and the organizations we worked with (larger) was similar to what we were seeing in the various sectors (largest). We were getting our first inkling there might be a breakdown fractal.

Paradigms. Third, Thomas Kuhn's book, *The Structure of Scientific Revolutions,* introduced us to paradigms. He described a paradigm as "a set of universally recognized principles, methodological processes and cultural concepts that refers to the work of the 'scientific community' of a certain era." (paradigm definition, ibsafoundation. org, online). And he suggested that scientific theories advance slowly until a discovery breaks with the past in some significant way, this is what he calls a "paradigm shift." The term is now widely used, and I think it can be applied more broadly to describe major social and cultural shifts.

The Industrial Paradigm. Fourth, Myrtle and I knew the industrial era was the context in which our program existed, succeeded, and then was killed. Since context is always important, we needed to know more about this era, which we thought of as a paradigm as well because it seemed to be an era defined by principles, methodologies, and cultural concepts.

When we discovered money was central in the problems being experienced throughout all the sectors of our society, we wondered how it gained such power. I believe even a brief glimpse of the industrial era can tell us how it happened.

The industrial era grew out of scientific discoveries that opened the way for new social structures and inventions as early as the sixteenth century. These in turn helped humanity move beyond the agrarian world of our distant ancestors.

Early on, as the industrial era gradually replaced the agrarian age, difficult challenges ensued as people moved from farms to cities, where new work beckoned. (This time around, as the industrial era wanes after making a mess of the planet and without a new era being clearly defined, the problems we face are much worse. Social paradigm shifts are always difficult, but this time there's a sense of urgency.)

Rules and regulations emerged to ensure things ran smoothly in the industrial paradigm and to protect its framework. The rules applied everywhere; they were based on the key assumptions guiding the paradigm, and they expressed its linearity. They took the form of laws, regulations, and policies at every level. This is how I ran into them. As you know, at Morrisania, our program was a pilot, an experiment, and it successfully met our patients' needs, whereas the old system failed them. The Joint Commission on Accreditation checked the records in the agencies, and they didn't like what they saw in our clinic.

Here's an example of our rule breaking. It was required that we use a separate chart to record the progress of each individual patient. But we used a family therapy model. Our patients were often families, not individuals. So we created a chart for each family, which ultimately wasn't acceptable. As our program neared the end of its pilot status, we experienced increased pressure to conform to existing rules. One of our families had 26 members: can you imagine how impossible it was for us to follow that rule? Furthermore, money was available for the old, individual treatment model. It was not uncommon for funding to be cut at the end of successful pilot programs if they didn't conform to existing rules. This was the reason our program was unsustainable.

We broke these rules deliberately since they didn't seem to apply to our situation. We did so naively, thinking if we were successful in helping our patients, our approach would be applauded, not rejected. We hadn't realized the power of the old system to make everything inside it toe the line. There was no way a program within that health system could survive if it violated the rules, no matter how excellent it was.

As the industrial era evolved, central ideas guided it: a major focus was on the individual, and emphasis was placed on achieving success. Progress became a ubiquitous goal. The rules, structures, assumptions, and beliefs characterizing this period led to prosperity and well-being at first. As time went on, manufacturing flourished and paved the way for technological advances, which have continued building on each other and are now bringing new waves of 'progress' to our society.

Ironically, the great, great, great "grandchildren" of the first inventions of this era pushed industrial operations out of the limelight, making the original paradigm somewhat obsolete. But its ideological bulwarks—its structures, rules, regulations, goals, and assumptions—remain in place, like zombies still holding sway over civilization. Laws, organizational structures, the assumption that progress follows a linear pathway into the future—these are aspects of the industrial paradigm that resist change.

Individualism and progress, coupled together, seemed at first to be principles beneficial to society. People were motivated to design new machines and create new methods to accomplish tasks with greater and greater efficiency. Their inventions made lives more comfortable, longer lasting, more productive, and even more enjoyable. But now these principles are taking on malignant characteristics. In an agrarian society, life is the highest value. People grow food to support life, and they follow the natural rhythms. The industrial paradigm subverted that value system, and money and power rose to the top as the most important goals an individual could achieve. Other values lost importance, even that of life itself, as strange as that may seem. As a result, money became a god.

The industrial paradigm is the context in which money rose to the top of the values pyramid; its trappings set the perfect stage for that to happen. And the power of money, with its compelling attraction, blinds people to the destructive ramifications of their behavior as they pursue its glitter. Everything about the industrial paradigm prods us to aim for individual success, to acquire wealth and power—in fact, to become wealthier and more powerful than anyone else. Those goals are inherent in the set of principles and rules that form the guidelines for this era. No one who's absorbed these precepts can be blamed for following them. It's not a black and white, linear situation. I've known many good and generous people who could also be hell-bent on acquiring wealth and power and rising to the top. It's what our society taught them. What they were NOT taught is to think about the ramifications of their behavior.

The industrial paradigm also bequeathed to us a mental model widely accepted today as a way to make sense of the world. In this mindset, we focus on separate items in our environment and pay less attention to the way they exist in relation to one another and to the ways they're interconnected and communicate with each other. The focus on separate items leads to fragmentation: I've often called the industrial paradigm the fragmentation paradigm because this characteristic is so pronounced and important. It's an out-of-balance perspective. We need both: to understand what items are and to know as well how they function together.

The description above is the way I characterize the world we're living in as the industrial paradigm slowly crumbles.

Although a new paradigm hasn't jumped out of a box completely formed and ready to be quickly accepted, one is slowly emerging, based on discoveries in the new scientific arenas of quantum, chaos, and complexity theories. These discoveries and the assumptions they give rise to inspire hope. They point to the need to restore the value of life and the well-being of all living systems as the highest value, which is bound to happen over time—if there is time. But our need for a turn-about is urgent: a centuries-long transition will culminate too late.

The four areas I've described mesh together in my mind. I see how the industrial era developed into a paradigm aligned with values that grew so powerful they became destructive, leading to breakdown everywhere, in groups of all sizes.

Breakdown is the inevitable result of the industrial era's value structure. Individualism's all-out competition separates us from each other and causes polarities everywhere: it pits people and resources against one another. "Rugged individualism" overrides the needs of community. It's all about individuals fighting to get a bigger piece of the pie for themselves.

A teacher-friend once told me she was worried about boys—she said they're hurting—and she wanted to find ways to help them. I'm sure she expected my compassionate support for this idea, but instead I said, "What about the girls? They're hurting too. What about everybody? Everybody's hurting. If we try to solve one problem and not the other, we create polarity, with a fight for resources and a failure to solve any problems. Addressing smaller problems separately leads to polarization. We have to solve the underlying problem behind all this hurting. We have to help everybody." She saw my point and agreed.

Polarity is a major product of the industrial paradigm; it operates in tandem with fragmentation. Everything gets separated into smaller parts and they compete, resulting in polarity. The paradigm necessitates this. So here we are, entangled in a web of the remaining rules, regulations, and fragmented structures of industrialization, guided by its assumptions and problem-solving methods, and we wonder why there's endless warfare on every level? We fight over rights, resources, ideologies, religions, philosophies, money, politics—you name it. Why? We can't blame it on the devil—the paradigm made us do it.

Until we can work our way out of this old mindset and embrace a set of values that prioritizes life and the well-being of all living systems, our problems will continue to metastasize until they engulf us.

I want to stress again that nobody is at fault for any of this, whether for creating the problems or because of their ineptitude in solving them. People are doing the only thing they know how to do. This concept is hard to accept because we want to blame others when we see them acting out in ways that make everything worse. It's challenging to keep remembering that everyone is doing their best within the limitations of their world view and the beliefs they've been taught. But it's largely true: even the people you most vehemently disagree with are for the most part trying to do what they think will work when they are engaged in problem-solving.

Roadmap to a Better World

Many of us want to make our world better, but we need to have a clear destination in mind before we figure out how to get there. What kind of world do we want to live in? While I'm sure people can imagine many different scenarios, I think most visions would have a few things in common. Also, our ongoing survival necessitates some specific characteristics. With that in mind, I suggest we try to create a world that values cooperation over conflict and harmony over hatred. A life-affirming value structure and a balance between individual and community needs would help re-establish the natural homeostatic balance in the world. I assume these qualities would appeal to most people.

How do we get there? We humans created the problems we're facing, but until people generally understand complexity, we won't be able to solve them. We're too stuck in our rigid, linear thinking and our polarizations to be able to focus on finding real solutions together.

I'd like to offer some suggestions for the process of moving forward based on my more than 40 years in the trenches. These aren't written in stone, but I know they work because they always have for me. And I'm quite sure that because they work with families, they'll be effective in groups of any size—because it's a fractal.

Here's one thing I'm clear about: with worldwide political chaos swirling, we can either begin a process of moving beyond the old ways of thinking and doing now—or wait until after the chaos spends itself. Which do you prefer?

What I'm about to suggest may sound naïve given the problems challenging the world. It is anything but. Naïve I am not after years of spending my entire career working with chaotic/complex families and organizations in settings ranging from the war zone of the South Bronx to affluent communities.

* * *

The successful launch of Sputnik by the Soviet Union on October 4, 1957 fed fears in the U.S. that we were falling behind in the space race, and the whole country geared up to teach more math and science. We now need a similarly focused approach to teaching about the new sciences of chaos and complexity and their implications for problem-solving in chaotic settings at all levels of scale. Before we can get there, we must find ways to convince enough people of the need to do this.

Building our new society must be a bottom-up process. The involvement of as many people as possible is needed because of their different perspectives. Nature thrives on variety. A national board could create an organization composed of satellite committees in individual communities across the country to work on transitioning into a new paradigm. Communities are the logical sites for this work because their unique situations would infuse the process with the necessary different perspectives.

That board could provide guidelines so all the committees would be working in tandem. Technology now offers ways for the committees to share information with each other. The board's guidelines would be most effective if they're based on systems thinking, mutual respect, openness, and striving for an ever-widening lens.

If I ran the zoo, I would give the following suggestions to those committees.

First, I would tell them they need to figure out the extent to which people in their community support change. They should involve as many people as possible in their work—a truly representative group. If they are to be successful, they must rule out blame. Remember, as soon as a person or a group is seen to be the skunk at the picnic, the picnic is over. This is hard but essential. A focus on relationships must be at the center of community building—relationships among everyone and everything in their system. And I do mean "system," because using a systems approach is necessary as each committee surveys their community and its context to identify their strengths and weaknesses and the challenges they're facing. Then they can see how to use their strengths to address their weaknesses to solve their problems.

The task for these committees will be to envision what their community would be like if the needs of all living beings were the top priority. If these committees try to solve more traditional problems, like repairing infrastructure or enlarging their tax base, before addressing the human problems, it won't work. They'll need to gather data describing the current state of their community first and identify the top priority needs for people and the planet. Then they'll need to use their imagination to figure out how to move their community from where it is now into their ideal vision.

These groups will have to consider how to end polarization within their communities. It starts with learning how to see the whole system, including the context. That makes it possible to see how all sides on polarized issues have a place within the whole, not unlike the blind men with the elephant. Then it's easier to see why people hold the positions they're advocating for, which ultimately allows everyone to move toward consensus. Getting to solutions absolutely depends on healing the polarities first.

I've mentioned patterns before. Because the major problems facing all communities these days are complex, the group will need to look for patterns that flow across their problems, helping to uncover hidden, underlying problems. These patterns will likely be the same or similar across communities. However, communities will differ in their ability to change.

Last, I would warn the board that solutions to problems are just the beginning since everything is in constant flux. They should plan for, and welcome resistance to their work (a normal part of the process), ongoing assessments, and future problem-solving.

* * *

There are, of course, many examples of community building taking place across the country. The three I list below have been or are currently successful: they are the Vision 2000 project, the ACLU's People Power organization, and Habitat for Humanity's Neighborhood Revitalization program.

- In the 1990s, Warwick, NY, did a visioning process based on one that was pioneered in Chattanooga, TN, called Vision 2000. A small group of leaders convened focus groups to brainstorm ideas about an ideal vision of their community. The leaders compiled and synthesized the results and held a large meeting (with entertainment and food) for community members to come and vote on their favorite ideas in each area of community life (e.g. education, commerce, etc.). They compiled the votes, and the top ideas were reported out to the community. A larger group then created an action plan that was circulated for more input. Finally, the community implemented the plan, and the area still bears its imprint.

- In 2019, the ACLU asked community leaders across the country to assemble people on a particular date who were from their region and who were interested in the plight of immigrants. The program was called, "People Power." On that date, everyone involved across the country watched a televised talk from one of ACLU's top lawyers describing the situation and asking each regional meeting to break into smaller groups according to their towns or cities. Each small group was asked to plan how to get their local leaders to pass an ordinance expressing how immigrants were protected and supported in their community.

- Habitat for Humanity has a Neighborhood Revitalization program that supports resident-led groups as they envision needed changes to their communities after long-term destabilization and as they make their vision a reality. Habitat for Humanity fosters collaboration among community partners as they rebuild and revitalize their communities.

* * *

Can we come together to restore the value for all living systems as our top national priority? We can if we have the will. We must if we want our planet to continue to support life. Understanding that humans have never been in this situation before should galvanize the American will. There've been stressful times in our past when many people were afraid authoritarian leaders would defeat the US and its allies and when it seemed imminent that nuclear weapons would end life as we know it on Earth. Authoritarian rulers still long to extend their reach and nuclear war remains possible, but now severe climate change is beginning to bring ramifications we still can't imagine. As these three threats intertwine, their strength together is greater than the sum of their parts. Let's stop thinking everything will probably get back to normal next week. We need to understand that everyone who is at all able MUST find a way to join in the effort to turn things around. What about you?

One of my contributions is to write this memoir, to spell out as best I can what the real underlying cause of our problems is and to describe an approach I believe has a chance of addressing it. We need people from all walks of life, all types of careers, all types of identities and families, to engage at all levels of participation to make the value of life and the well-being of all living systems our most important value. People everywhere, joining together, must shift our societal focus from individual acquisition of money and power to the well-being of families and communities. In the process, we can popularize a mindset that will facilitate worldwide communication, co-existence, cooperation, and collaboration, starting in our various small communities. The three examples above show that communities can be brought together to solve problems.

* * *

Nutshell

What follows here is a concise summary of the message I want to share: I summarize it hoping to make it easier for these thoughts to reach a broad audience.

We live in an unprecedented time of peril. Humans have unintentionally caused dire, complex, global problems that have so far evaded solution. I believe the underlying root of this crisis stems from the breakdown of the industrial paradigm and its emphasis on acquiring individual money and power that became the hallmark of the industrial era.

The problems we face during this time of chaos occur with fractal-like similarity across all the groupings in which we organize ourselves—families, organizations, communities, and nations—as do the many attempts to address them. Without understanding that the values of the industrial paradigm, whose dictates still structure our lives, are the underlying cause of our most urgent problems, we will continue to spin our wheels and waste critical time trying to address those problems separately, and we will fail. We must move from a conflict model to one that fosters collaboration.

I suggest a bottom-up approach to address all these problems by speeding up the natural process of shifting to a new paradigm. Twentieth century scientific discoveries gave rise to quantum, chaos, and complexity theories, which transform our view of the world and reaffirm the old agrarian assumption that our highest value must be life itself.

The approach I suggest requires wide-spread participation, a welcoming of inputs from multiple perspectives, and using communities as the base for sharing and gathering ideas and then taking collaborative action. A central organizing body would coordinate the process of creating a renaissance. The process used to give birth to this renaissance would be inclusive, respectful, welcoming, creative, cooperative, inspiring, and hopefully, global.

It is gratifying to me to share what I hope you will find useful as you see events unfolding in your own life, around you, and on the world stage. If you want to participate in this effort, please contact us through our website, www.chaosinstitute.org.

* * *

307

Reflections

While writing this memoir, as I dug up memories and emotions I buried long ago, brain fog would descend at times, especially when I was searching for particularly meaningful or painful experiences. It lasted for days, weeks, or sometimes a couple of months. I learned to surrender to that fog, because I came to realize it meant that my mental energy was actively focused on my unconscious mind, trying to organize what I hid there and bring it to the surface.

And when the fog suddenly lifted, information would burst into my consciousness. There it would be, and I felt elated, both because I remembered something important and because clarity was restored.

Things are clear now. It's as if the blind men and I have our sight restored, and we can finally see the whole elephant. The blind men see the animal itself—legs, trunk, tail, tusks, ears—the whole body. What they see is one of the glorious, intelligent, gentle, herbivorous giants that used to number around five million and are now dwindling toward extinction.

For me, the elephant is a magnificent shapeshifter, reflecting different landscapes when light hits it from new angles, throwing off images of what I accumulated throughout this lifetime.

* * *

When the elephant takes on a personal hue, I see what I finally learned about my family. I can see that my family was a group of people doing their best given their serious limitations, even though their best wasn't good enough for me and Mac.

My family was caught up in the promises of the industrial era—my father was an industrial icon; his dream was to live like the robber barons. But he also helped people, being the generous man he was. I see that Mac and Fred never had a chance; that sometimes the mountains people must climb are too high. And Katie, who was always tentative about being on this planet, tried hard and managed to stay until her children were thriving adults before she let go.

This elephant shows me that intensity is an important pattern in my life. I was driven to succeed in everything: in sports, academics, finding answers to big questions about my family and the program at Morrisania, working with patients, and the biggest challenge of all—figuring out how we can solve intractable global problems.

It's clear to me now I had a choice from the very beginning. I could become resilient and survive, or I could fail the test I was given and depart. But I'm oppositional, and I can't resist a challenge, so I developed grit—and understanding—and I'm still here.

* * *

There's another version of my elephant; this one is a complex being. For most of my life, I've been riding on this beast, who comprises knowledge, understanding, frustration, and patience. This elephant has taken me exploring in the primeval forest of human dynamics and in the jungle of complexity. I've learned that ultimate survival on our planet requires a widespread understanding of how to solve complex problems, from the smallest settings up to the largest. I see the importance of relationships in complex situations: not just among people, but between and among everything.

* * *

When the light shifts, I see an elephant of the future. This matriarch is a creature of harmony and balance, of wholeness and maturity. She belongs in a world where humans have learned to manage complexity and balance individual and community needs. This is a world where people everywhere place the highest value on the well-being of everything that is alive.

* * *

I also see that we're all blind. We're all trying to see the whole elephant, but we each have limitations. We're faced with a huge, immediate challenge: to try as hard as we can to identify what's holding us back and to find ways to turn things around on our planet. If we reach this goal in time, the remaining elephants will have a chance to survive, and so will we.

I look forward to a time when our society puts the highest value on the environment and on life, and when rebuilding families and communities is progressing at a rapid pace. I will continue doing everything I can to further this cause, and I intend to post updates on our website: www.chaosinstitute.org. I hope to see you there.

This whole experience of bringing up buried treasure and then trying to piece it all together has been intense, as befits my nature. It's been exhausting and exhilarating and frightening at the same time. I've been living with these ideas for over 35 years. The experience of writing this memoir made me determined to stay with the process in whatever way I can. I feel a sense of peace with its completion. But I'm not stopping here.

One of my next interests is applying this systems model, which I call "The Fractal Model of Relationships," to show how the patterns of interaction that take place in complex families get played out in the immune system. My hope is that disease amelioration has a better chance of success if we don't find ourselves with successful operations in which the patient dies.

* * *

"There is no more neutrality in the world. You either have to be part of the solution, or you're going to be part of the problem."
—**Eldridge Cleaver**

Me with Judy: Collaborators going forward, 2021

Made in United States
North Haven, CT
04 March 2024

49559065R00173